D1405728

Prima's Official Strategy Guide

Mark Cohen

Prima Games
A Division of Random House, Inc.

3000 Lava Ridge Court
Roseville, CA 95661
1-800-733-3000
www.primagames.com

SEP 19 2013

* Requires *The Sims™*, *The Sims™ Deluxe Edition*, or *The Sims™ Double Deluxe* to play.

The Prima Games logo is a registered trademark of Random House, Inc., registered in the United States and other countries. Primagames.com is a registered trademark of Random House, Inc., registered in the United States. Prima Games is a division of Random House, Inc.

© 2003 Electronic Arts Inc. Electronic Arts, The Sims, EA, EA GAMES, the EA GAMES logo, Maxis and the Maxis logo are trademarks or registered trademarks of Electronic Arts Inc. in the U.S. and/or other countries. All Rights Reserved. All other trademarks are the property of their respective owners. EA GAMES™ and Maxis™ are Electronic Arts™ brands.

No part of this book may be reproduced or transmitted in any form or by any means, electronic or mechanical, including photocopying, recording, or by any information storage or retrieval system without written permission from Electronic Arts Inc.

Associate Product Manager: Christy L. Curtis
Project Editor: Tamar Foster

Please be advised that the ESRB rating icons, "EC", "K-A", "E", "T", "M", "AO" and "RP" are copyrighted works and certification marks owned by the Entertainment Software Association and the Entertainment Software Rating Board and may only be used with their permission and authority. Under no circumstances may the rating icons be self-applied or used in connection with any product that has not been rated by the ESRB. For information regarding whether a product has been rated by the ESRB, please call the ESRB at 1-800-771-3772 or visit www.esrb.org. For information regarding licensing issues, please call the ESA at (212) 223-8936. Please note that ESRB ratings only apply to the content of the game itself and does NOT apply to the content of this book.

Important:
Prima Games has made every effort to determine that the information contained in this book is accurate. However, the publisher makes no warranty, either expressed or implied, as to the accuracy, effectiveness, or completeness of the material in this book; nor does the publisher assume liability for damages, either incidental or consequential, that may result from using the information in this book. The publisher cannot provide information regarding game play, hints and strategies, or problems with hardware or software. Questions should be directed to the support numbers provided by the game and device manufacturers in their documentation. Some game tricks require precise timing and may require repeated attempts before the desired result is achieved.

ISBN: 0-7615-4452-6
Library of Congress Catalog Card Number: 2003111134
Printed in the United States of America

03 04 05 06 BB 10 9 8 7 6 5 4 3 2

A very special thanks to the amazing creative team at Maxis:
Charles Gast: Software Engineer, Gabe Gils Carbó: Assistant Producer, Jeannie Yang: Assistant Producer, Jenna Chalmers: Associate Designer, Jonathan Knight: Producer, Juan Custer: Software Engineer, Lyndsay McGaw: Assistant Producer, Peter Fargo: Sr. Product Manager, Sean Hugunin: Lead Tester, Shannon Copur: Associate Producer, and Waylon Wilsonoff: Software Engineer.

TABLE OF CONTENTS

Introduction

The life of a Sim is not as easy as it looks. Between making food, climbing the career ladder, cleaning, and emptying your bladder (preferably not on the floor), there's barely enough time to get eight hours of sleep. Wouldn't it be nice to have a shortcut once in a while? Perhaps a little spell to clean up the bathrooms, prepare a sumptuous feast, or make the object of your affection feel the same way about you—without all the small talk?

Well, your wish is our command. With a snap of the wand, *Makin' Magic* is here to save the day. It all begins when the MagiCo Mystery Man delivers a package on your front lawn, giving you the necessary ingredients to make your first spell, charge your wand, and turn your neighbor into a toad.

But, this is just the beginning. You'll need to hone your Logic and Mechanical skills, then scour every inch of Magic Town, looking for secret ingredients to add to your Family Spellbook. Along the way you'll complete quests, compete in duels, and perform magic on stage. And, of course, as your inventory fills with magical spells and charms, you'll be tempted to practice on other Sims. But, be careful how you point your wand. If you cast a spell on another magical Sim, you're likely to be the unwilling recipient of your own good (or bad) magic.

Makin' Magic introduces more than 200 new items, including magic stages, vendor stands, carnival games, and a complete Fun House design kit. At home, you'll find new objects to aid in your production of magic, including a Nectar Press, Spinning Wheel (for Golden Thread), and the EverAfter Crafter, where you make your own magical charms. And, of course, no magical household can be without its very own Skeleton Maid. She isn't much to look at, but she cleans like the devil.

This strategy guide covers the many new features of *Makin' Magic*, including a glossary of new objects, complete magic tutorials for beginning and advanced sorcerers, and detailed tables of spell and charm ingredients. You'll also find a complete guide to the original *Sims*, with interaction tables and tutorials on all aspects of Sim life. So, whether you're a veteran or a newbie, everything you need to find happiness and fulfillment as a Sim is within these pages. Here is a preview of what you'll find in this guide.

Part I: The Sims

The first part takes you on a detailed tour through the original *Sims* game. We explain how a Sim thinks, acts, and reacts in various situations; and we teach you how to select and blend your Sim's personality traits. Next are the Motives, the eight primal urges that drive all Sims. We cover each one in detail, and show you how to manipulate your Sim's world to create happiness and contentment.

Sims are very social creatures, and this can be a blessing or a curse. We show you how and why a Sim interacts with others, and explain the benefits and pitfalls that accompany every short-term and long-term relationship. If marriage and children are in your Sim's future, you can find out what to expect when the blessed day arrives.

Sims spend simoleans at a staggering rate, so ou'll need to think about a job, and hopefully a uccessful career. We cover all the career paths, vith extensive tables detailing salaries, work chedules, and promotion requirements.

After analyzing the Sim psyche from all lirections, we shift our focus to the physical world, vhich consists of a home and its many objects. Our building tutorials take you through every step of the construction process, from putting up the raming to slapping on the final coat of paint. Our topics include walls, windows, doors, wall overings, stairways and second stories, pools, and landscaping.

A Sim home is empty until you fill it with lots of tuff, and we provide facts and statistics on every ingle object you can buy. In addition to data and lescriptions, we use detailed lists and tables to how how items relate to each other, and how ome objects can even alter the effectiveness of other objects.

Part 2: The Sims Makin' Magic

We begin the second section of our guide with Welcome to Magic Town, including a tour of the ollowing all-new commercial lots:

- **Clowntastic Land**
- **Coldwind Meadow**
- **Forest Edge Camp**
- **Serra Glen**
- **Vernon's Vault**
- **A Spooktacular Spot**

Next, we introduce you to the world of magic, lescribing the MagiCo Mystery Box, and taking you through your first spell. We show you how to find special ingredients, blend them in your Wand Charger, and charge your wand.

In The Complete Book of Magic, we delve deeper into the mysteries of *Makin' Magic*, with valuable tips on creating spells and charms, and finding rare ingredients. Just because you mix up a spell correctly does not guarantee positive results, and we have all the inside information on how to increase your chances for success. We also cover all the backfires, so you'll know what to expect when your casting goes bad.

In Quests, Duels, and Performances, we take you through Magic Town's toughest challenges. We show you how to win duels, wow the audiences with your stage magic, and complete special quests. We also introduce you to the mysterious Magic Growth objects, including Crystals, Beanstalks, Roots, and Flowers.

We finish up with chapters on Dragons, and Magical Friends and Toys (every magician needs an animated Gnome). Last but not least, you'll find complete interaction tables for *The Sims*.

All that's left for you to do is grab your wand and come up swinging. Remember, the more spells you cast, the more mysteries are revealed, so whatever you do, don't stop *Makin' Magic*!

PART I:

The Sims™

CHAPTER 1: WHAT'S YOUR SIM SIGN?

Introduction

When you are charged with the solemn task of creating a Sim from scratch, you have 25 points to distribute over five traits: Neat, Outgoing, Active, Playful, and Nice. Whether we admit it or not, all of us have an inherent wish to be perfectly balanced people (or Sims). Of course, you can take the easy way out and award five points in every category, creating a generic Sim. You'll spend less time managing a middle-of-the-road Sim because in most situations, he or she will do the right thing. If you'd rather play it safe, skip this chapter and move right to "Motives: I Want, I Need; Therefore, I Am a Sim." If not, read on as we describe the subtle (and sometimes dramatic) outcomes that your Sim's personality ratings will inspire.

It's in the Stars

As you play with the personality bars, you'll note the changing zodiac sign that appears on the screen. Of course, a serious astrologer would argue that a true personality profile is based on much more than five traits. However, if you have a basic understanding of newspaper horoscopes, you'll be able to recognize yourself, or someone close to you, as you create a Sim personality. In the next section we'll look at each trait and examine the potential effects of your ratings in various game situations. But first, let's take a look at basic interpersonal compatibility as seen through the eyes of the zodiac. The following table gives you the best and worst matchups for friends and lovers. This doesn't necessarily imply that any other Relationship outside of the table is doomed; it is merely an indication of how hard you'll have to work on it.

Sims Zodiac Compatibility Table

SIGN	ATTRACTED TO	REPELLED BY
Aries	Gemini/Taurus	Cancer/Libra
Taurus	Aries/Libra	Virgo/Cancer
Gemini	Pisces/Virgo	Capricorn/Aries
Cancer	Taurus/Scorpio	Gemini/Aries
Virgo	Aquarius/Sagittarius	Leo/Taurus
Libra	Virgo/Cancer	Pisces/Scorpio
Scorpio	Pisces/Leo	Libra/Aquarius
Sagittarius	Pisces/Capricorn	Libra/Scorpio
Leo	Sagittarius/Cancer	Capricorn/Gemini
Capricorn	Aquarius/Taurus	Leo/Gemini
Aquarius	Capricorn/Sagittarius	Scorpio/Virgo
Pisces	Scorpio/Gemini	Leo/Aries

Personality Traits

The following sections review what you can expect from each type of Sim, with examples of how different personality traits will manifest during the game. For our purposes, we'll divide the ratings bar into three sections: Low (1–3), Average (4–7), and High (8–10). These numbers correspond to the number of light blue bars to the right of each trait.

Neat

Low

Don't expect these Sims to pick up their dirty dishes, wash their hands after using the bathroom, or take timely showers. They are perfectly content to let others clean up their messes.

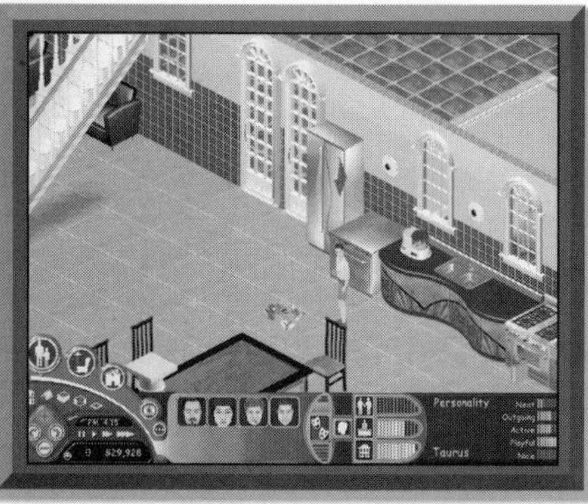
Fig. 1-1. The kitchen floor is a perfect place for this messy Sim's snack leavings.

Medium

At least these Sims keep themselves relatively clean, and you can depend on them to clean up their own messes. Occasionally, they'll even clean up another Sim's garbage, but you might have to intervene if you have several cleanup items that need attention.

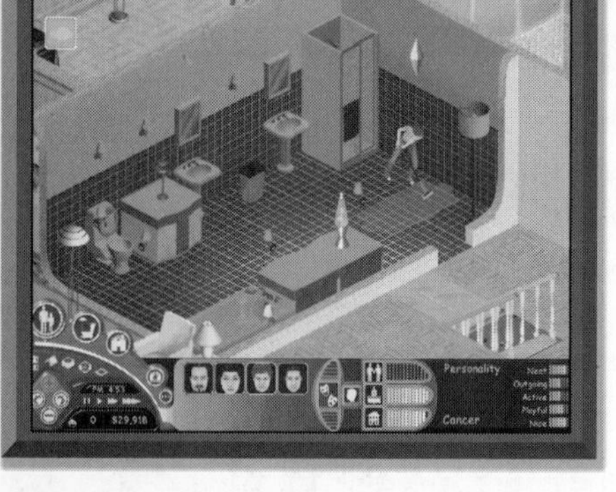
Fig. 1-2. After slopping water all over the bathroom during his shower, this moderately Neat Sim mops up his mess before leaving the room.

High

A super-Neat Sim always checks the vicinity for dirty dishes and old newspapers, and of course, personal hygiene is a big priority. One of these Sims can compensate for one or two slobs in a household.

Fig. 1-3. This fastidious Sim goes straight to the bathtub after a hard day's work.

Outgoing

Low

Shy, reserved, Sims have less pressing needs for Social interaction, so it will be more difficult to pursue friendships with other Sims, although they can still carry on stimulating conversations. Within their own home, a shy Sim may be less interested in receiving hugs, kisses, and back rubs, so if you are looking for romance, it would be a good idea to find a compatible target (see zodiac chart on p. 9).

Fig. 1-4. This Sim cringes at the thought of a back rub—poor guy.

Medium

It will be a little easier to get this Sim to mix with strangers and enjoy a little intimacy from his housemates. Don't expect a party animal, but you'll be able to entice your guests into most activities.

Fig. 1-5. Come on everyone, let's hit the pool!

High

This Sim needs plenty of Social stimulation to prevent his or her Social score from plummeting. You'll have no trouble throwing parties or breaking the ice with just about any personality type.

Fig. 1-6. This outgoing Sim is still unconscious from last night's pool party, and she has inspired the close friendship of another man. Hmmm.

Active

Low

Forget about pumping iron or swimming 100 laps at 5:00 a.m. These Sims prefer a soft easy chair to a hard workout. A sofa and a good TV are high on their priority list. In fact, if they don't get their daily ration of vegging, their Comfort scores will suffer.

Fig. 1-7. This Sim says "No way!" to a session on the exercise bench.

Medium

These Sims strike a good balance between relaxing and breaking a sweat. They dance, swim, and even shoot hoops without expressing discomfort.

Fig. 1-8. His Active rating is only a four, but that doesn't stop this Sim from shooting hoops in his jammies.

High

Active Sims like to pick up the pace rather than fall asleep on the sofa in front of the TV. Get these Sims a pool, basketball hoop, or exercise bench, and plan on dancing the night away with friends.

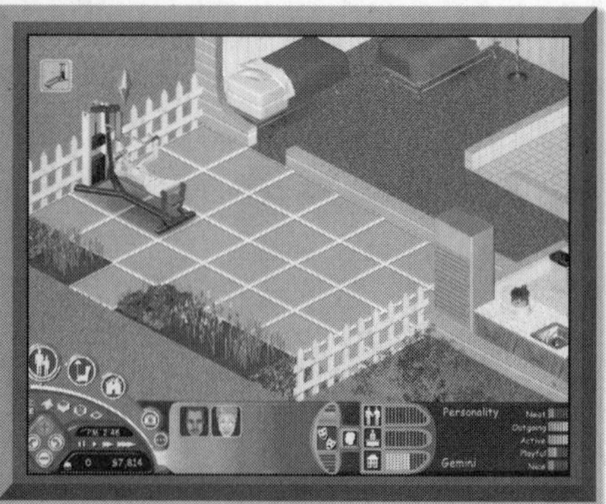

Fig. 1-9. Even in her business suit, this active Sim will gladly leave Mortimer on the sofa and pump some iron in the backyard.

Playful

Low

Get these Sims a bookcase, a comfortable chair, and plenty of books. If reading isn't an option, looking at a painting or playing a game of chess will do just fine.

Fig. 1-10. There's always time to watch the fish, for this less-than-playful Sim.

Medium

These well-rounded Sims are usually receptive to a good joke and don't mind a little tickling. They may not be the first ones on the dance floor, but they'll join in with a good crowd.

Fig. 1-11. This Sim is Playful enough to dance, even though she is overdue for a shower.

High

Can you spell P-A-R-T-Y? These Sims love to have a few drinks, dance to good music, and invite lots of guests over to the house. They love telling jokes, and they are usually ready to laugh at others' stories.

Fig. 1-12. This Playful kid would get the Maid in the pool for a game of chicken, if only she would respond.

Nice

Low

There is nothing redeeming about a grouchy Sim. They are always ready to tease or insult their friends, and they love to brag. A Sim with a low Nice rating should be dropped from your guest list immediately, or asked to leave if he or she shows up.

Fig. 1-13. Usually a compliment elicits a nice response, but not so with with sourpuss.

Medium

This Sim keeps an even keel about most things. Of all the traits, Nice is the least destructive if you award at least four points. Only the nastiest Sims can get under a medium-Nice Sim's skin.

Fig. 1-14. This Sim has time for a good tickle, even while mopping up the bathroom.

High

These Sims just want to make the world a better place for everyone. If there was a Sim beauty contest, the winner would be extremely "Nice."

Fig. 1-15. Even after spending the night on the kitchen floor, this Sim still knows how to compliment her mate.

Personality Tables

The following tables demonstrate how personality traits affect Fun scores and Skill development.

Traits that Raise Max Fun Value

PERSONALITY TRAIT	RAISES MAX FUN SCORE FOR
Playful	Aquarium, Chess Table, Computer, Doll House, Flamingo, Pinball, TV (Cartoon Channel), VR Glasses
Serious (Low Playful)	Newspaper (Read)
Active	Basketball Hoop, Play Structure, TV (Action Channel)
Outgoing	Hot Tub, TV (Romance Channel)
Grouchy (Low Nice)	TV (Horror Channel)

Skills Accelerated by Personality

SKILL	OBJECTS USED TO INCREASE SKILL	TRAIT ACCELERATOR
Creativity	Easel, Piano	Playful
Body	Exercise Machine, Swimming Pool	Active
Charisma	Medicine Cabinet, Mirrors	Outgoing

CHAPTER 2: MOTIVES—I WANT, I NEED; THEREFORE, I AM A SIM!

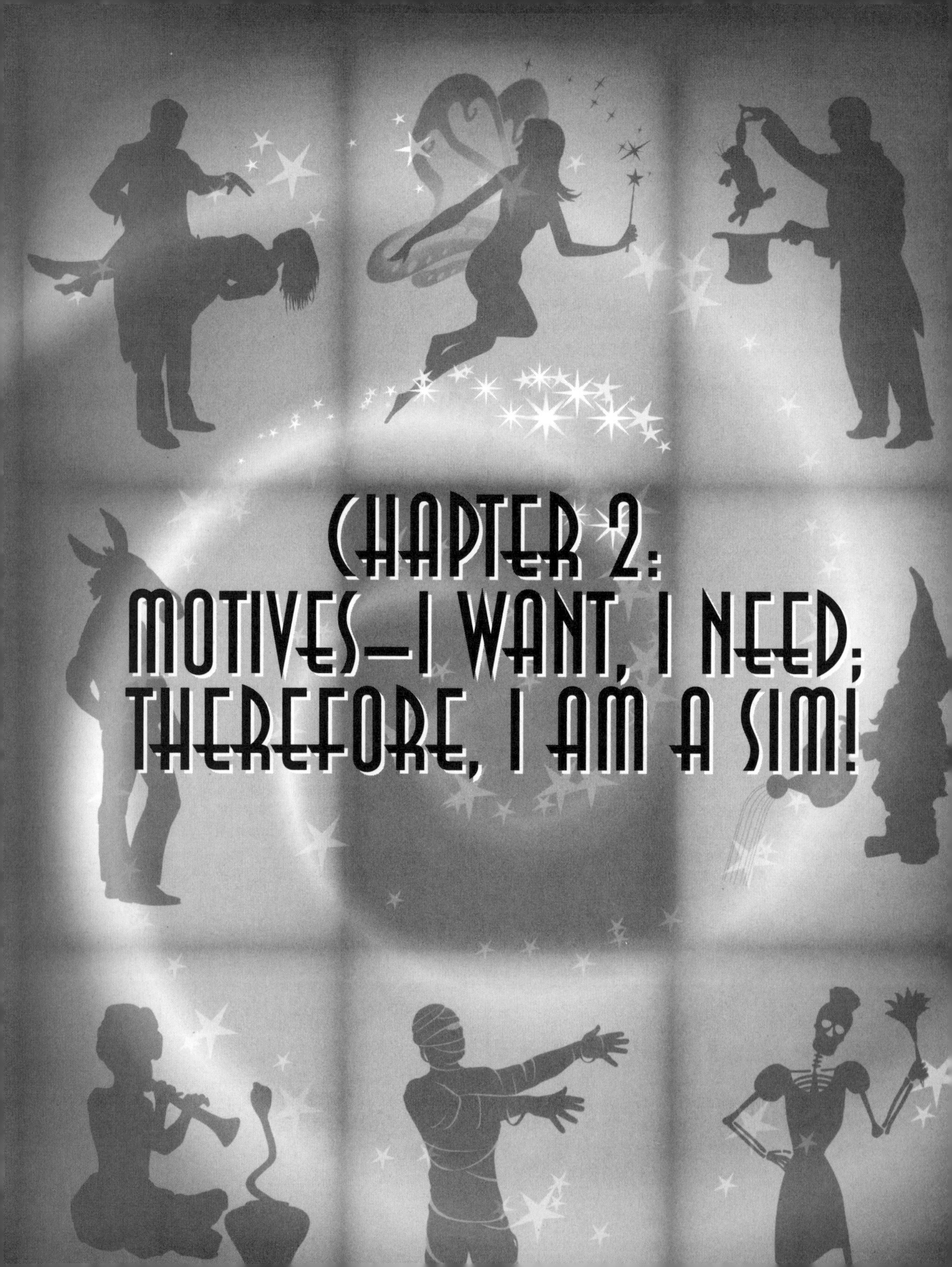

Introduction

When you consider how many needs, traits, and desires make up a Sim's personality, it would be an injustice to call it AI. Never before has a computer-generated character interacted so completely with both the game and the gamer while maintaining a unique (and ever-changing) personality. Is it any wonder that *The Sims* has topped the PC sales chart for nearly two years running?

In the previous chapter we discussed a Sim's personality traits. It painted a broad picture of the various types of Sims you might encounter in the game, much the same as a newspaper horoscope tells a superficial story of a person's life. In this chapter, we advance from broad-brush personality traits to the eight powerful Motives that drive a Sim's every action. We cover each Motive in detail, but first, let's begin with a few basic definitions.

What Is a Motive?

A Motive is, very simply, a need. Your Sims follow these needs, based on their own instincts and a little help from you. If you activate Free Will in the Options menu, your Sims will also make their own decisions, based on changing needs. After selecting a Motive to fulfill, be it Hunger or Hygiene, the Sim is "rewarded" with Motive points. These points raise the corresponding Motive score.

The eight Motive scores are displayed on the right side of the control panel. A Motive rating is considered positive if the bar is green, and negative if it is red. Internally, the game uses a 200-point system, with positive (green) ratings between 0 and 100, and negative (red) ratings from 0 to -100.

TIP

When any of the Sims' eight Motives drop below a certain level, a Sim will cease an activity that doesn't improve the Motive in distress. So, you'll see low-priority items drop out of the activity queue, or your Sim will add an activity that addresses the critical need.

CAUTION

Without Free Will, your Sims depend entirely on your input to keep them alive. If you don't tell them to eat, they will starve, and eventually die.

Mood Rating

The game control panel also displays a Mood Rating, just to the right of the Sim character icons. If the rating is positive, you see up to five green bars displayed above the comedy/tragedy masks. When the Mood Rating is negative, it displays up to five red bars below the masks.

In calculating the Mood Rating, each of the eight Motives is weighted, based on how critical it is to sustaining a Sim's life. Hence, Hunger, Bladder, and Energy, which are all related to a Sim's physical well-being, carry more weight than the noncritical Motives such as Social, Fun, or Room. So, if a Sim is hungry and tired, as pictured in figure 2-1, the overall Mood Rating will be relatively low, even if several other Motives are high.

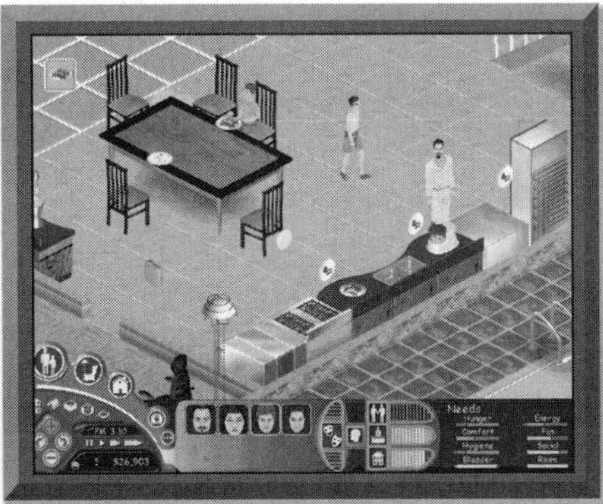

Fig. 2-1. This Sim kid's overall Mood Rating is barely positive, due to the fact that he is starving and low on Energy.

The Motives

In the following sections we describe the eight Motives, using several tables to show you how and why a Sim reacts to different objects in the environment. By recognizing the relationships between Motives and objects, you'll begin to understand how a Sim considers a perpetual barrage of options. Once you do this, the only remaining question is, "Who is really in charge here, you or the Sim?"

Fig. 2-2. This Sim family enjoys a meal together. Mom's Hunger bar is in the worst shape, so she has a second meal plate at the ready.

NOTE

Aside from the overall Motive weighting system, each Sim suffers different rates of Motive depreciation based on personality traits. For example, a Playful Sim must have more "rewards" to maintain the Fun Motive bar. Similarly, an Outgoing Sim requires more interaction with other Sims to maintain the Social score.

Hunger Score for Each Meal, Snack, or Gift

MEAL TYPE	HUNGER MOTIVE BAR POINTS
Snack	9
Quick Meal	16
Full Meal	16
Group Meal (per serving)	16
Pizza (per serving)	33
Candy Box (gift)	3 (per serving, 12 servings per box)
Fruitcake (gift)	7 (per slice, 6 slices per box)

Hunger

For obvious reasons, a Sim cannot survive for very long without food. We'll cover the details of food preparation in a later chapter, but for now let's focus on the basics. As long as you have a refrigerator, a Sim can enjoy a Snack, Quick Meal, Full Meal, or Group Meal (same as a Full Meal, except one of the Sims prepares several servings). In addition to preparing food, a Sim with a telephone can order out for Pizza, or enjoy food that was brought as a gift (Candy Box or Fruitcake). The Hunger Motive bar points awarded with each meal are outlined in the following table.

Comfort

The next category listed in the Needs section of the control panel is considerably less important than Hunger. Sims like to be comfortable, and they love cushy chairs, oversized sofas, and supportive beds. Spending more money on these objects translates into greater Motive rewards. However, if your budget is tight, you must still furnish the house with basic furniture or your Sims will express their discomfort.

Fig. 2-3. With only a cheap chair and loveseat, this Sim's Comfort score is mired in the red.

Fig. 2-4. Three out of four Motive scores are on the way up while this couple enjoys a hot tub soak.

Hunger, Bladder, Energy, and Comfort are the most demanding of Motives, because if any one score drops below a certain level, the Sim will immediately exit his or her current activity to remedy the deficit. The following table lists the exit triggers for each category.

Mandatory Exit Factors

MOTIVE	SIM TYPE	EXITS CURRENT INTERACTION WHEN MOTIVE DROPS BELOW
Bladder	Resident	-85
Bladder	Visitor	-80
Comfort	Resident	-90
Comfort	Visitor	-60
Energy	Resident	-80
Energy	Visitor	-70
Hunger	Resident	-80
Hunger	Visitor	-40

Hygiene

Bad Hygiene will never kill a Sim, although it may seriously gross out others in the immediate vicinity. Solving this problem is easy—have your Sims wash their hands or take a shower. You can also combine Hygiene with other Motives. Taking a bath boosts the Hygiene and Comfort scores, while a soak in the hot tub (with friends) rewards the Hygiene, Comfort, Social, and Fun Motive bars.

Bladder

If you can't satisfy the Bladder urge, you'll be cleaning up puddles on the floor. Just make sure you find a bathroom before the Motive bar turns full red. A Sloppy Sim creates an additional risk by not regularly flushing the toilet. If you don't issue timely reminders, the toilet could get clogged, causing a major mess.

TIP

Pay special attention to the Bladder bar when your Sim spends time at the Beverage Bar or drinks a lot of coffee.

CAUTION

The Hygiene score takes a nose dive if a Sim can't get to the bathroom in time and pees on the floor.

Fig. 2-5. This Sim's Bladder is not quite full, but unless his guest vacates the bathroom soon, he could be in trouble.

Energy

We're talking sleep, pure and simple. Ideally, a good night's sleep should turn the bar completely green. This will happen at varying rates, depending upon the quality of the mattress, so you can get by on less sleep if you splurge for an expensive bed. If your Sim can't get to the bedroom or a couch before the Energy bar turns completely red, the floor becomes your only option. If this happens, wake your Sim and find the closest bed. A night on the hard floor will degrade your Sim's Comfort level to zero, while only restoring partial energy.

If your Sim stays up too late playing computer games, a shot of espresso provides a temporary Energy boost, although it will also fill the Bladder at an increased rate. Espresso has a powerful effect, but it takes longer to consume, which could be a problem if the car pool driver is honking.

Fig. 2-6. It never hurts to send your kids to bed early, because if they are tired in the morning, a coffee jolt is not an option.

Fun

Sims like to cut loose from the daily grind and have Fun, but depending upon their personalities, they prefer different activities. For example, a Playful Sim leans toward computer games, pinball machines, and train sets; while a more Serious Sim would rather sit down to a quiet game of chess or spend a few minutes gazing at a painting.

Fig. 2-7. These two Sims enjoy a game of pool after work.

Kids need to have more Fun than adults, and the effects of a single play session deteriorate faster for kids than for their older counterparts. Hence, it is a good idea to fill the house with plenty of juvenile diversions if you have children.

There are four different types of Fun activities: Extended, One-Time, Timed, and Endless. The following lists and tables provide additional information, including exit factors, for these pursuits.

Extended Fun Activities

Sims exit the following extended activities after reaching the maximum Fun score for their personality types. Hence, a Playful, Active Sim will stay on the basketball court longer than a Serious Sim.

- Basketball Hoop
- Bookshelf (reading)
- Dollhouse
- Computer (playing games)
- Pinball Machine
- Play Structure
- Stereo
- Toy Box
- Train Set
- TV
- VR Glasses

One-Time Fun Activities

The following activities raise a Sim's Fun score once with each interaction. It may take several interactions with the same activity for a Sim to reach the maximum Fun level.

OBJECT	ACTION
Aquarium	Feed or watch fish
Baby	Play
Diving Board	Dive into the pool
Espresso Machine	Drink espresso
Fountain	View
Lava Lamp	View
Painting	View
Sculpture	View

Timed (Pre-set) Fun Activities

As with the one-time activities listed above, a Sim may need to repeat the following activities to achieve maximum Fun points.

- Chess Set
- Pool Table

Endless Fun

- Hot Tub: A Sim will stay in the tub until Fun, Comfort, Social, and Hygiene numbers reach maximum levels.
- Swimming Pool: A Sim will keep doing laps until another Motive takes effect, or until you assign him or her to another activity.

Social

Sims crave other Sims, especially if they are Outgoing. Although they won't die without socializing, it is a good idea to devote a portion of each day to a group activity, even if it is a simple hot tub session with your Sim's mate, or a family meal.

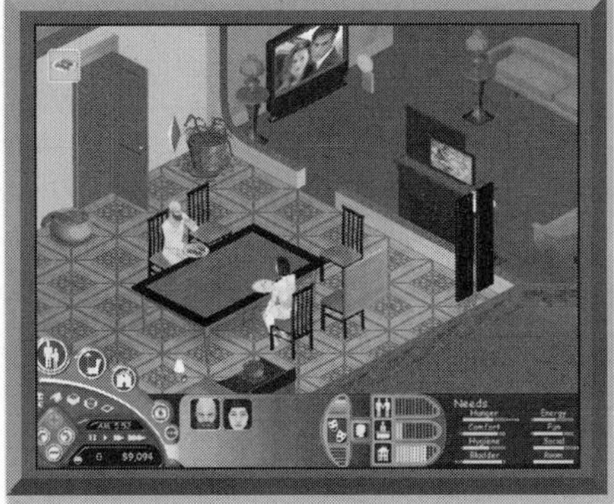

Fig. 2-8. A casual conversation during breakfast raises this Sim's Social score.

The following table summarizes all of the possible Social interactions between adults and children. We take this one step further in the next chapter, "Interacting with Other Sims," where we examine Relationships.

Adult-Child Interactions

Action	Adult to Adult	Child to Child	Adult to Child	Child to Adult
Apologize	X	—	—	—
Attack	X	X	—	—
Brag	X	X	X	X
Call Here	X	X	X	X
Cheer Up	X	X	X	X
Compliment	X	—	—	—
Dance	X	—	—	—
Entertain	X	X	X	X
Flirt	X	—	—	—
Give Back Rub	X	—	—	—
Give Gift	X	X	X	X
Hug	X	X	X	X
Insult	X	X	X	X
Joke	X	X	X	X
Kiss	X	—	—	—
Say Goodbye	X	X	X	—
Scare	X	X	X	X
Slap	X	—	—	—
Tag	—	X	—	—
Talk	X	X	X	X
Tease	X	X	X	X
Tickle	X	X	X	X

Social Outcome Modifiers

You didn't expect a Sim Social encounter to be simple, did you? When one Sim communicates with another, several calculations determine the outcome. Factors include age (adult or child), sex, mood, and personality traits, not to mention the current state of their Relationship. Also, a Sim with strong Social needs (but few friends) may expect more from an encounter with a Sim who has similar needs.

The following table lists the factors that govern the choices that appear on a Social actions menu. For example, two Sims who are strangers are not likely to have the options to kiss or hug. Additionally, the table lists key factors that determine the eventual outcome.

rel = Relationship	age = Adult/Child
out = Outgoing	social = Social Motive Value
play = Playful	vis = Visitor
ff = Friend Flag	budget = Household Budget
ss = Same Sex	nice = Nice
rom = Romance Flag	body = Body

Social Outcome Factors

Interaction	Factors That Determine Appearance on the Menu	Factors That Determine Outcome
Apologize	rel	mood
Attack	age, nice, mood, rel	body
Back Rub	age, nice, mood, rel, out, ss	rel, out, ss
Brag	nice, out, social, rel	rel, mood
Cheer Up	ff, mood (of friend), nice	rel
Compliment	age, nice, out, mood, rel	rel, mood
Dance	age, mood, out, rel	rel, out, mood
Entertain	social, out, play, mood, rel	play, rel
Flirt	age, social, ss, out, mood, rel, rom	rel, mood, ss
Gift	vis, budget, nice, mood, rel	rel, mood
Hug	age, out, mood, rel, ss	rel, out, mood, ss
Insult	nice, mood, rel	nice
Joke	play, mood, rel	play, mood, rel
Kiss	ss, mood, rel, age	rel, mood, ss
Scare	nice, mood, play, rel	play, mood
Slap	age, nice, mood, rel	nice, mood
Talk	mood, rel, out	topics match
Tease	nice, mood, rel	rel, mood
Tickle	social, out, play, active, mood, rel	rel, play

Room

This is a combined rating that analyzes the design and contents of the current room, and translates it into a Room score. Of all the Motives, Room is the least important. However, if you love your Sim, you'll want to create the best possible environment. The most important contributing factors to Room score are:

- **Light: Sims hate dark rooms, so fill your house with sunlight (windows and paned doors), lamps, and wall lights.**
- **Room Size: Don't cramp your Sims into tiny rooms.**
- **Corners: As mentioned in the "Building a House" chapter, Sims love corners.**
- **State of Repair: Any items that are not functioning properly detract from the Room score (see following list).**

Fig. 2-9. Who wouldn't love a kitchen like this? It's bright, roomy, nicely furnished, and packed with high-tech appliances.

Negative Impact on Room Score

- **Trash**
- **Floods**
- **Dirty plates**
- **Meals with flies**
- **Full trash cans/compactors**
- **Dead plants**
- **Puddle or ash pile**
- **Dead fish in aquariums**
- **Dirty objects (shower, toilet, tub)**

The following table lists the positive or negative value of every object in *The Sims*.

Room Score

OBJECT	STATE/TYPE	ROOM SCORE
Aquarium	Fish Alive	25
	Dirty	-25
	Dirty and/or Dead	-50
Ash	N/A	-10
Bar	N/A	20
Bed	Unmade (Any Bed)	-10
	Made Mission	30
	Made (Other than Mission)	10
Chair	Parisienne	25
	Empress	10
Clock (Grandfather)	N/A	50
Computer	Broken	-25
Counter	Barcelona	15
Desk	Redmond	15
Dresser	Antique Armoire	20
	Oak Armoire	10
Fire	N/A	-100

OBJECT	STATE/TYPE	ROOM SCORE
Fireplace	Library Edition (No Fire)	20
	Library Edition (Fire)	75
	Worcestershire (No Fire)	15
	Worcestershire (Fire)	60
	Bostonian (No Fire)	10
	Bostonian (Fire)	45
	Modesto (No Fire)	5
	Modesto (Fire)	30
Flamingo	N/A	10
Flood	N/A	-25
Flowers (Outdoor)	Healthy	20
	Dead	-20
Flowers/Plants (Indoor)	Healthy	10
	Wilted	0
	Dead	-10
Food	Snack (Spoiled)	-15
	Fruitcake (Empty Plate)	-5
	BBQ Group Meal (Spoiled)	-20
	BBQ Single Meal (Spoiled)	-15
	Empty Plate	-10
	Pizza Slice (Spoiled)	-10
	Pizza Box (Spoiled)	-25
	Candy (Spoiled)	-5
	Group Meal (Spoiled)	-20
	Meal (Spoiled)	-25
	Quick Meal (Spoiled)	-20
Fountain	N/A	25
Flowers (Gift)	Dead	-10
	Alive	20
Lamp	Not Broken	10
Lava Lamp	N/A	20
Newspaper	Old Newspapers	-20
Piano	N/A	30
Pinball Machine	Broken	-15
Shower	Broken	-15
Sofa (Deiter or Dolce)	N/A	20
Stereo	Strings	25
Table	Mesa	15
	Parisienne	25
Toilet	Clogged	-10
Train Set	Small	25
Trash Can (Inside)	Full	-20
Trash Compactor	Full	-25
Trash Pile	N/A	-20
TV	Soma	20
	Broken (Any TV)	-15

Object Advertising Values

Earlier in the chapter we mentioned that Sims receive Motive rewards when they select an activity. If you are in complete control of your Sims (Free Will is off), you determine their choices. However, with Free Will on, Sims constantly poll their surroundings to compare which objects are "advertising" the most attractive rewards. The following table includes a Motive profile of every object in *The Sims*.

Object Advertising Values

Object Type	Possible Interactions	Object Variations	Advertised Motive	Advertised Value	Personality Trait Modifier	Reduced Effects (Over Distance)
Aquarium	Clean & Restock	N/A	Room	30	Neat	Medium
	Feed Fish	N/A	Room	10	Nice	High
		N/A	Fun	10	Playful	High
	Watch Fish	N/A	Fun	10	Playful	High
Ash	Sweep Up	N/A	Energy	23	N/A	Medium
		N/A	Room	50	Neat	Medium
Baby	Play	N/A	Fun	50	Playful	Medium
Bar	Have Drink	N/A	Room	30	N/A	Low
	Grill	Barbecue	Energy	-10	N/A	Low
			Hunger	40	Cooking	Low
Basketball Hoop	Join	N/A	Fun	30	Active	High
		N/A	Social	20	N/A	Medium
		N/A	Energy	-20	N/A	Medium
	Play	N/A	Fun	30	Active	High
		N/A	Energy	-20	N/A	High
Bed	Make Bed	All Beds	Room	25	Neat	High
	Sleep	Double Bed (Cheap Eazzzzze)	Energy	65	N/A	None
		Double Bed (Napoleon)	Energy	67	N/A	None
		Double Bed (Mission)	Energy	70	N/A	None
		Single Bed (Spartan)	Energy	60	N/A	None
		Single Bed (Tyke Nyte)	Energy	63	N/A	None
	Tuck in Kid	All Beds	Energy	160	Nice	None

Object Type	Possible Interactions	Object Variations	Advertised Motive	Advertised Value	Personality Trait Modifier	Reduced Effects (Over Distance)
Bookcase	Read a Book	Bookcase (Pine)	Fun	10	Serious	High
		Bookcase (Amishim)	Fun	20	Serious	High
		Bookcase (Libri di Regina)	Fun	30	Serious	High
Chair (Living Room)	Sit	Wicker	Comfort	20	N/A	Medium
		Country Class	Comfort	20	N/A	Medium
		Citronel	Comfort	20	N/A	Medium
		Sarrbach	Comfort	20	N/A	Medium
Chair (Dining Room)	Sit	Werkbunnst	Comfort	25	N/A	Medium
		Teak	Comfort	25	N/A	Medium
		Empress	Comfort	25	N/A	Medium
		Parisienne	Comfort	25	N/A	Medium
Chair (Office/Deck)	Sit	Office Chair	Comfort	20	N/A	Medium
		Deck Chair	Comfort	20	N/A	Medium
Chair (Recliner)	Nap	Both Recliners	Energy	15	Lazy	High
		Both Recliners	Comfort	20	Lazy	Medium
	Sit	Both Recliners	Comfort	30	Lazy	Medium
Chess	Join	Chess Set	Fun	40	Outgoing	High
			Social	40	N/A	Medium
	Play		Fun	35	Serious	High
Clock (Grandfather)	Wind	N/A	Room	40	Neat	High
Coffee (Espresso Machine)	Drink Espresso	N/A	Energy	115	N/A	Medium
		N/A	Fun	10	N/A	High
		N/A	Bladder	-10	N/A	High
Coffeemaker	Drink Coffee	N/A	Bladder	-5	N/A	High
		N/A	Energy	115	N/A	Medium

OBJECT TYPE	POSSIBLE INTERACTIONS	OBJECT VARIATIONS	ADVERTISED MOTIVE	ADVERTISED VALUE	PERSONALITY TRAIT MODIFIER	REDUCED EFFECTS (OVER DISTANCE)
Computer	Play	Moneywell	Fun	30	Playful	High
		Microscotch	Fun	35	Playful	High
		Brahma	Fun	40	Playful	High
		Marco	Fun	50	Playful	High
	Turn Off	All Computers	Energy	220	Neat	Medium
Dollhouse	Play	N/A	Fun	30	Playful	High
	Watch	N/A	Fun	30	Playful	Medium
		N/A	Social	30	N/A	Medium
Easel	Paint	N/A	Fun	20	N/A	High
Flamingo	Kick	N/A	Mood	15	Grouchy	High
	View	N/A	Fun	10	Playful	High
Flood	Clean	N/A	Room	80	Neat	High
Flowers (Outdoor)	Stomp On	N/A	Mood	10	Grouchy	High
	Water	N/A	Room	20	Neat	Medium
Flowers/Plants (Indoor)	Throw Out	N/A	Room	50	Neat	Medium
	Water	N/A	Room	25	Neat	Medium
Food	Clean	All Meal/ Snack Types	Room	20	Neat	Medium
	Prepare and Eat	BBQ Group Meal	Hunger	90	N/A	Low
		BBQ Single	Hunger	80	N/A	Low
		Candy	Hunger	30	N/A	Low
		Fruitcake (Group Meal)	Hunger	30	N/A	Low
		Fruitcake (Slice)	Hunger	80	N/A	Low
		Light Meal	Hunger	80	N/A	Low
		Pizza Box	Hunger	90	N/A	Low
		Pizza Slice	Hunger	80	N/A	Low
		Regular Group Meal	Hunger	90	N/A	Low
		Regular Single Meal	Hunger	80	N/A	Low
		Snack	Hunger	25	N/A	Low

OBJECT TYPE	POSSIBLE INTERACTIONS	OBJECT VARIATIONS	ADVERTISED MOTIVE	ADVERTISED VALUE	PERSONALITY TRAIT MODIFIER	REDUCED EFFECTS (OVER DISTANCE)
Fountain	Play	N/A	Fun	10	Shy	High
Refrigerator	Have Meal	All Fridges	Hunger	65	N/A	Low
	Have Snack	Llamark	Hunger	20	N/A	Low
		Porcina	Hunger	30	N/A	Low
		Freeze Secret	Hunger	40	N/A	Low
	Have Quick Meal	All Fridges	Hunger	55	N/A	Low
	Serve Meal	All Fridges	Hunger	70	Cooking	Low
		All Fridges	Energy	-10	N/A	Low
Gift (Flowers)	Clean	N/A	Room	30	Neat	Medium
Hot Tub	Get In	N/A	Fun	45	Lazy	High
		N/A	Comfort	50	N/A	High
		N/A	Social	25	Outgoing	Medium
		N/A	Hygiene	5	N/A	Medium
	Join	N/A	Comfort	30	N/A	Low
		N/A	Fun	50	Outgoing	Low
		N/A	Social	50	N/A	Low
		N/A	Hygiene	5	N/A	Medium
Lava Lamp	Turn On	N/A	Room	5	N/A	High
		N/A	Fun	5	N/A	High
Mailbox	Get Mail	N/A	Comfort	10	N/A	High
		N/A	Hunger	10	N/A	High
		N/A	Hygiene	10	N/A	High
		N/A	Room	10	N/A	High
Medicine Cabinet	Brush Teeth	N/A	Hygiene	25	Neat	Medium
Newspaper	Clean Up	N/A	Room	50	Neat	Medium
	Read	N/A	Fun	5	Serious	High
Painting	View	N/A	Fun	5	Serious	High
Phone	Answer	N/A	Fun	50	N/A	Medium
		N/A	Comfort	50	N/A	Medium
		N/A	Social	50	N/A	Medium
Piano	Play	N/A	Fun	40	Strong Creativity	High
	Watch	N/A	Fun	70	N/A	Medium
		N/A	Social	10	N/A	Medium

Object Type	Possible Interactions	Object Variations	Advertised Motive	Advertised Value	Personality Trait Modifier	Reduced Effects (Over Distance)
Pinball Machine	Join	N/A	Fun	50	N/A	Medium
		N/A	Social	30	N/A	Medium
	Play	N/A	Fun	40	Playful	High
Play Structure	Join	N/A	Fun	60	Playful	Medium
		N/A	Social	40	N/A	Medium
	Play	N/A	Fun	60	Playful	Medium
Pool Diving Board	Dive In	N/A	Fun	35	Active	High
		N/A	Energy	-10	N/A	High
Pool Table	Join	N/A	Fun	50	Playful	Low
		N/A	Social	40	N/A	Low
	Play	N/A	Fun	45	Playful	High
Sculpture	View	Scylla and Charybdis	Fun	6	Serious	High
		Bust of Athena	Fun	5	Serious	High
		Large Black Slab	Fun	8	Serious	High
		China Vase	Fun	7	Serious	High
Shower	Clean	N/A	Room	20	Neat	High
	Take a Shower	N/A	Hygiene	50	Neat	Medium
Sink	Wash Hands	N/A	Hygiene	10	Neat	High
Sofa/Loveseat	Nap	All Sofas/ Loveseats	Energy	40	Lazy	High
		All Sofas/ Loveseats	Comfort	5	Lazy	High
	Sit	All Sofas/ Loveseats	Comfort	30	Lazy	Medium
		Garden Bench	Comfort	30	Lazy	Medium
Stereo	Dance	Boom Box	Social	40	Outgoing	High
			Fun	50	Active	High
		Zimantz Hi-Fi	Social	50	Outgoing	High
			Fun	60	Active	High
		Strings Theory	Social	60	Outgoing	High
			Fun	70	Active	High
	Join	Boom Box	Social	40	Outgoing	Low

OBJECT TYPE	POSSIBLE INTERACTIONS	OBJECT VARIATIONS	ADVERTISED MOTIVE	ADVERTISED VALUE	PERSONALITY TRAIT MODIFIER	REDUCED EFFECTS (OVER DISTANCE)
Stereo			Fun	40	Outgoing	Low
		Zimantz Hi-Fi	Social	50	Outgoing	Low
			Fun	40	Outgoing	Low
		Strings Theory	Social	60	Outgoing	Low
			Fun	40	Outgoing	Low
	Turn Off	All Stereos	Energy	220	Neat	Medium
	Turn On	Boom Box	Fun	25	Playful	High
		Zimantz Hi-Fi	Fun	25	Playful	High
		Strings Theory	Fun	30	Playful	High
Toilet	Clean	Both Toilets	Room	40	Neat	High
	Flush	Hygeia-O-Matic	Room	30	Neat	High
	Unclog	Both Toilets	Room	50	Neat	High
	Use	Hygeia-O-Matic	Bladder	50	N/A	Low
		Flush Force	Bladder	70	N/A	Low
Tombstone/ Urn	Mourn (first 24 hours)	N/A	Bladder	5	N/A	Low
		N/A	Comfort	50	N/A	Low
		N/A	Energy	5	N/A	Low
		N/A	Fun	50	N/A	Low
		N/A	Hunger	5	N/A	Low
		N/A	Hygiene	50	N/A	Low
		N/A	Social	50	N/A	Low
		N/A	Room	50	N/A	Low
	Mourn (second 48 hours)	N/A	Bladder	0	N/A	Low
		N/A	Comfort	30	N/A	Low
		N/A	Energy	0	N/A	Low
		N/A	Fun	30	N/A	Low
		N/A	Hunger	0	N/A	Low
		N/A	Hygiene	30	N/A	Low
		N/A	Social	30	N/A	Low
		N/A	Room	30	N/A	Low
Toy Box	Play	N/A	Fun	55	Playful	Medium

Object Type	Possible Interactions	Object Variations	Advertised Motive	Advertised Value	Personality Trait Modifier	Reduced Effects (Over Distance)
Train Set (Large)	Play	N/A	Fun	40	N/A	Medium
	Watch	N/A	Fun	40	N/A	Low
		N/A	Social	40	N/A	Low
Train Set (Small)	Play	N/A	Fun	45	Playful	Medium
	Watch	N/A	Fun	20	N/A	Medium
		N/A	Social	30	N/A	Medium
Trash Can (Inside)	Empty Trash	N/A	Room	30	Neat	Medium
Trash Compactor	Empty Trash	N/A	Room	30	N/A	High
Trash Pile	Clean	N/A	Room	75	Neat	Medium
Bathtub	Clean	All Tubs	Room	20	Neat	High
	Bathe	Justa	Hygiene	50	Neat	Medium
		Justa	Comfort	20	N/A	Medium
		Sani-Queen	Hygiene	60	Neat	Medium
		Sani-Queen	Comfort	25	N/A	Medium
		Hydrothera	Hygiene	70	Neat	Medium
		Hydrothera	Comfort	30	N/A	Medium
TV	Join	Monochrome	Fun	20	Lazy	High
		Trottco	Fun	30	Lazy	High
		Soma Plasma	Fun	45	Lazy	High
	Turn Off	All TVs	Energy	220	Neat	Medium
	Turn On	Monochrome	Fun	18	Lazy	High
		Trottco	Fun	35	Lazy	High
		Soma Plasma	Fun	49	Lazy	High
	Watch TV	Monochrome	Fun	18	Lazy	High
		Trottco	Fun	28	Lazy	High
		Soma Plasma	Fun	42	Lazy	High
VR Glasses	Play	N/A	Fun	60	Playful	High

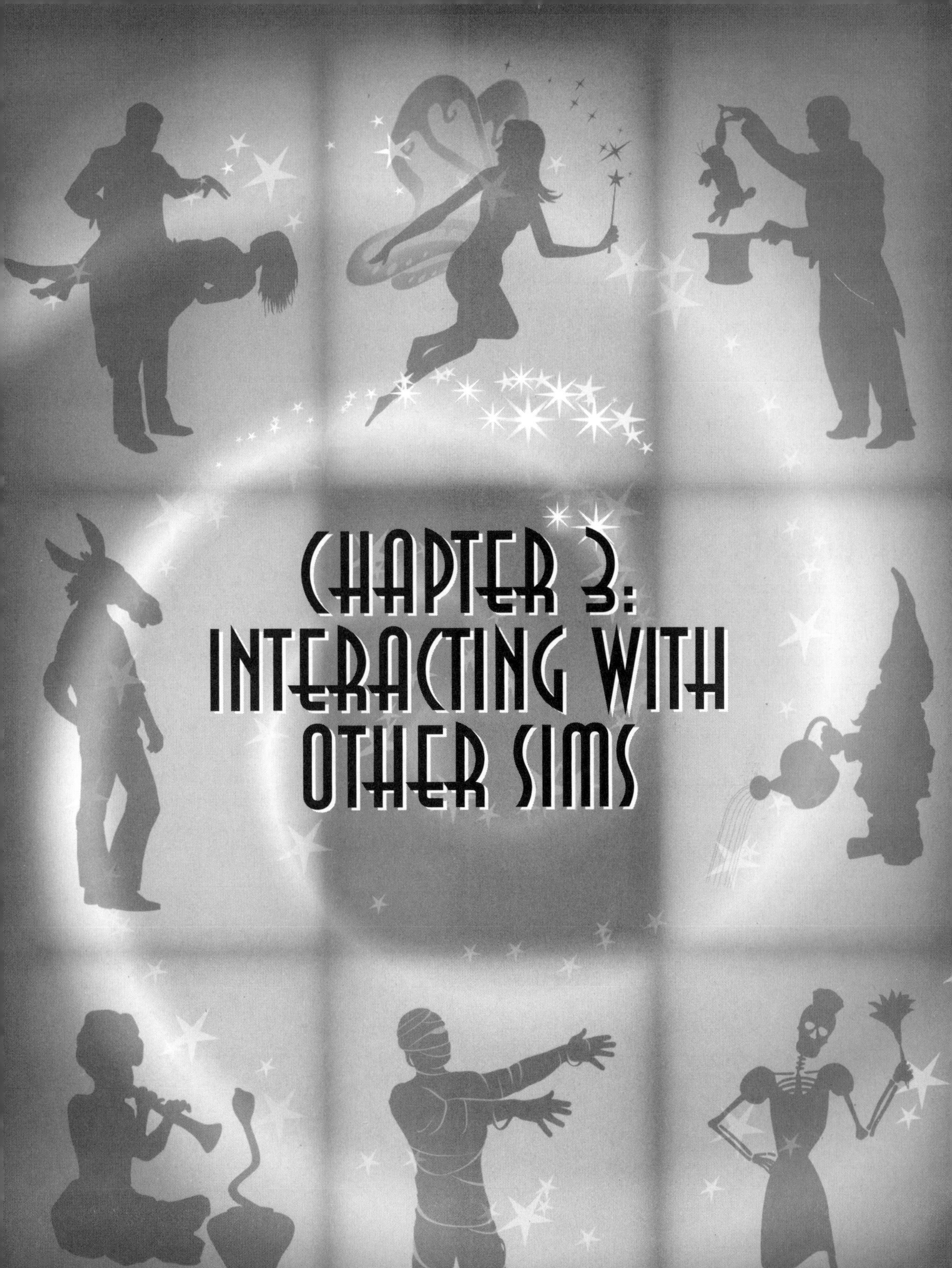
CHAPTER 3:
INTERACTING WITH
OTHER SIMS

Introduction

Once you get beyond the dark attraction of watching jilted Sims slap their rivals, or obnoxious Sims insulting their friends, you realize that Relationships are very important to your Sims' quality of life, and even to the advancement of their careers. In this chapter, we introduce you to the world of Relationships, covering the possible events that occur when two Sims come together verbally or physically. Our goal here is to lay down the ground rules. We'll offer hands-on tips for building and maintaining Relationships in the "All in the Family" chapter.

Relationship Scores

Icons representing a Sim's friendships, or lack thereof, appear in the screen's lower-right corner when you click on the Relationships icon (just above the Job icon). The scoring system ranges from below 0 (not good) to 100, which is reserved for one or more significant others. A relationship is considered a true friendship if the score climbs above 50. Only these Relationships are considered when the game calculates career advancements. Consult the next chapter, "9 to 5—Climbing the Career Ladder," for more information on promotion requirements.

Fig. 3-1. This Sim Dad is clicking on all cylinders with his wife, but he needs to spend more time with the kids.

Social Interactions

All Sim Relationships develop from Social interactions. If you don't spend quality time with your friends, the Relationships will deteriorate on their own, at a rate of two points per day. Of course, if you interact poorly, the rate accelerates dramatically. In the following sections, we review the myriad communication choices that are available during the game (grouped alphabetically by the active action). At any given time, your choice will vary, depending upon the level of your friendship, and whether or not your Sim is acting like a jerk!

Good Old Conversation

The easiest way to cultivate a new friendship is to talk. Sims communicate with each other using Sim-Speak, a delightful chatter that you actually begin to understand (yes, we have played this game way too much!). Adults and kids have favorite topics within their peer groups. These topics are randomly assigned by the game during the Sim creation process. Additionally, kids and adults have special cross-generational topics that are only used with each other. Active topics are displayed in thought balloons during the game, as shown in figure 3-2.

Fig. 3-2. Pets are a good common ground for conversation between adults and kids.

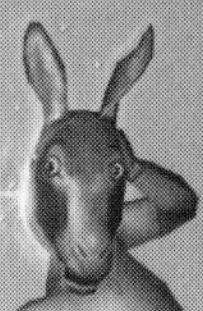

When a conversation is going well, you see a green plus sign over one or both of the Sims. Conversely, when talk deteriorates into the gutter, you'll see red minus signs. The following tables list positive and negative communications, including each potential outcome and the corresponding effect on Social and Relationship scores. For our purposes, an outcome is positive if it produces an increase in one or both scores. When scores drop or stay the same, it is considered a negative outcome.

Fig. 3-3. When two or more people enter a hot tub, the conversations begin spontaneously.

Positive Communications

Interaction	Response	Relationship Change	Social Score Change
Apologize	Accept	10	15
Be Apologized To	Accept	10	15
Brag	Good	5	13
Be Bragged To	Good	5	7
Cheer Up	Good	5	7
Cheer Up	Neutral	0	5
Be Cheered Up	Good	10	10
Be Cheered Up	Neutral	0	5
Compliment	Accept	5	5
Be Complimented	Accept	5	11
Entertain	Laugh	4	7
Be Entertained	Laugh	8	13
Flirt	Good	5	13
Be Flirted With	Good	10	13
Joke	Laugh	5	13
Joke	Giggle	2	7
Listen to Joke	Laugh	7	13
Listen to Joke	Giggle	3	7
Scare	Laugh	5	10
TalkHigh Interest	Topic	3	5
TalkLike	Topic	3	5
Group Talk	N/A	1	8
Tease	Giggle	5	7

Negative Communications

INTERACTION	RESPONSE	RELATIONSHIP CHANGE	SOCIAL SCORE CHANGE
Apologize	Reject	-10	0
Be Apologized To	Reject	-10	0
Brag	Bad	-5	0
Be Bragged To	Bad	-5	0
Cheer Up	Bad	-3	0
Be Cheered Up	Bad	-10	0
Compliment	Reject	-10	0
Be Complimented	Reject	-7	0
Entertain	Boo	-15	0
Be Entertained	Boo	-7	0
Flirt	Refuse	-10	-17
Flirt	Ignore	-5	0
Be Flirted With	Refuse	-10	0
Be Flirted With	Ignore	0	0
Insult	Cry	5	0
Insult	Stoic	0	3
Insult	Angry	-10	7
Be Insulted	Cry	-12	-13
Be Insulted	Stoic	-5	-5
Be Insulted	Angry	-14	-7
Joke	Uninterested	-6	0
Listen to Joke	Uninterested	-7	0
Scare	Angry	-5	0
Be Scared	Angry	-10	0
TalkDislike	Topic	-3	3
TalkHate	Topic	-3	3
Tease	Cry	-4	0
Be Teased	Cry	-13	-7

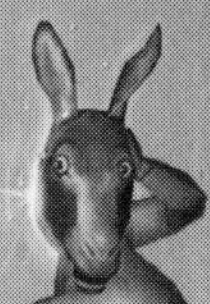

Physical Contact

When a Relationship moves past the 50-point threshold, you begin to see new options on the Social interaction menu. Instead of just talking, you find new items including Hug, Give Back Rub, Flirt, and Kiss. It all depends upon how your Relationship is progressing and what the other Sim is looking for in the current interaction. The following tables include information on positive and negative physical events.

Positive Physical Events

Interaction	Response	Relationship Change	Social Score Change
Give Back Rub	Good	5	7
Receive Back Rub	Good	9	13
Dance	Accept	8	13
Be Danced With	Accept	10	13
Give Gift	Accept	5	7
Receive Gift	Accept	10	13
Hug	Good	7	15
Hug	Tentative	2	7
Be Hugged	Good	8	15
Be Hugged	Tentative	4	7
Kiss	Passion	12	20
Kiss	Polite	5	10
Be Kissed	Passion	12	20
Be Kissed	Polite	5	10
Tickle	Accept	5	13
Be Tickled	Accept	8	13

Negative Physical Events

INTERACTION	RESPONSE	RELATIONSHIP CHANGE	SOCIAL SCORE CHANGE
Attack	Win Fight	-5	10
Attack	Lose Fight	-10	-20
Give Back Rub	Bad	-7	0
Receive Back Rub	Bad	-10	0
Dance	Refuse	-5	0
Be Danced With	Refuse	-5	0
Give Gift	Stomp	-15	0
Receive Gift	Stomp	-5	0
Hug	Refuse	-10	0
Be Hugged	Refuse	-10	0
Kiss	Deny	-15	5
Be Kissed	Deny	-10	0
Slap	Cry	0	3
Slap	Slap Back	-10	-7
Be Slapped	Cry	-20	-17
Be Slapped	Slap Back	-15	7
Tickle	Refuse	-5	0
Be Tickled	Refuse	-8	0

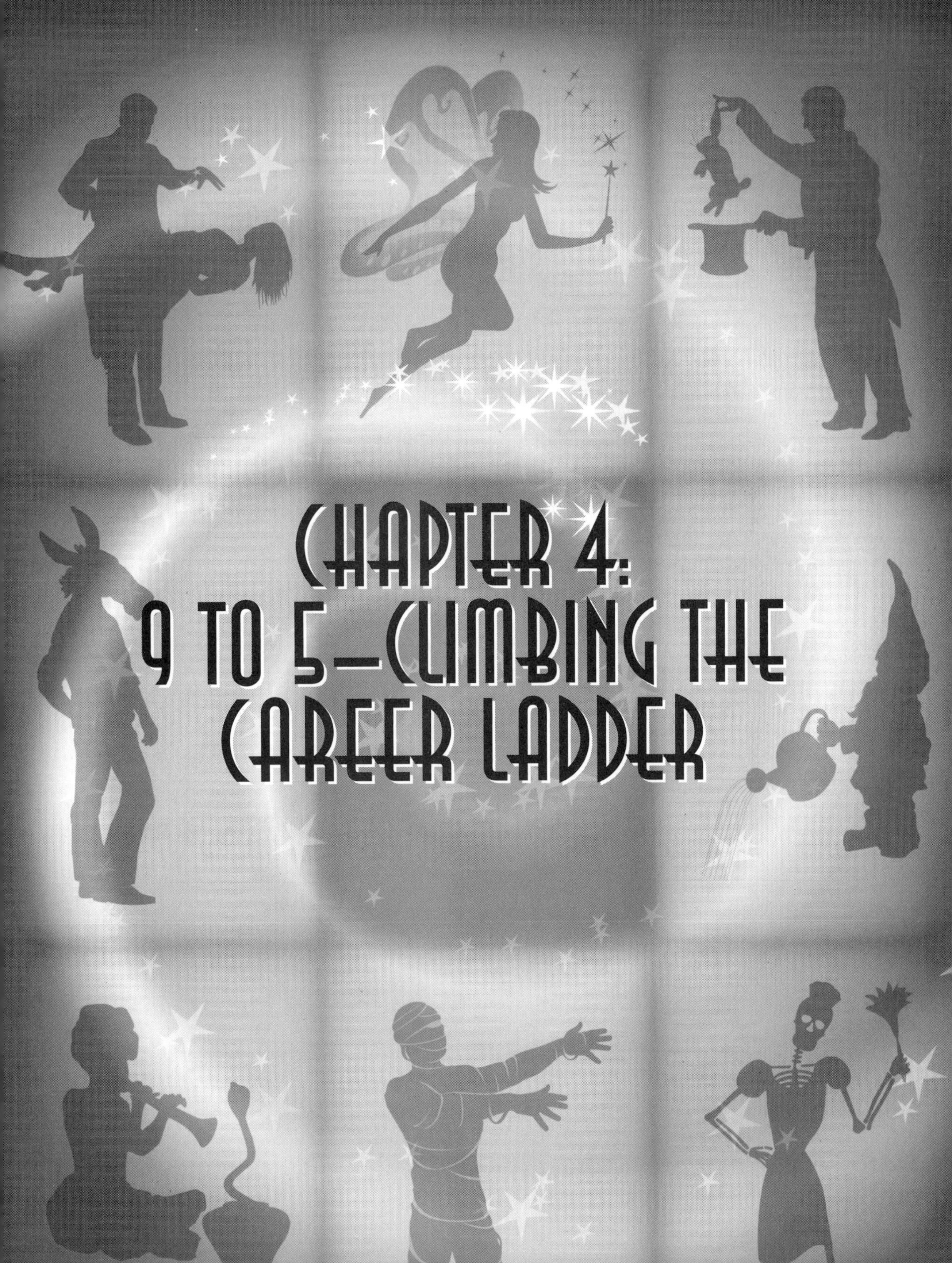

CHAPTER 4:
9 TO 5—CLIMBING THE CAREER LADDER

Introduction

When you first start playing *The Sims*, it's easy to get lost in the element. There's so much to explore and experience, and with more than enough money to furnish your house and buy a few toys, you can just hang out and live the good Sim-life. But, reality sets in sooner than you would like, and you must find a job. In this chapter we show you how to select a career, nurture the Skills necessary to earn the first few promotions, and finally, stockpile enough friends (it's called networking) to make the big bucks and zoom to the top of your field. For easy reference, we include comprehensive career tables that contain everything you need to know about the 10 Sim careers, including advancement requirements for all 10 pay levels.

Your First Job

Every Sim house receives a daily copy of the *Sim City Times* that includes a single job posting. You can take the first job you see, or buy a computer and view three jobs a day. There is no rush—you have enough money to get by for several days.

Fig. 4-1. Today's job posting is for a test driver.

TIP

You can enjoy the free use of a computer by buying it, checking the want ads, and then returning it the same day for a full refund. Keep this up until you find the job you want. Then, later when you have more disposable cash, you can buy—and keep—a computer.

A Military job is usually available on the computer. This is an excellent first career, with a starting salary of §250. Furthermore, it remains the highest paying of the 10 careers through the first three advances. A Law Enforcement position is a close second.

Fig. 4-2. This two-commando family takes home §325 each as members of the Elite Forces (Level 2—Military Career).

If you would rather take your time and sort through all 10 job tracks, the following table will help you choose a career that is suited to your Sim's personality traits.

Career Choices

CAREER TRACK	NECESSARY SKILLS	RELATED PERSONALITY TRAITS
Business	Logic, Charisma	Outgoing
Entertainment	Charisma, Creativity	Outgoing, Playful
Law Enforcement	Logic, Body	Active
Life of Crime	Creativity, Charisma	Playful, Outgoing
Medicine	Logic, Body	Active
Military	Repair, Body	Active
Politics	Charisma, Logic	Outgoing
Pro Athlete	Body, Charisma	Active, Outgoing
Science	Logic, Creativity	Playful
Xtreme	Creativity, Body/Charisma (tie)	Playful, Active, Outgoing

Developing Your Skills

After you decide on a career, focus on developing the appropriate Skills needed for advancement. It is important to remember that Sims do not study on their own. You need to direct your Sim to one of the activities listed in the Skill Enhancement table on the following page.

TIP

On the control panel, click on the Job icon to display your Sim's current Skill bars (see figure 4-3). A white line designates the minimum level of Skill needed for the next promotion. Other factors contribute to earning a promotion, but without the Skill requirement, you have absolutely no chance for advancement to the next level.

Fig. 4-3. This Sim needs to boost his Body Skill one more notch, so he is scheduled for a session on the exercise machine right after lunch.

Skill Enhancement

SKILL	METHOD OF ENHANCEMENT	NOTES
Cooking	Bookshelf (Study Cooking)	Any type of bookshelf will suffice.
Mechanical	Bookshelf (Study Mechanical)	Any type of bookshelf will suffice.
Body	Exercise Machine (Work Out)	Exercise machine increases Skill four times faster than the pool. Active Sims improve their Skill at a higher rate.
	Pool (Swim)	See above.
Charisma	Mirrors or Medicine Cabinet (Practice Speech)	Outgoing Sims acquire Skill more quickly.
	Easel (Paint)	Playful Sims acquire Skill more quickly.
	Piano (Play)	Playful Sims acquire Skill more quickly.
Logic	Chessboard (Play)	Playing with another Sim generates Social points.

Fig. 4-4. A session on the exercise bench nets a Body point for this Sim.

Sim Career Tracks

The following tables include the salaries, hours, car pool vehicles, and job level requirements for each level of the 10 Sim career tracks. The Daily Motive Decay value shows which Motives deteriorate while the Sim is on the job.

equirements for Level 1 Positions

REER ACK	POSITION	PAY	HOURS	CAR POOL VEHICLE	COOKING	REPAIR	CHARISMA	BODY	LOGIC	CREATIVITY	FAMILY/ FRIENDS	DAILY MOTIVE DECAY HUNGER	COMFORT	HYGIENE	BLADDER	ENERGY	FUN	SOCIAL
siness	Mail Room	§120	9 a.m. –3 p.m	Junker	0	0	0	0	0	0	0	0	0	0	0	-30	0	0
tertainment	Waiter Waitress	§100	9 a.m. –3 p.m.	Junker	0	0	0	0	0	0	0	0	0	0	0	-30	0	0
w forcement	Security Guard	§240	12 a.m. –6 a.m.	Squad Car	0	0	0	0	0	0	0	0	0	0	0	-30	0	0
fe of Crime	Pickpocket	§140	9 a.m. –3 p.m.	Junker	0	0	0	0	0	0	0	0	0	0	0	-30	0	0
edicine	Medical Technician	§200	9 a.m. –3 p.m.	Junker	0	0	0	0	0	0	0	0	0	0	0	-30	0	0
ilitary	Recruit	§250	6 a.m. –12 p.m.	Military Jeep	0	0	0	0	0	0	0	0	0	-15	0	-30	0	0
litics	Campaign Work	§220	9 a.m. –6 p.m.	Junker	0	0	0	0	0	0	0	0	0	0	0	-30	0	0
o Athlete	Team Mascot	§110	12 p.m. –6 p.m.	Junker	0	0	0	0	0	0	0	0	0	-5	0	-35	0	0
ience	Test Subject	§155	9 a.m. –3 p.m.	Junker	0	0	0	0	0	0	0	0	0	0	0	-30	0	0
treme	Daredevil	§175	9 a.m. –3 p.m.	Junker	0	0	0	0	0	0	0	0	0	0	0	-30	0	0

equirements for Level 2 Positions

AREER ACK	POSITION	PAY	HOURS	CAR POOL VEHICLE	COOKING	REPAIR	CHARISMA	BODY	LOGIC	CREATIVITY	FAMILY/ FRIENDS	DAILY MOTIVE DECAY HUNGER	COMFORT	HYGIENE	BLADDER	ENERGY	FUN	SOCIAL
siness	Executive Assistant	§180	9 a.m. –4 p.m	Junker	0	0	0	0	0	0	0	0	0	0	0	-34	-2	0
ntertainment	Extra	§150	9 a.m. –3 p.m.	Junker	0	0	0	0	0	0	0	0	0	0	0	-34	-2	0
aw nforcement	Cadet	§320	9 a.m. –3 p.m.	Squad Car	0	0	0	0	0	0	0	0	0	0	0	-34	-2	0
fe of Crime	Bagman	§200	11 p.m. –7 a.m.	Junker	0	0	0	0	0	0	0	0	0	0	0	-34	-2	0
edicine	Paramedic	§275	11 p.m. –5 a.m.	Junker	0	0	0	0	0	0	0	0	0	0	0	-34	-2	0
ilitary	Elite Forces	§325	7 a.m. –1 p.m.	Military Jeep	0	0	0	0	0	0	0	0	0	-15	0	-34	-2	0
olitics	Intern	§300	9 a.m. –3 p.m.	Junker	0	0	0	0	0	0	0	0	0	0	0	-34	-2	0
ro Athlete	Minor Leaguer	§170	9 a.m. –3 p.m.	Junker	0	0	0	0	0	0	0	0	0	-10	0	-40	-2	0
cience	Lab Assistant	§230	11 p.m. –5 a.m.	Junker	0	0	0	0	0	0	0	0	0	0	0	-34	-2	0
treme	Bungee Jump Instructor	§250	9 a.m. –3 p.m.	Junker	0	0	0	0	0	0	0	0	0	0	0	-34	-2	0

Requirements for Level 3 Positions

Career Track	Position	Pay	Hours	Car Pool Vehicle	Cooking	Repair	Charisma	Body	Logic	Creativity	Family/ Friends	Daily Motive Decay: Hunger	Comfort	Hygiene	Bladder	Energy	Fun	Social
Business	Field Sales Rep	§250	9 a.m. –4 p.m.	Junker	0	2	0	0	0	0	0	-3	0	-5	0	-38	-4	0
Entertainment	Bit Player	§200	9 a.m. –3 p.m.	Junker	0	0	2	0	0	0	0	-3	0	-5	0	-38	-4	0
Law Enforcement	Patrol Officer	§380	5 p.m. –1 a.m.	Squad Car	0	0	0	2	0	0	0	-3	0	-5	0	-38	-4	0
Life of Crime	Bookie	§275	12 p.m. –7 p.m.	Standard Car	0	0	0	2	0	0	0	-3	0	-5	0	-38	-4	0
Medicine	Nurse	§340	9 a.m. –3 p.m.	Standard Car	0	2	0	0	0	0	0	-3	0	-5	0	-38	-4	0
Military	Drill Instructor	§250	8 a.m. –2 p.m.	Military Jeep	0	0	0	2	0	0	0	-3	0	-20	0	-38	-4	0
Politics	Lobbyist	§360	9 a.m. –3 p.m.	Standard Car	0	0	2	0	0	0	0	-3	0	-5	0	-38	-4	0
Pro Athlete	Rookie	§230	9 a.m. –3 p.m.	Junker	0	0	0	2	0	0	0	-3	0	-15	0	-45	-2	0
Science	Field Researcher	§320	9 a.m. –3 p.m.	Standard Car	0	0	0	0	2	0	0	-3	0	-5	0	-38	-4	0
Xtreme	Whitewater Guide	§325	9 a.m. –3 p.m.	SUV	0	0	0	2	0	0	1	-3	0	-10	0	-45	-4	0

Requirements for Level 4 Positions

Career Track	Position	Pay	Hours	Car Pool Vehicle	Cooking	Repair	Charisma	Body	Logic	Creativity	Family/ Friends	Daily Motive Decay: Hunger	Comfort	Hygiene	Bladder	Energy	Fun	Social
Business	Junior Executive	§320	9 a.m. –4 p.m.	Standard Car	0	2	2	0	0	0	1	-7	0	-10	0	-42	-7	0
Entertainment	Stunt Double	§275	9 a.m. –4 p.m.	Standard Car	0	0	2	2	0	0	2	-7	0	-10	0	-42	-7	0
Law Enforcement	Desk Sergeant	§440	9 a.m. –3 p.m.	Squad Car	0	2	0	2	0	0	1	-7	0	-10	0	-42	-7	0
Life of Crime	Con Artist	§350	9 a.m. –3 p.m.	Standard Car	0	0	1	2	0	1	2	-7	0	-10	0	-42	-7	0
Medicine	Intern	§410	9 a.m. –6 p.m.	Standard Car	0	2	0	2	0	0	2	-7	0	-10	0	-42	-7	0
Military	Junior Officer	§450	9 a.m. –3 p.m.	Military Jeep	0	1	2	2	0	0	0	-7	0	-20	0	-42	-8	0
Politics	Campaign Manager	§430	9 a.m. –6 p.m.	Standard Car	0	0	2	0	1	0	2	-7	0	-10	0	-42	-7	0
Pro Athlete	Starter	§300	9 a.m. –3 p.m.	Standard Car	0	0	0	5	0	0	1	-7	0	-20	0	-50	-2	0
Science	Science Teacher	§375	9 a.m. –4 p.m.	Standard Car	0	0	1	0	3	0	1	-7	0	-10	0	-40	-7	0
Xtreme	Xtreme Circuit Pro	§400	9 a.m. –3 p.m.	SUV	0	1	0	4	0	0	2	-7	0	-20	0	-50	-2	0

Requirements for Level 5 Positions

reer ack	Position	Pay	Hours	Car Pool Vehicle	Cooking	Repair	Charisma	Body	Logic	Creativity	Family/ Friends	Daily Motive Decay: Hunger	Comfort	Hygiene	Bladder	Energy	Fun	Social
usiness	Executive	§400	9 a.m. –4 p.m.	Standard Car	0	2	2	0	2	0	3	-10	0	-15	0	-46	-10	0
tertainment	B-Movie Star	§375	10 a.m. –5 p.m.	Standard Car	0	0	3	3	0	1	4	-10	0	-15	0	-46	-10	0
w nforcement	Vice Squad	§490	10 p.m. –4 a.m.	Squad Car	0	3	0	4	0	0	2	-10	0	-15	0	-46	-10	0
fe of Crime	Getaway Driver	§425	5 p.m. –1 a.m.	Standard Car	0	2	1	2	0	2	3	-10	0	-10	0	-46	-10	0
edicine	Resident	§480	9 p.m. –4 a.m.	Standard Car	0	3	0	2	2	0	3	-10	0	-15	0	-46	-10	0
ilitary	Counter-Intelligence	§500	9 a.m. –3 p.m.	Military Jeep	1	1	2	4	0	0	0	-10	0	-25	0	-46	-12	0
litics	City Council Member	§485	9 a.m. –3 p.m.	Town Car	0	0	3	1	1	0	4	-10	0	-15	0	-46	-8	0
o Athlete	All-Star	§385	9 a.m. –3 p.m.	SUV	0	1	1	6	0	0	3	-10	0	-25	0	-55	-3	0
cience	Project Leader	§450	9 a.m. –5 p.m.	Standard Car	0	0	2	0	4	1	3	-10	0	-12	0	-43	-8	0
treme	Bush Pilot	§475	9 a.m. –3 p.m.	SUV	1	2	0	4	1	0	3	-10	0	-15	0	-46	-5	-10

Requirements for Level 6 Positions

areer rack	Position	Pay	Hours	Car Pool Vehicle	Cooking	Repair	Charisma	Body	Logic	Creativity	Family/ Friends	Daily Motive Decay: Hunger	Comfort	Hygiene	Bladder	Energy	Fun	Social
usiness	Senior Manager	§520	9 a.m. –4 p.m.	Standard Car	0	2	3	0	3	2	6	-14	0	-20	0	-50	-13	0
ntertainment	Supporting Player	§500	10 a.m. –6 p.m.	Limo	0	1	4	4	0	2	6	-14	0	-20	0	-50	-13	0
aw nforcement	Detective	§540	9 a.m. –3 p.m.	Squad Car	1	3	1	5	1	0	4	-14	0	-20	0	-50	-13	0
ife of Crime	Bank Robber	§530	3 p.m. –11 p.m.	Town Car	0	3	2	3	1	2	4	-14	0	-15	0	-50	-13	-5
edicine	GP	§550	10 a.m. –6 p.m.	Town Car	0	3	1	3	4	0	4	-14	0	-20	0	-50	-13	0
ilitary	Flight Officer	§550	9 a.m. –3 p.m.	Military Jeep	1	2	4	4	1	0	1	-14	0	-28	0	-50	-15	0
olitics	State Assembly-person	§540	9 a.m. –4 p.m.	Town Car	0	0	4	2	1	1	6	-14	0	-20	0	-50	-12	-3
ro Athlete	MVP	§510	9 a.m. –3 p.m.	SUV	0	2	2	7	0	0	5	-14	0	-30	0	-60	-4	0
cience	Inventor	§540	10 a.m. –7 p.m.	Town Car	0	2	2	0	4	3	4	-14	0	-15	0	-45	-9	-8
treme	Mountain Climber	§550	9 a.m. –3 p.m.	SUV	1	4	0	6	1	0	4	-14	0	-30	0	-60	0	0

Requirements for Level 7 Positions

Career Track	Position	Pay	Hours	Car Pool Vehicle	Cooking	Repair	Charisma	Body	Logic	Creativity	Family/ Friends	Daily Motive Decay: Hunger	Comfort	Hygiene	Bladder	Energy	Fun	Social
Business	Vice President	§660	9 a.m. –5 p.m.	Town Car	0	2	4	2	4	2	8	-18	0	-25	0	-54	-16	0
Entertainment	TV Star	§650	10 a.m. –6 p.m.	Limo	0	1	6	5	0	3	8	-18	0	-25	0	-54	-16	0
Law Enforcement	Lieutenant	§590	9 a.m. –3 p.m.	Limo	1	3	2	5	3	1	6	-18	0	-25	0	-54	-16	0
Life of Crime	Cat Burglar	§640	9 p.m. –3 a.m.	Town Car	1	3	2	5	2	3	6	-18	0	-20	0	-54	-16	0
Medicine	Specialist	§625	10 p.m. –4 a.m.	Town Car	0	4	2	4	4	1	5	-18	0	-25	0	-54	-16	0
Military	Senior Officer	§580	9 a.m. –3 p.m.	Military Jeep	1	3	4	5	3	0	3	-18	0	-31	0	-55	-20	0
Politics	Congress-person	§600	9 a.m. –3 p.m.	Town Car	0	0	4	3	3	2	9	-18	0	-25	0	-54	-18	-7
Pro Athlete	Superstar	§680	9 a.m. –4 p.m.	SUV	1	2	3	8	0	0	7	-18	0	-35	0	-65	-5	0
Science	Scholar	§640	10 a.m. –3 p.m.	Town Car	0	4	2	0	6	4	5	-18	0	-20	0	-48	-10	-10
Xtreme	Photo-journalist	§650	9 a.m. –3 p.m.	SUV	1	5	2	6	1	3	5	-18	0	-25	0	-54	-16	0

Requirements for Level 8 Positions

Career Track	Position	Pay	Hours	Car Pool Vehicle	Cooking	Repair	Charisma	Body	Logic	Creativity	Family/ Friends	Daily Motive Decay: Hunger	Comfort	Hygiene	Bladder	Energy	Fun	Social
Business	President	§800	9 a.m. –5 p.m.	Town Car	0	2	5	2	6	3	10	-22	0	-30	0	-58	-19	0
Entertainment	Feature Star	§900	5 p.m. –1 a.m.	Limo	0	2	7	6	0	4	10	-22	0	-30	0	-58	-19	0
Law Enforcement	SWAT Team Leader	§625	9 a.m. –3 p.m.	Limo	1	4	3	6	5	1	8	-22	0	-30	0	-58	-19	0
Life of Crime	Counterfeiter	§760	9 p.m. –3 a.m.	Town Car	1	5	2	5	3	5	8	-22	0	-25	0	-58	-19	-15
Medicine	Surgeon	§700	10 p.m. –4 a.m.	Town Car	0	4	3	5	6	2	7	-22	0	-30	0	-58	-19	0
Military	Commander	§600	9 a.m. –3 p.m.	Military Jeep	1	6	5	5	5	0	5	-22	0	-33	0	-60	-25	0
Politics	Judge	§650	9 a.m. –3 p.m.	Town Car	0	0	5	4	4	3	11	-22	0	-30	0	-58	-22	-11
Pro Athlete	Assistant Coach	§850	9 a.m. –2 p.m.	SUV	2	2	4	9	0	1	9	-22	0	-40	0	-70	-6	0
Science	Top Secret Researcher	§740	10 a.m. –3 p.m.	Town Car	1	6	4	0	7	4	7	-22	0	-25	0	-52	-12	-13
Xtreme	Treasure Hunter	§725	10 a.m. –5 p.m.	SUV	1	6	3	7	3	4	7	-22	0	-34	0	-60	-15	-5

'equirements for Level 9 Positions

REER ACK	POSITION	PAY	HOURS	CAR POOL VEHICLE	COOKING	REPAIR	CHARISMA	BODY	LOGIC	CREATIVITY	FAMILY/ FRIENDS	DAILY MOTIVE DECAY HUNGER	COMFORT	HYGIENE	BLADDER	ENERGY	FUN	SOCIAL
siness	CEO	§950	9 a.m. –4 p.m.	Limo	0	2	6	2	7	5	12	-26	0	-35	0	-62	-22	0
tertainment	Broadway Star	§1100	10 a.m. –5 p.m.	Limo	0	2	8	7	0	7	12	-26	0	-35	0	-62	-22	0
w forcement	Police Chief	§650	9 a.m. –5 p.m.	Limo	1	4	4	7	7	3	10	-26	0	-35	0	-62	-22	0
fe of Crime	Smuggler	§900	9 a.m. –3 p.m.	Town Car	1	5	5	6	3	6	10	-26	0	-30	0	-62	-22	-20
edicine	Medical Researcher	§775	9 p.m. –4 a.m.	Limo	0	5	4	6	8	3	9	-26	0	-35	0	-62	-22	0
litary	Astronaut	§625	9 a.m. –3 p.m.	Limo	1	9	5	8	6	0	6	-26	0	-35	0	-65	-30	0
litics	Senator	§700	9 a.m. –6 p.m.	Limo	0	0	6	5	6	4	14	-26	0	-35	0	-62	-26	-15
o Athlete	Coach	§1,000	9 a.m. –3 p.m.	SUV	3	2	6	10	0	2	11	-26	0	-45	0	-75	-8	0
ience	Theorist	§870	10 a.m. –2 p.m.	Town Car	1	7	4	0	9	7	8	-26	0	-30	0	-56	-16	-16
reme	Grand Prix Driver	§825	10 a.m. –4 p.m.	Bentley	1	6	5	7	5	7	9	-26	0	-35	0	-62	-5	-10

equirements for Level 10 Positions

REER ACK	POSITION	PAY	HOURS	CAR POOL VEHICLE	COOKING	REPAIR	CHARISMA	BODY	LOGIC	CREATIVITY	FAMILY/ FRIENDS	DAILY MOTIVE DECAY HUNGER	COMFORT	HYGIENE	BLADDER	ENERGY	FUN	SOCIAL
usiness	Business Tycoon	§1,200	9 a.m. –3 p.m.	Limo	0	2	8	2	9	6	14	-30	0	-40	0	-66	-25	0
ntertainment	Super-star	§1,400	10 a.m. –3 p.m.	Limo	0	2	10	8	0	10	14	-30	0	-40	0	-66	-25	0
aw nforcement	Captain Hero	§700	10 a.m. –4 p.m.	Limo	1	4	6	7	10	5	12	-20	-80	-45	-25	-60	0	0
fe of Crime	Criminal Mastermind	§1,100	6 p.m. –12 a.m.	Limo	2	5	7	6	4	8	12	-30	0	-35	0	-66	-25	-25
edicine	Chief of Staff	§850	9 p.m. –4 a.m.	Hospital Limo	0	6	6	7	9	4	11	-30	0	-40	0	-66	-25	0
ilitary	General	§650	9 a.m. –3 p.m.	Staff Sedan	1	10	7	10	9	0	8	-30	0	-40	0	-70	-35	0
olitics	Mayor	§750	9 a.m. –3 p.m	Limo	0	0	9	5	7	5	17	-30	0	-40	0	-66	-30	-20
ro Athlete	Hall of Famer	§1,300	9 a.m. –3 p.m.	Limo	4	2	9	10	0	3	13	-30	0	-50	0	-80	-10	0
cience	Mad Scientist	§1,000	10 a.m. –2 p.m.	Limo	2	8	5	0	10	10	10	-30	0	-35	0	-60	-20	-20
treme	International	§925	11 a.m. –5 p.m.	Bentley	2	6	8	8	6	9	11	-30	0	-30	0	-70	-20	-15

The Daily Grind

A working Sim needs to follow a schedule that is conducive to good job performance. Review the following tips as you devise a work schedule for your household.

Get Plenty of Sleep

Sims need to awake refreshed in order to arrive at work in a good mood. Send your Sims to bed early, and make sure there are no distractions (stereos, TVs, computers, etc.) that might interrupt their beauty sleep.

Fig. 4-5. Make sure your Sims get to bed early enough to restore maximum Energy before the alarm rings.

Set Your Alarm Clock

When set, the clock wakes your Sims two hours before the car pool arrives (one alarm clock takes care of the entire house). This is plenty of time to take care of Hunger, Bladder, and Hygiene Motive bars. If you still have time, improve your Sim's mood with a little non-strenuous fun like watching TV, or use the extra time to improve a Skill.

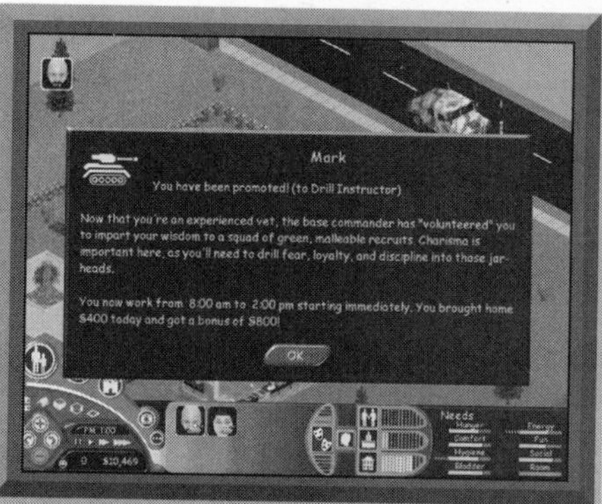

Fig. 4-6. That last set on the exercise bench paid off!

CAUTION

If two or more Sims in the house have jobs, the alarm clock rings for the earliest riser. Unfortunately, this wakes everyone else, regardless of when they have to be ready for the car pool. If you send the other Sims back to bed, you'll need to wake them manually, because the alarm clock only rings once each day.

Eat a Hearty Breakfast

When you're angling for a promotion, you need to arrive at work with all cylinders firing. When the alarm rings, send the designated house chef (the Sim with the highest Cooking Skill) to the kitchen to "Prepare a Meal." By the time your Sim is finished emptying his Bladder and completing necessary Hygiene, breakfast will be on the counter. There should be plenty of time to complete the meal and head to work with a full Hunger bar.

TIP

Make sure that your Sim is on the first floor and relatively close to the car pool within 15 minutes of departure to be sure he or she catches his or her ride. If you meet this deadline, your Sim will change clothes on the fly and sprint to the curb.

Aake Friends and Influence Your Boss

.dvancing through the first three levels does not arry a friendship requirement; however this ramps p very quickly. It helps to have a stay-at-home nate to concentrate on making friends. Remember hat the career friendship requirement is for your ousehold, not your Sim. So, if your mate or hildren have friends, they count toward your romotions, too.

Fig. 4-7. This Sim is just about out of Energy, but his Social score is maxed out and he's just made two new friends.

'ake an Occasional Day Off to Recharge

f you find that your Sim is unable to have enough un or Social events to maintain a positive mood, kip a day of work and indulge. See a friend or wo, work on Skills, or have some Fun. Just don't niss two days in a row or your Sim will be utomatically fired!

Aajor Decisions

As you work your way up the career ladder, you encounter "major decisions" that involve various degrees of risk. They are winner-take-all, loser-gets-nada events that force you to gamble with 'our salary, integrity, or even your job. The ollowing sections include a sample "major decision" for each career.

Business

Major decision: "Stock Option"

Player is given the choice of accepting a portfolio of company stock instead of salary for that pay period. The stock could double or tank. As a result, the player receives twice his salary or nothing at all for the pay period.

Entertainment

Major decision: "The Remake"

Your agent calls with an offer: Sim Studios wants you for the lead in a remake of *Citizen Kane*. Accepting will either send your Charisma sky high when the film succeeds wildly...or send it crashing if the turkey flops.

Law Enforcement

Major decision: "The Bribe"

A mobster you're investigating offers a huge bribe to drop the case. The charges won't stick without your testimony and you *could* suddenly "lose the evidence" and quietly pocket a nice nest egg...or get busted by Internal Affairs and have to start over on a new career track.

Life of Crime

Major decision: "The Perfect Crime"

You've just been handed a hot tip that an informant claims will be an easy knockover with loads of cash for the taking. Either the tip is gold, or it's a police sting. An arrest means your family is left at home alone while you're sent off to cool your heels in Sim City Prison for a while. If you succeed, your Charisma and Creativity Skills are enhanced.

Medicine

Major Decision: "Malpractice"

A former patient has slapped you with a massive malpractice suit. You can settle immediately by offering a payment equal to 50 percent of the cash in your household account. Or, take the bum to court. Lose, and all your furniture and household goods are repossessed. Win, and you receive a settlement equal to 100 percent of the cash in your household account.

Military

Major decision: "Gung Ho"

The general needs volunteers for a highly dangerous mission. You can refuse without penalty. If you accept, and succeed on the mission, you are decorated and immediately promoted to the next level. Failure means a demotion, soldier—you're broken down to the previous level.

Politics

Major decision: "Scandal"

An attractive young member of your team also happens to be heir to a fortune. He or she will finance your career advancement if you agree to "private consultations." You can refuse, with no change in status. Otherwise, there are two possible outcomes. You might get away with it and immediately advance *two* levels. If you're caught, you'll lose your friends when the scandal breaks in the media, and you'll be tossed from the career track to seek another.

Pro Athlete

Major Decision: "The Supermatch"

A one-on-one, pay-per-view contest pitting you against your greatest local rival is offered. If you win, it's worth double your paycheck. If you lose, the indignity comes complete with an injury costing you a reduction in your Body Skill along with a drop in Charisma. The player can always refuse at no penalty.

Science

Major decision: "The Experiment"

A science research firm is willing to pay you a fat bonus for conducting a complex experiment. However, the work must be conducted at your home, using rats as test subjects. Success means you collect the fee, with a bonus increase in your Logic Skill level. A failed experiment results in a dozen rats escaping into your home. That means a major bill from both your exterminator and your electrician (the rats have chewed through power cords.) Financial damage could be reduced if the Player's Repair Skills are strong.

Xtreme

Major decision: "Deep Freeze"

An arctic expedition is holding a spot open for you. It's a risky enterprise, so you may refuse. However, for a person in your particular line of work, that refusal will lower your Charisma. If you join the team, and they reach their goal, you will be rewarded with a considerable rise in Charisma. If the mission goes awry, your Sim is "lost on an iceberg" for a period of game time.

CHAPTER 5:
BUILDING A HOUSE

Introduction

Anyone who has ever built a home knows that the best laid plans of architects can sometimes turn into a house of horrors when the walls start going up. The same holds true in *The Sims*, where you have enough power to build a magnificent dream house or your worst residential nightmare. Limited only by your bank account, you can build a conservative dwelling that is functional above all else, or you can drop a family of eight in the middle of a meadow with only a bathroom and a refrigerator. It's all possible in *The Sims*, but rest assured that your family will deliver a quick—and sometimes scathing—critique when the clock starts ticking on their simulated lives.

In this chapter, we take you through the house design process from terrain preparation to landscaping. For demonstration purposes, we will use just about every building option available. Obviously, you would need a pile of Simoleans to do this in the game. However, we also cover important design considerations that enable you to maximize your Room score, regardless of your budget. In this chapter, we limit our discussion to the available options in Build Mode only. For detailed descriptions of more than 150 *Sims* objects, see the next chapter.

Of course, our suggestions are just the beginning. Sims thrive on the individuality of their creator, and if you want to build dungeons, sprawling compounds, or one-room huts, you have our support and encouragement. Remember, a bad house is no match for the bulldozer—your next house is only a click away!

TIP

Don't try to build your dream house at the beginning of the game. It's easier to tear down your original house and start over after you've fattened up your bank account.

Design Considerations

Before we introduce you to the various options available in Build Mode, here is a checklist for your basic floor plan. Invariably, your unique family of Sims will make their needs known to yo as the game progresses. However, if you follow these house design basics, you should get your family off to a positive start with a minimum of emotional outbursts.

- **Don't worry about having room to expand. Build your first house to match the number of Sims in your family.**
- **Keep the bathroom centrally located. A door on either side allows quick access for emergencies.**
- **If you start with three Sims or more, build one or more half-bathrooms (toilet and sink only) to ease the crunch.**
- **Place the house close to the street, so you don't have to do the hundred yard dash to meet your car pool.**
- **Allow enough open wall for your kitchen countertops and appliances.**
- **Make your kitchen large enough to accommodate a small table and chairs.**
- **If you don't want a separate den or family room, make one of the bedrooms large enough to handle a computer desk and chair.**

'errain Tools

ı most locations you can build a roomy house on flat piece of land without having to level the ɜrrain. However, if you want to build a house near ıe water or at the edge of a hill, you'll need to mooth the sloping tiles before building a wall or lacing an object. You can also use the Terrain ools to place lush, green grass over patches of dirt. ee the pictures below for examples of each tool.

TIP

The grid lines become noticeably darker when a previously elevated or lowered terrain becomes level.

Grass Tool: Simply click, hold, and drag the Grass Tool to create lawn. You can change back to dirt by holding CTRL + SHIFT and dragging the tool back over the same area.

Level Terrain: Click, hold, and drag the Level Terrain Tool to smooth out one or more tiles of land.

Lower Terrain: When you select the Lower Terrain Tool, each time you click on a tile, the terrain is lowered (so, don't hold the button down unless you want a very deep gully). This tool can have drastic effects on a landscape, so you should use it carefully, one click at a time.

Raise Terrain: The Raise Terrain Tool also works one click at a time, lifting the terrain up. If you hold down the button, the selected tile will rise quickly to its maximum height.

NOTE

Each time you use the Level, Lower, or Raise Terrain Tools, you turn any grass back into dirt. When you are finished altering the terrain, you can use the Grass Tool to quickly restore your beautiful lawn.

Wall and Fence Tools

There are several tools here, but your first step is to "frame" your house. Simply place the cursor at any tile intersection. Then click, hold, and drag to place your wall (figure 5-4). When you release the mouse button, the wood framing will change to the type of wall you selected on the Control Panel (see page 52 for descriptions of wall types).

Fig. 5-4. Drag and release to place a wall.

Although you must start a wall at an intersection, you are not limited to square walls. Simply drag the cursor at an angle to create an interesting corner (figure 5-5). However, don't make the angled walls too long. You cannot place doors, windows, or objects on these walls. Also, you cannot connect an angled wall to an existing straight wall inside your house.

TIP

To delete a wall, hold down the Ctrl key, then click and drag on a section of wall.

Fig. 5-5. Angled corners help you transform a boring box into a custom home.

TIP

Don't worry if you end up with a tree inside the walls of your house. You can build an atrium and keep the tree where it is, or use the Hand Tool to select the tree, and then move or delete it.

Wall Tool

Wall Types

NAME	COST (PER SECTION)	DESCRIPTION
White Picket Fence	§10	Outdoor fencing
Privacy Fence	§35	8-foot outdoor fence
Monticello Balustrade	§45	Railings for balconies and stairs
Wrought Iron Balustrade	§45	Railings for balconies and stairs
Tumbleweed Wooden Column	§70	Support columns for second stories or patio covers
Wall Tool	§70	Basic unfinished wall
The Zorba Ionic Column	§80	Classic, white Graeco-Roman column
Chester Brick Column	§100	All brick, squared off column

TIP

Columns are not restricted to outside use. Try using the Zorba Ionic Column to create a beautiful entry from the living room into a formal dining room.

Door and Window Tools

Door Tool

ims are very active. They seek the best path for their current task, and they think nothing of going out one exterior door and back in through another, if it's the best route. The least expensive Walnut Door (figure 5-6) is only §100, but because it is solid, your Room score does not benefit from outside light. If at all possible, invest in one of the windowed doors, and ideally, pick the multi-paned Monticello Door for maximum light.

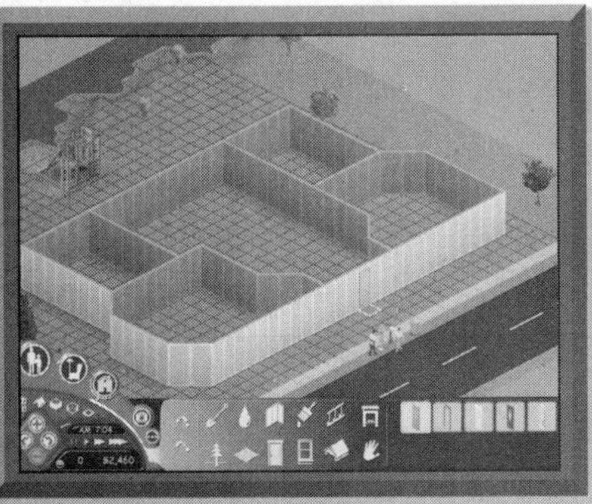

Fig. 5-6. The Walnut Door gives your Sims privacy, but it doesn't allow outside light to improve your Room score.

Door Types

NAME	COST	NOTES
Walnut Door	§100	Solid door without windows
Maple Door Frame	§150	Wooden door frame for rooms that do not require total privacy
Federal Lattice Window Door	§200	Glass panes in the upper half of door
Windsor Door	§300	Designer leaded glass door
Monticello Door	§400	7 rows of 3 panes, topped with a 6-pane half circle, allow maximum light to flow into your home

Window Tool

Let the sun shine in to pump up your Room score. Sims love light, so install plenty of windows from the start. Simply click on the selected window and place it on any right-angle wall (remember, you cannot place doors, windows, or objects on a diagonal wall). Window style is strictly personal—all windows exert the same positive effect on the Room score.

TIP

For aesthetic value, match your windows to your door style, such as the Monticello Door with Monticello Windows, as pictured in figure 5-7.

Fig. 5-7. Monticello Doors and Windows provide maximum light.

Window Types

NAME	COST	DESCRIPTION
Single-Pane Fixed Window	§50	This economy window still lets in the sun.
Single-Hung Window	§55	This looks good over the kitchen sink.
Privacy Window	§60	Tired of the neighborhood peeping Toms? This window is positioned higher on the wall.
Plate Glass Window	§65	This one's strictly glass from floor to ceiling.
El Sol Window	§80	This round ornamental window is a nice change from square and rectangular styles.
Monticello Window	§110	Use as a bedroom window to complement the Monticello door.
Windsor Window	§120	This ornamental natural wood window adds turn-of-the-century character to your home.
Monticello Window Full-Length	§200	This dramatic window looks beautiful on either side of a Monticello door.

Floor Tool

Unless you like grass in your living room, use the Floor Tool to lay some flooring inside your house. *The Sims* also includes outdoor flooring that works well in patios, backyard barbecue areas, or as pathways to a pool or play area. One tile covers a single grid, and you can quickly finish an entire room with a single shift-click. The price range for floor coverings is §10–§20, and you have a selection of 29 different styles/colors.

TIP

When you lay flooring inside a room with angled walls, half of the floor tiles appear on the other side of the wall, in another room or outside the house (see figure 5-8). To remove these outside tiles, place any floor type over the tiles, hold down the Ctrl key, and then click to delete them. The flooring on the other side of the wall remains undisturbed.

Fig. 5-8. After you finish the inside flooring, go back and delete the external tiles.

NOTE

You can use any type of flooring inside or outside.

Flooring Types

- Carpeting (7)
- Cement (1)
- Ceramic Tile-Small Tiles (3)
- Checkerboard Linoleum (1)
- Clay Paver Tiles (1)
- Colored Pavement (1)
- Granite (2)
- Gravel (1)
- Hardwood Plank (1)
- Inlaid Hardwood (1)
- Italian Tile (1)
- Poured Concrete (1)
- Shale (1)
- Striped Pavement (2, Both Directions)
- Tatami Mats (2)
- Terracotta Tile (1)
- Wood Parquet (2)

Wallpaper Tool

Fig. 5-9. Use the Wallpaper Tool to create a different mood in every room.

There are 30 different indoor/outdoor wall coverings in *The Sims,* and just as with floor coverings, you are limited only by your budget and sense of style. Prices range from §4 for basic wallpaper to §14 for granite block. If you change your mind after putting up the wallpaper, you can rip it down and get your money back by holding down the Ctrl key and clicking on the ugly panel.

Wallpaper Types

- Adobe (1)
- Aluminum Siding (1)
- Brick (2)
- Granite (1)
- Interior Wall Treatments (6 Fabric and Paint Combinations)
- Japanese Paper/Screens (4)
- Paint (4)
- Plaster (1)
- Stucco (1)
- Tudor (1)
- Wainscoting (1)
- Wallpaper (4)
- Wood Clapboard (1)
- Wood Paneling (1)
- Wood Shingles (1)

Stair Tool

You may not plan to build a second story immediately, but it's still a good idea to place your staircase before you start filling your house with objects. Choose from four staircases, two at §900 and two at §1,200. But, no matter how much you spend, they still get your Sims up and down the same way.

Style is considerably less important than function. You don't want to interrupt the traffic flow inside your house, especially to critical rooms such as the bathroom and kitchen. For this reason, staircases work well against a wall, where they are out of the way, or between two large, open rooms, such as the kitchen and family room (figure 5-10).

Fig. 5-10. Both of these placements keep the staircases out of the main traffic patterns.

If you don't have the money to finish the second story, just place the staircase and forget about it. The Sims won't go upstairs until you add a second story. After the staircase is positioned, the process for building a second story is exactly the same as building the first floor. The only obvious difference is that the buildable wall space extends out one square beyond the walls on the first floor. This allows you to squeeze a little extra space for a larger room or balcony.

Roof Tool

Although it is much easier to play *The Sims* using the Walls Cutaway or Walls Down options on the Control Panel, you will want to step back and enjoy your masterpiece in all of its crowning glory. The Roof Tool allows you to select a Shallow, Medium, or Steep Pitch for your roof, and choose from a selection of four roof patterns.

Water Tools

Pool Tool

Now that you have walls, floors, and doors, it's time to add a pool. Of course, this isn't a necessity, but your Sims love to swim, and it's an easy way to add important Body points. After placing your pool, don't forget to add a ladder so your Sims can get in and out of the pool (diving board is optional). The Pool Tool also places light-colored cement squares as decking around your pool. You can go back and cover these tiles with the outdoor surface of your choice, as displayed in figure 5-11. You can also add fencing around your deck to give your pool a more finished look.

Fig. 5-11. With the pool and decking in place, you have room to add an outdoor barbecue and beverage cart.

Vater Tool

Fig. 5-12.

f you want to add decorative, free form pools on our property, use the Water Tool to place oval-haped sections of pond. You can drag the tool to lace a long oval pond, or connect several small onds to form an irregular pattern, as pictured in igure 5-12. Your Sims can't swim in ponds, and hey cannot walk on water, so don't forget to nclude a pathway.

Fireplace Tool

Fig. 5-13. It looks innocent enough, but a roaring fire can turn nearby objects or Sims into a deadly inferno.

Vhen placed safely out of the way of flammable bjects, a fireplace adds a major boost to the Room score. However, it can be a dangerous fire azard if Sims wander too close, so give it a wide erth when a fire is roaring.

Plant Tool

Now, it's time to put the finishing touches on the exterior of your house. Using the Plant Tool, you can select from 14 different plants, priced from §5 for Wildflowers to §300 for an Apple Tree. The following types of vegetation are included:

Plant Types

- **Flowers (4)**
- **Bushes (1)**
- **Hedges (2)**
- **Shrubs (2)**
- **Trees (5)**

Let your green thumb go wild, but don't forget that only trees and shrubs will thrive without regular watering. If you want colorful flowers, you'll probably need to hire a Gardener.

Fig. 5-14. This colorful landscaping will require the services of a Gardener, or a Sim with a lot of time to kill.

Special Editing Tools

In addition to the building tools described above, there are two other options on the Build Mode Control Panel. The curved arrows pictured at the bottom corner of figure 5-15 allow you to undo or repeat your last action(s). This is a quick way to delete unwanted items.

Fig. 5-15. Click Undo Last to reverse your most recent actions.

If the undo button is unavailable, you can click on the Hand Tool, select any object, and then press the Delete key to sell it back. For directions on how to delete walls, wall coverings, and floor coverings, see the appropriate sections in this chapter.

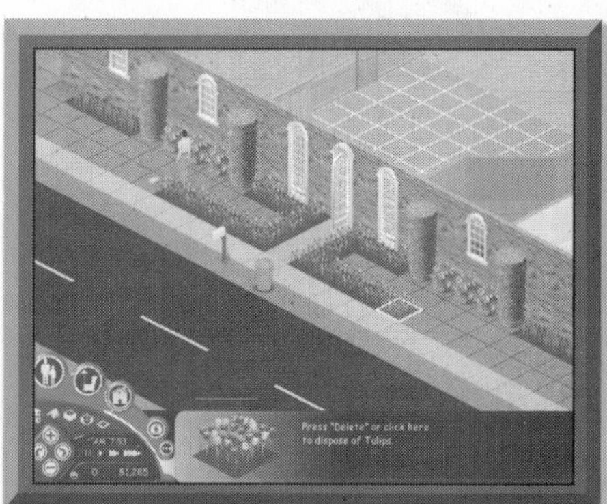

Fig. 5-16. Select an item with the Hand Tool, then press Delete to make it go away.

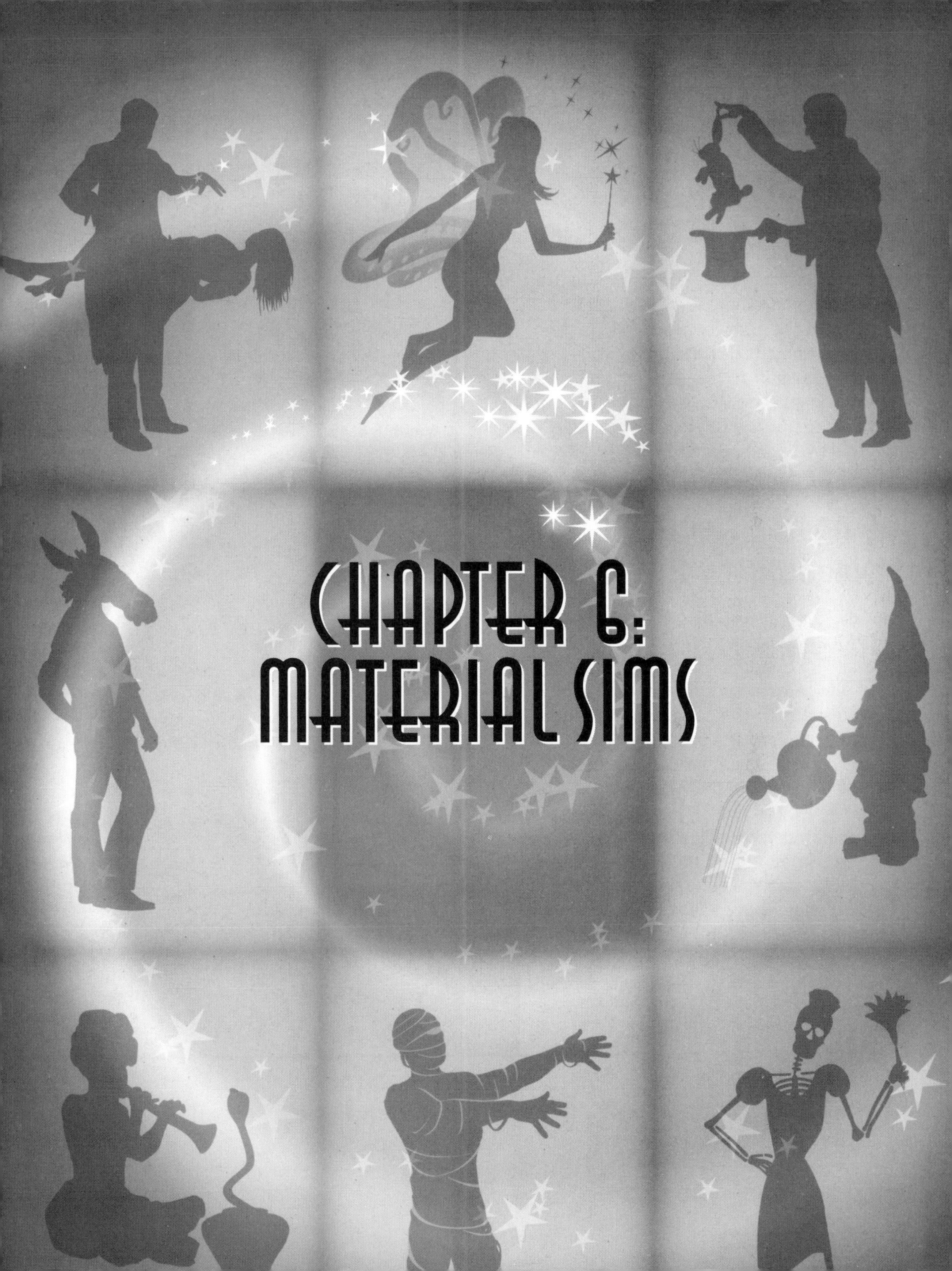
CHAPTER 6:
MATERIAL SIMS

Introduction

This chapter covers the eight categories of objects available in Buy Mode: Seating, Surfaces, Decorative, Electronics, Appliances, Plumbing, Lighting, and Miscellaneous. Every object is listed with its purchase price, related Motives, and Efficiency ratings. You can shop 'til you drop, but it's more important to buy smart than to buy often. Our comprehensive Buying Guide is just ahead, but first let's study some important factors that impact your spending habits.

Buying for Needs, Instead of Needing to Buy

If you select a ready-made house for your new Sim family, you acquire walls, floors, and a roof, but little else. The house is empty, with nary a toilet, bed, or refrigerator in sight. Depending upon how much you spent on the house, you'll have a few thousand Simoleans to use in Buy Mode, where you can purchase more than 150 objects. Most objects affect your Sims' environment in positive ways. However, not every object is a necessity. In fact, if you are a recovering shopping channel addict, this is not a good time to fall off your wallet. Make your first purchases with The Sims' Motives (or Needs) in mind. You can review your Sims' current Needs state by clicking on the Mood icon. We provide detailed descriptions in the Motives chapter, but for now, here is a basic shopping list that will help you get your Sims' Need bars out of the red zone during the early stages of a game.

TIP

In most instances, an expensive item has a greater impact on the related Need bar than an economy model. For example, a §300 cot gives your Sim a place to crash, but a §3,000 Mission Bed provides more Comfort and lets your Sim get by on less sleep. As an added bonus, the top-of-the-line bed also adds to the overall Room score.

Fig. 6-1. Despite logging only five hours of sleep, Bella is feeling pretty good, thanks to her §3000 Mission bed.

Fig. 6-2. A big-screen TV is fun for your Sims, but also for the neighbors, who will often hang out, and boost your Social score.

Need	Item	Explanation
Hunger	Refrigerator, Food Processor, Stove	A refrigerator alone will sustain life, but you will greatly improve the quality of Sim meals by using a food processor and stove. However, there is a risk of fire if your Sim doesn't have at least two Cooking Skill points.
Comfort	Bed, Chairs	Sims will sleep anywhere when they are tired, but a bed is highly recommended for sleeping, and you'll need chairs (for eating and working at the computer), and a couch for napping. A bathtub provides a little extra comfort for your Sims, but it isn't critical, provided you have a shower.
Hygiene	Sink, Shower	Dirty Sims spend a lot of time waving their arms in the air to disperse their body odor. Not a pretty sight. Fortunately, a sink and shower go a long way toward improving their state of mind (not to mention the smell).
Bladder	Toilet	When you gotta go, you gotta go. Sims prefer using a toilet, but if one is not available, they will relieve themselves on the floor. This not only causes great shame and embarrassment, but someone in your family will have to clean up the mess. It's also very bad for your Hygiene levels.
Energy	Bed	If you don't want to spawn a family of insomniacs, buy a sufficient number of beds for your Sims. A shot of coffee or espresso provides a temporary Energy boost, but it is definitely not a long-term solution.
Fun	TV	The boob tube is the easiest and cheapest way to give your Sims a break from their daily grinds. You can add other, more exciting, items later, but this is your best choice early on.
Social	Telephone	Ignore this for a short time while you focus on setting up your house. However, don't force your Sims into a solitary lifestyle. Other Sims may walk by the house, but you'll have better results after buying a telephone, so that you can invite people over and gain Social points when they arrive.
Room	Windows, Lamps, Decorations, Landscaping	Sims like plenty of light, from windows during the day and artificial lighting at night. Table Lamps are the cheapest, but they can only be placed on raised surfaces. As your game progresses, you can add decorations and landscaping to boost the Room score.

Sims Can Be Hard to Please

Given a fat bank account, it would seem that you can always cheer up your Sims with a few expensive purchases. Not exactly. While you are spending your hard-earned Simoleans, the Sims are busy comparing everything that you buy to everything they already own. If you fail to keep your Sims in the manner to which they are accustomed, their responses to your new objects may be indifferent or even downright negative. Every time you make a purchase, the game uses an assessment formula to calculate your Sim's response. The logic goes like this:

- Calculates the average value of everything in your house (including outdoor items).
- Subtracts 10 percent of the new object's value for each existing copy of the same item. Don't expect your family members to jump for joy if you add a hot tub to every room in the house.
- Compares the value of the new object with all existing objects in your house. If the new purchase is worth 20 percent or more above the average value of current items, the Sim exhibits a positive response by clapping.
- If the new object is within 20 percent (above or below) of the current average value of all items in your household, the Sim gives you an uninspired shrug.
- If the new object is less than 20 percent below the average value, your Sim waves it off and you'll see a red X through the object.

Fig. 6-3. Compared to the §2,100 "Snails With Icicles in Nose," this §45 clown picture doesn't quite stack up.

Your Diminishing Net Worth

When times are tough, you may need to raise cash by selling objects in your house. With rare exception, you will never match your initial investment, thanks to instant depreciation, and as time goes on, your belongings continue to lose value until they reach their depreciation limits. The following table lists every object in *The Sims* (alphabetically), including purchase price and depreciated values.

TIP

Although depreciation reduces the value of your furnishings over time, there is a buyer's remorse period when you can return the item for full value (if it has been less than 24 hours since you purchased it). So, if you have second thoughts about that new hot tub, simply select the item and hit the Delete key to get your money back.

Fig. 6-4. This Pyrotorre Gas Range is §1,000 new, but after depreciation it's worth only §300.

Object Depreciation

NAME	PURCHASE PRICE	INITIAL DEPRECIATION	DAILY DEPRECIATION	DEPRECIATION LIMIT
Alarm: Burglar	§250	§62	§2	§50
Alarm: Smoke	§50	§12	§0	§10
Aquarium	§200	§30	§2	§80
Bar	§800	§120	§8	§320
Barbecue	§350	§70	§4	§105
Basketball Hoop (Cheap Eaze)	§650	§98	§6	§260
Bed: Double	§450	§68	§4	§180
Bed: Double (Mission)	§3,000	§450	§30	§1,200
Bed: Double (Napoleon)	§1,000	§150	§10	§400
Bed: Single (Spartan)	§300	§45	§3	§120
Bed: Single (Tyke Nyte)	§450	§68	§4	§180
Bench: Garden	§250	§38	§2	§100
Bookshelf: Amishim	§500	§75	§5	§200
Bookshelf: Libri di Regina	§900	§135	§9	§360
Bookshelf: Pine	§250	§38	§2	§100
Chair: Deck (Survivall)	§150	§22	§2	§60
Chair: Dining (Empress)	§600	§90	§6	§240
Chair: Dining (Parisienne)	§1,200	§180	§12	§480
Chair: Dining (Teak)	§200	§30	§2	§80
Chair: Dining (Werkbunnst)	§80	§12	§1	§32
Chair: Living Room (Citronel)	§450	§68	§4	§180
Chair: Living Room (Country Class)	§250	§38	§2	§100
Chair: Living Room (Sarrbach)	§500	§75	§5	§200
Chair: Living Room (Wicker)	§80	§12	§1	§32
Chair: Office	§100	§15	§1	§40

NAME	PURCHASE PRICE	INITIAL DEPRECIATION	DAILY DEPRECIATION	DEPRECIATION LIMIT
Chair: Recliner (Back Slack)	§250	§38	§2	§100
Chair: Recliner (Von Braun)	§850	§128	§8	§340
Chess Set	§500	§75	§5	§200
Clock: Alarm	§30	§4	§0	§12
Clock: Grandfather	§3,500	§525	§35	§1,400
Coffee: Espresso Machine	§450	§90	§4	§135
Coffeemaker	§85	§17	§1	§26
Computer (Brahma 2000)	§2,800	§700	§28	§560
Computer (Marco)	§6,500	§1,625	§65	§1,300
Computer (Microscotch)	§1,800	§450	§18	§360
Computer (Moneywell)	§999	§250	§10	§200
Counter: Bath (Count Blanc)	§400	§60	§4	§160
Counter: Kitchen (Barcelona: In)	§800	§120	§8	§320
Counter: Kitchen (Barcelona: Out)	§800	§120	§8	§320
Counter: Kitchen (NuMica)	§150	§22	§2	§60
Counter: Kitchen (Tiled)	§250	§38	§2	§100
Desk (Cupertino)	§220	§33	§2	§88
Desk (Mesquite)	§80	§12	§1	§32
Desk (Redmond)	§800	§120	§8	§320
Dishwasher (Dish Duster)	§550	§110	§6	§165
Dishwasher (Fuzzy Logic)	§950	§190	§10	§285
Dollhouse	§180	§27	§2	§72
Dresser (Antique Armoire)	§1,200	§180	§12	§480
Dresser (Kinderstuff)	§300	§45	§3	§120

NAME	PURCHASE PRICE	INITIAL DEPRECIATION	DAILY DEPRECIATION	DEPRECIATION LIMIT
Dresser (Oak Armoire)	§550	§82	§6	§220
Dresser (Pinegulcher)	§250	§38	§2	§100
Easel	§250	§38	§2	§100
Exercise Machine	§700	§105	§7	§280
Flamingo	§12	§2	§0	§5
Food Processor	§220	§44	§2	§66
Fountain	§700	§105	§7	§280
Fridge (Freeze Secret)	§2,500	§500	§25	§750
Fridge (Llamark)	§600	§120	§6	§180
Fridge (Porcina)	§1,200	§240	§12	§360
Hot Tub	§6,500	§1,300	§65	§1,950
Lamp: Floor (Halogen)	§50	§8	§0	§20
Lamp: Floor (Lumpen)	§100	§15	§1	§40
Lamp: Floor (Torchosteronne)	§350	§52	§4	§140
Lamp: Garden	§50	§7	§1	§20
Lamp: Love n' Haight Lava	§80	§12	§1	§32
Lamp: Table (Antique)	§300	§45	§3	§120
Lamp: Table (Bottle)	§25	§4	§0	§10
Lamp: Table (Ceramiche)	§85	§13	§1	§34
Lamp: Table (Elite)	§180	§27	§2	§72
Medicine Cabinet	§125	§19	§1	§50
Microwave	§250	§50	§2	§75
Mirror: Floor	§150	§22	§2	§60
Mirror: Wall	§100	§15	§1	§40
Phone: Tabletop	§50	§12	§0	§10
Phone: Wall	§75	§19	§1	§15
Piano	§3,500	§525	§35	§1,400
Pinball Machine	§1,800	§450	§18	§360
Plant: Big (Cactus)	§150	§22	§2	§60
Plant: Big (Jade)	§160	§24	§2	§64
Plant: Big (Rubber)	§120	§18	§1	§48

NAME	PURCHASE PRICE	INITIAL DEPRECIATION	DAILY DEPRECIATION	DEPRECIATION LIMIT
Plant: Small (Geranium)	§45	§7	§0	§18
Plant: Small (Spider)	§35	§5	§0	§14
Plant: Small (Violets)	§30	§4	§0	§12
Play Structure	§1,200	§180	§12	§480
Pool Table	§4,200	§630	§42	§1,680
Shower	§650	§130	§6	§195
Sink: Bathroom Pedestal	§400	§80	§4	§120
Sink: Kitchen (Double)	§500	§100	§5	§150
Sink: Kitchen (Single)	§250	§50	§2	§75
Sofa (Blue Pinstripe)	§400	§60	§4	§160
Sofa (Contempto)	§200	§30	§2	§80
Sofa (Country)	§450	§68	§4	§180
Sofa (Deiter)	§1,100	§165	§11	§440
Sofa (Dolce)	§1,450	§218	§14	§580
Sofa (Recycled)	§180	§27	§2	§72
Sofa (SimSafari)	§220	§33	§2	§88
Sofa: Loveseat (Blue Pinstripe)	§360	§54	§4	§144
Sofa: Loveseat (Contempto)	§150	§22	§2	§60
Sofa: Loveseat (Country)	§340	§51	§3	§136
Sofa: Loveseat (Indoor-Outdoor)	§160	§24	§2	§64
Sofa: Loveseat (Luxuriare)	§875	§131	§9	§350
Stereo (Strings)	§2,550	§638	§26	§510
Stereo (Zimantz)	§650	§162	§6	§130
Stereo: Boom Box	§100	§25	§1	§20
Stove (Dialectric)	§400	§80	§4	§120
Stove (Pyrotorre)	§1,000	§200	§10	§300
Table: Dining (Colonial)	§200	§30	§2	§80
Table: Dining (Mesa)	§450	§68	§4	§180

NAME	PURCHASE PRICE	INITIAL DEPRECIATION	DAILY DEPRECIATION	DEPRECIATION LIMIT
Table: Dining (NuMica)	§95	§14	§1	§38
Table: Dining (Parisienne)	§1,200	§180	§12	§480
Table: End (Anywhere)	§120	§18	§1	§48
Table: End (Imperious)	§135	§20	§1	§54
Table: End (KinderStuff)	§75	§11	§1	§30
Table: End (Mission)	§250	§38	§2	§100
Table: End (Pinegulcher)	§40	§6	§0	§16
Table: End (Sumpto)	§300	§45	§3	§120
Table: End (Wicker)	§55	§8	§1	§22
Table: Outdoor (Backwoods)	§200	§30	§2	§80
Toaster Oven	§100	§20	§1	§30
Toilet (Flush Force)	§1,200	§240	§12	§360
Toilet (Hygeia-O-Matic)	§300	§60	§3	§90
Tombstone/Urn	§5	§1	§0	§2
Toy Box	§50	§8	§0	§20
Train Set: Large	§955	§239	§10	§191
Train Set: Small	§80	§20	§1	§16
Trash Compactor	§375	§75	§4	§112
Tub (Hydrothera)	§3,200	§640	§32	§960
Tub (Justa)	§800	§160	§8	§240
Tub (Sani-Queen)	§1,500	§300	§15	§450
TV (Monochrome)	§85	§21	§1	§17
TV (Soma)	§3,500	§875	§35	§700
TV (Trottco)	§500	§125	§5	§100
VR Glasses	§2,300	§575	§23	§460

The Sims Buying Guide

The following sections represent the eight item categories that appear when you click the Buy Mode button on the control panel. We've added a few subcategories to make it easier to find a specific object. The Efficiency Value (1–10) indicates how well the item satisfies each Motive. You get what you pay for in *The Sims*, so an §80 chair doesn't quite stack up to an §850 recliner when it comes to boosting your Comfort level, and it cannot restore Energy.

Seating

Chairs

There are three types of chairs in *The Sims*: movable, stationary, and reclining. Any chair will function at a desk or table for eating and using objects. If your budget is tight, you can also use cheaper chairs for watching TV or reading, but their Comfort ratings are very low. You can use high-ticket dining room chairs at the computer, but that is probably overkill. You are better off placing them in the dining room where you receive greater benefit from their enhanced Room ratings.

Stationary chairs are cushier and nicely upholstered (depending on your taste, of course), and they usually provide more comfort. Finally, the reclining chairs are top of the line, giving you increased comfort and the added benefit of being able to catch a few Zs in the reclining position.

TIP

Chair placement is critical, especially around tables. A Sim will not move a chair sideways, only forward and backward. So, position the chair properly or the Sim will not be able to use the table (or what is on it). Also, be careful not to trap a Sim in a corner when a chair is pulled out. For example, if a child is playing with a train set in the corner of the room, and another Sim pulls out a chair to use the computer, the child would be trapped in the corner until the computer user is finished.

Werkbunnst All-Purpose Chair

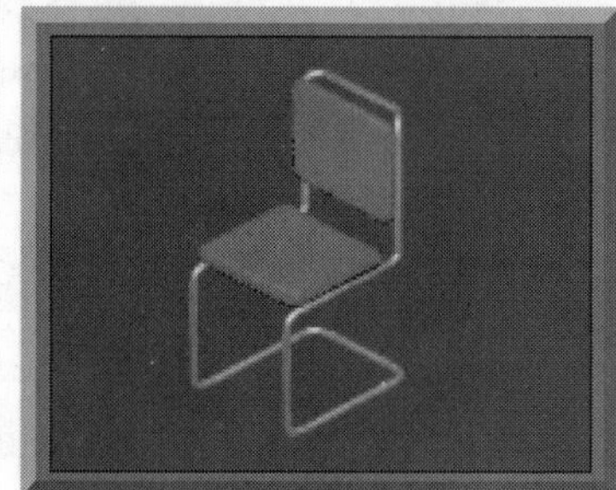

Type: Movable

Cost: §80

Motive: Comfort (2)

Posture Plus Office Chair

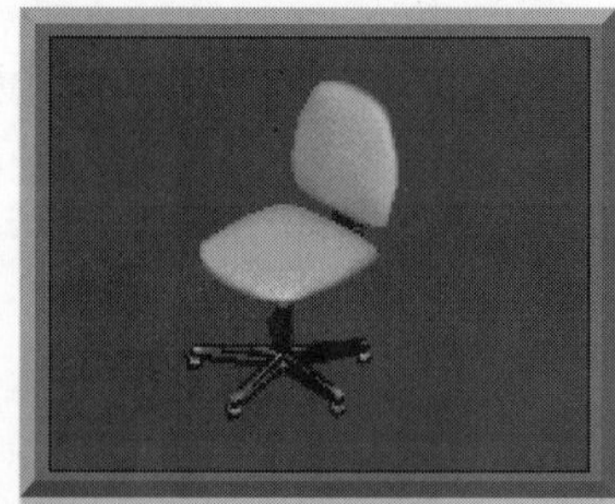

Type: Movable

Cost: §100

Motive: Comfort (3)

Deck Chair by Survivall

Type: Movable

Cost: §150

Motive: Comfort (3)

Touch of Teak Dinette Chair

Type: Movable

Cost: §200

Motive: Comfort (3)

Empress Dining Room Chair

Type: Movable

Cost: §600

Motives: Comfort (4), Room (2)

Parisienne Dining Chair

Type: Movable

Cost: §1,200

Motives: Comfort (6), Room (3)

Sioux City Wicker Chair

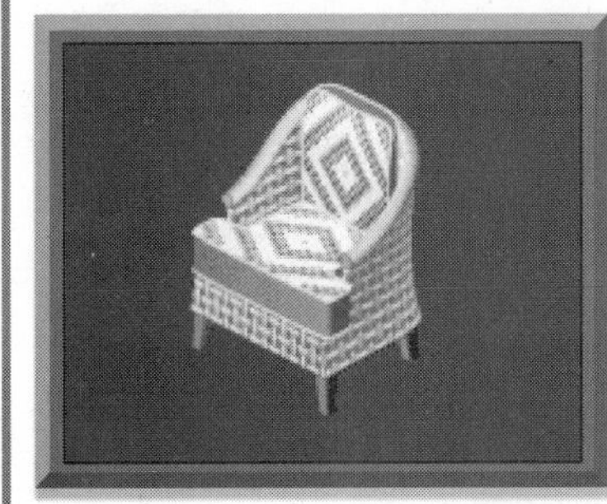

Type: Stationary

Cost: §80

Motive: Comfort (2)

Country Class Armchair

Type: Stationary

Cost: §250

Motive: Comfort (4)

"Citronel" from Chiclettina Inc.

Type: Stationary

Cost: §450

Motive: Comfort (6)

"The Sarrbach" by Werkbunnst

Type: Stationary

Cost: §500

Motive: Comfort (6)

"Back Slack" Recliner

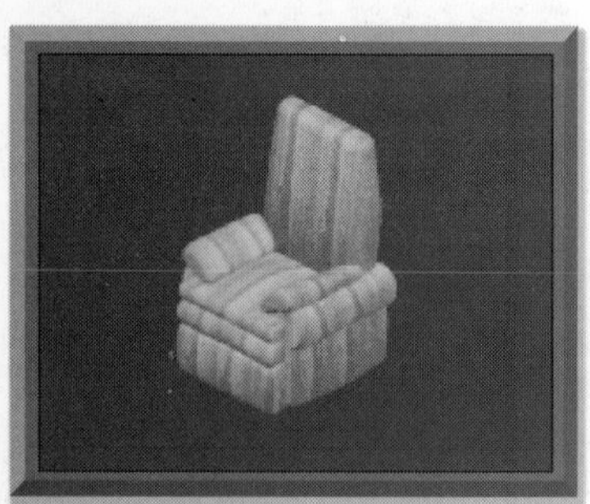

Type: Recliner

Cost: §250

Motives: Comfort (6), Energy (3)

"Von Braun" Recliner

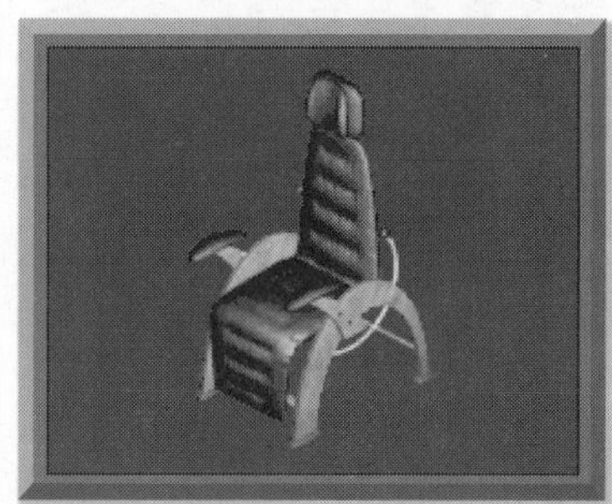

Type: Recliner

Cost: §850

Motives: Comfort (9), Energy (3)

Couches

Sitting down is fine for reading, eating, or working, but for serious vegging, your Sims need a good couch. When selecting a couch, function is more important than quality. If you are looking for a place to take naps, pay more attention to the Energy rating than the Comfort or Room ratings. A multipurpose couch should have good Energy and Comfort ratings. However, if you are furnishing your party area, select one that looks good, thereby enhancing your Room rating. Stay away from the cheapest couches (under §200). For a few extra dollars, a medium-priced couch will make your Sims a lot happier. When you're flush with Simoleans, don't forget to dress up your garden with the outdoor bench. You can't sleep on it, but it looks great.

Contempto Loveseat

Cost: §150

Motives: Comfort (3), Energy (4)

Indoor-Outdoor Loveseat

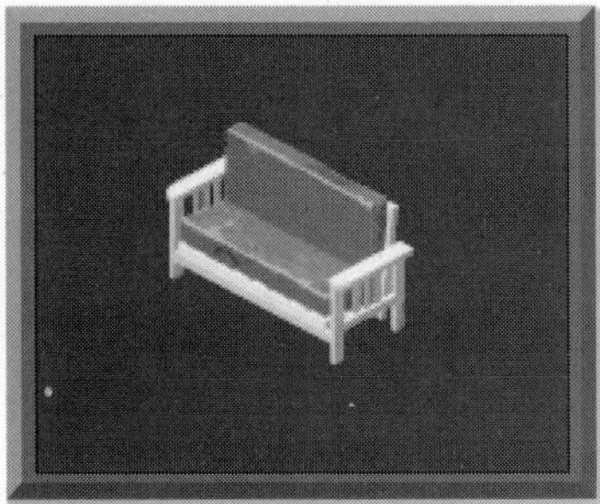

Cost: §160

Motives: Comfort (3), Energy (4)

Recycled Couch

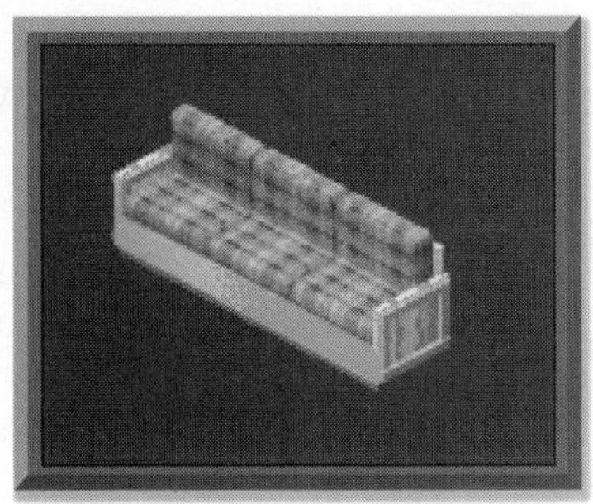

Cost: §180

Motives: Comfort (2), Energy (5)

Contempto Couch

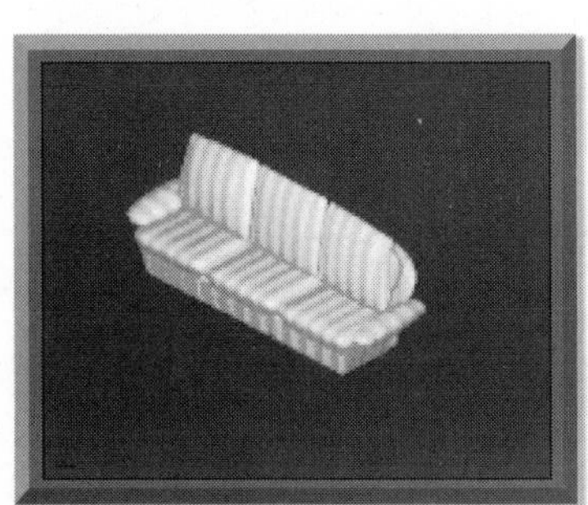

Cost: §200

Motives: Comfort (3), Energy (5)

SimSafari Sofa

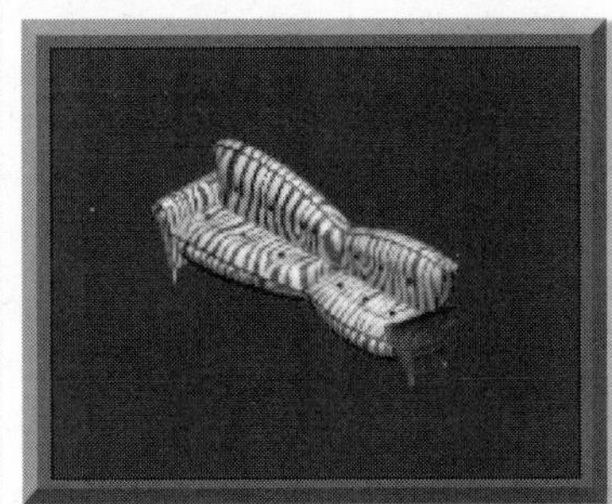

Cost: §220

Motives: Comfort (3), Energy (5)

Parque Fresco del Aire Bench

Cost: §250

Motive: Comfort (2)

Country Class Loveseat

Cost: §340

Motives: Comfort (5), Energy (4)

Pinstripe Loveseat from Zecutime

Cost: §360

Motives: Comfort (5), Energy (4)

Pinstripe Sofa from Zecutime

Cost: §400

Motives: Comfort (5), Energy (5)

Country Class Sofa

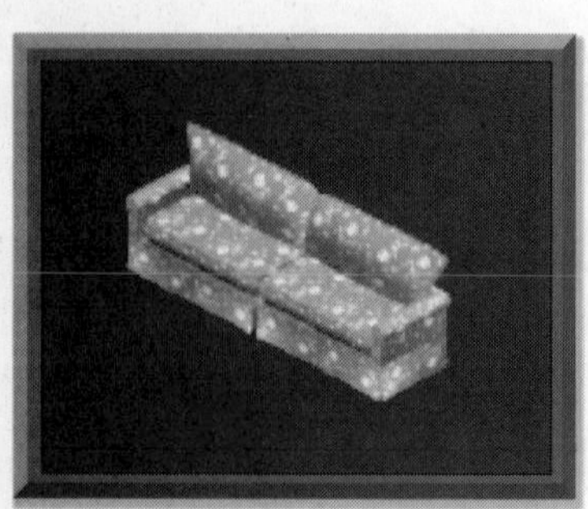

Cost: §450

Motives: Comfort (5), Energy (5)

Luxuriare Loveseat

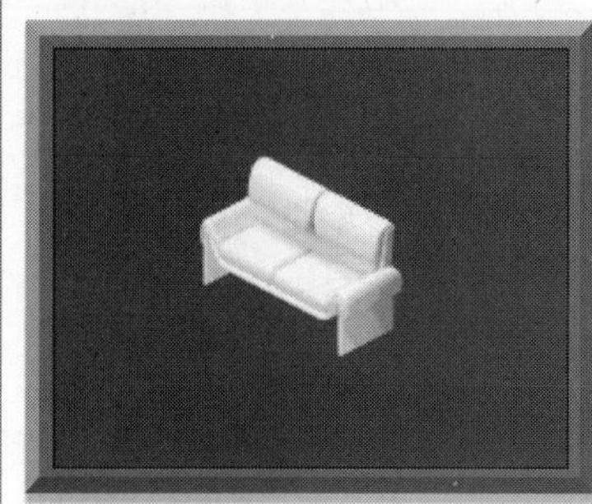

Cost: §875

Motives: Comfort (8), Energy (4), Room (2)

"The Deiter" by Werkbunnst

Cost: §1,100

Motives: Comfort (8), Energy (5), Room (3)

Dolce Tutti Frutti Sofa

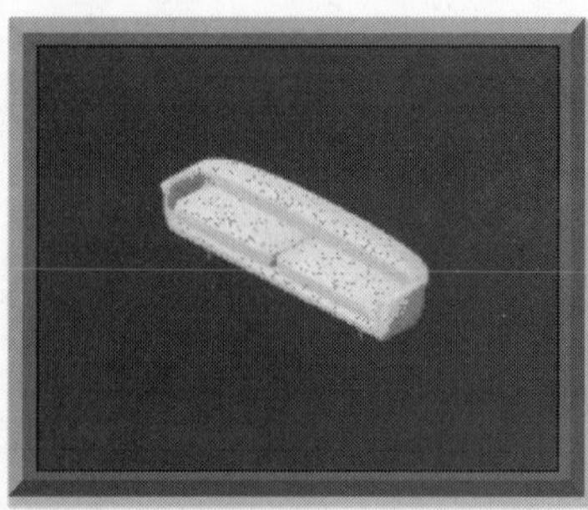

Cost: §1,450

Motives: Comfort (9), Energy (5), Room (3)

Beds

Getting enough sleep can be one of the most frustrating goals in *The Sims*, especially if there is a new baby in the house, or your car pool arrives at some ungodly hour of the morning. In the early stages of a game, it is not important to spend a bundle of money on a designer bed. However, an upgrade later on is well worth the money, because a top-of-the-line bed recharges your Energy bar faster.

Spartan Special

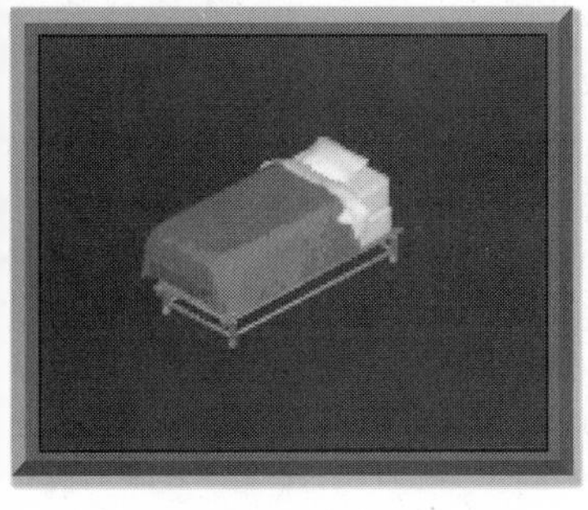

Cost: §300

Motives: Comfort (6), Energy (7)

Cheap Eazzzzze Double Sleeper

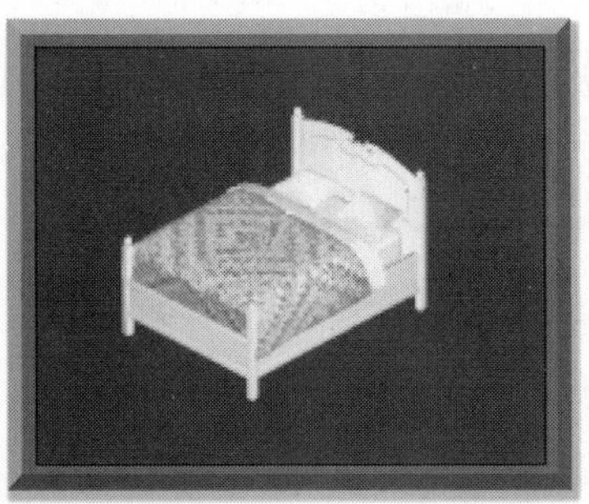

Cost: §450

Motives: Comfort (7), Energy (8)

Tyke Nyte Bed

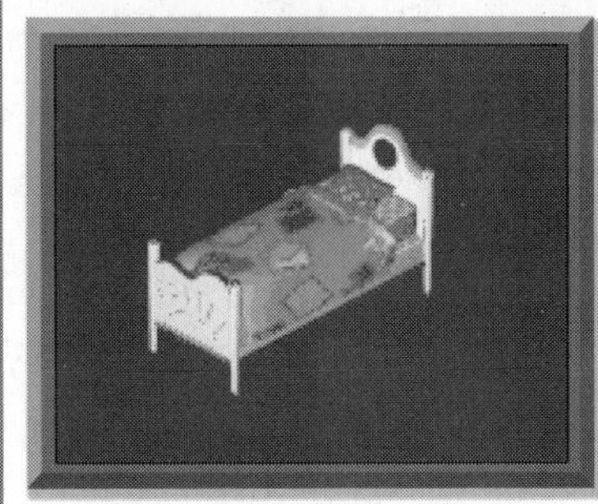

Cost: §450

Motives: Comfort (7), Energy (7)

Napoleon Sleigh Bed

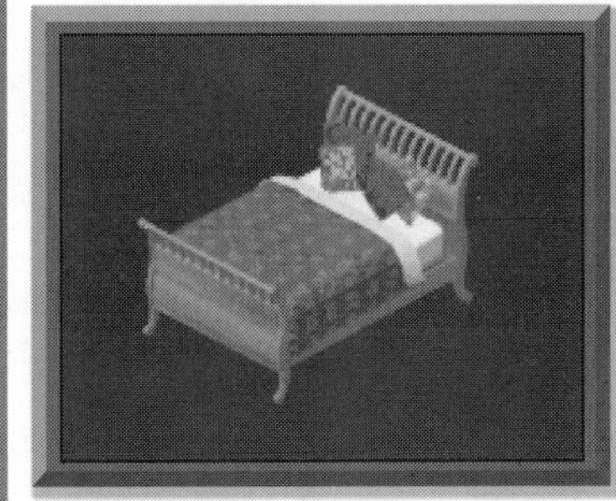

Cost: §1,000

Motives: Comfort (8), Energy (9)

Modern Mission Bed

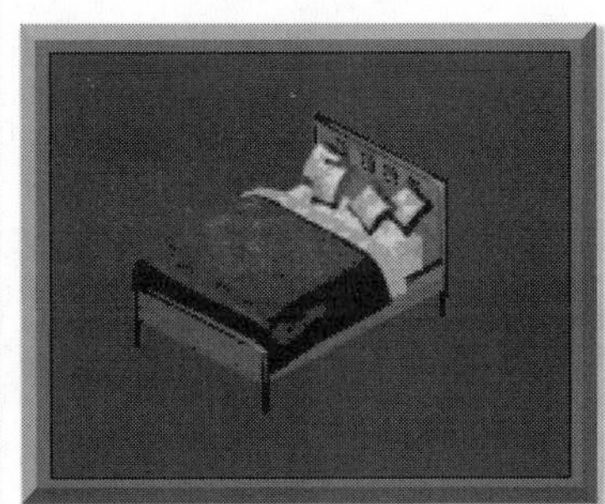

Cost: §3,000

Motives: Comfort (9), Energy (10), Room (3)

Surfaces

Sims will eat or read standing up if they have to, but they won't be particularly happy about it. Sitting at a table while eating a meal bolsters a Sim's Comfort. Since your Sims have to eat to satisfy Hunger, they might as well improve Comfort, too. Many objects require elevated surfaces, so allow enough room for nightstands (alarm clock, lamps), tables (computer), and countertops (microwave, coffeemaker, etc.), when you design the interior of your house. Also, your Sims cannot prepare food on a table, so provide ample countertop space in the kitchen, or you may find them wandering into the bathroom to chop veggies on the counter (hair in the soup—yummy!).

Countertops

NuMica Kitchen Counter

Cost: §150

Motive: None

Tiled Counter

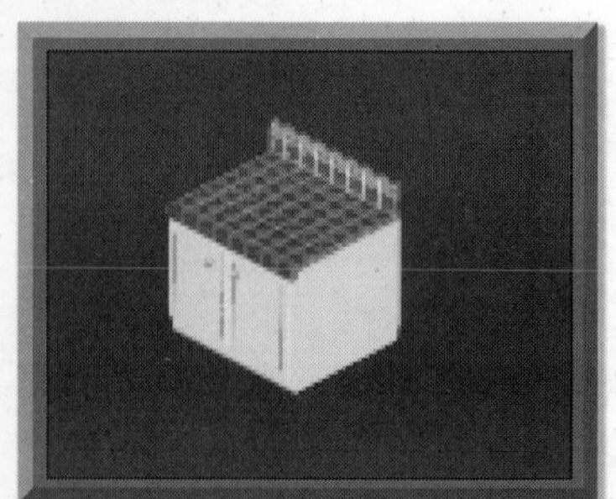

Cost: §250

Motive: None

Count Blanc Bathroom Counter

Cost: §400

Motive: None

"Barcelona" Outcurve Counter

Cost: §800

Motive: Room (2)

"Barcelona" Incurve Counter

Cost: §800

Motive: Room (2)

End Tables

Pinegulcher End Table

Cost: §40

Motive: None

Wicker Breeze End Table

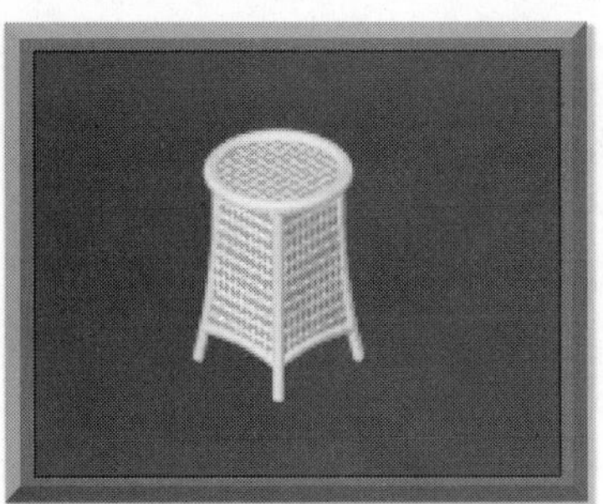

Cost: §55

Motive: None

"Anywhere" End Table

Cost: §120

Motive: None

Imperious Island End Table

Cost: §135

Motive: None

Modern Mission End Table

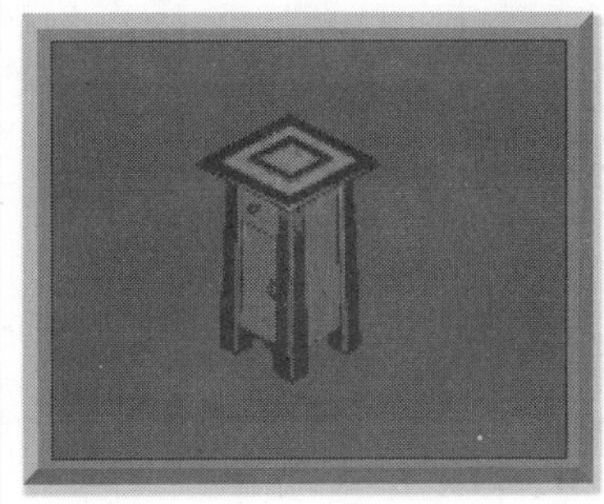

Cost: §250

Motive: Room (1)

Sumpto End Table

Cost: §300

Motive: Room (1)

KinderStuff Nightstand

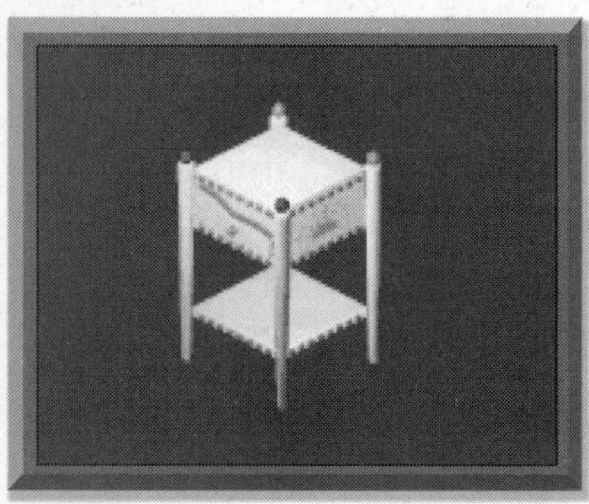

Cost: §75

Motive: None

Desks/Tables

Mesquite Desk/Table

Cost: §80

Motive: None

NuMica Folding Card Table

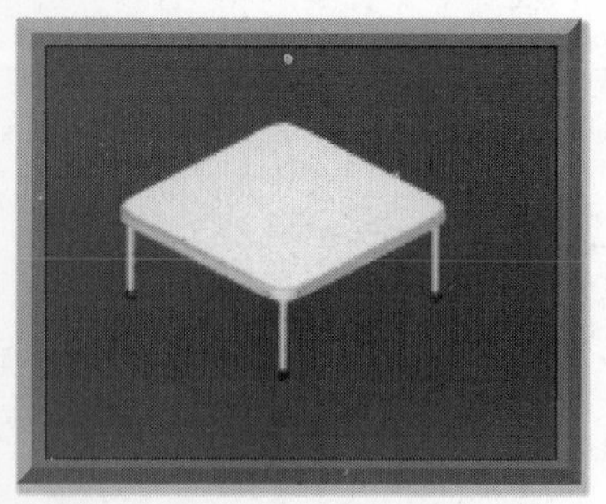

Cost: §95

Motive: None

"Colonial Legacy" Dining Table

Cost: §200

Motive: None

Backwoods Table by Survivall

Cost: §200

Motive: None

London "Cupertino" Collection Desk/Table

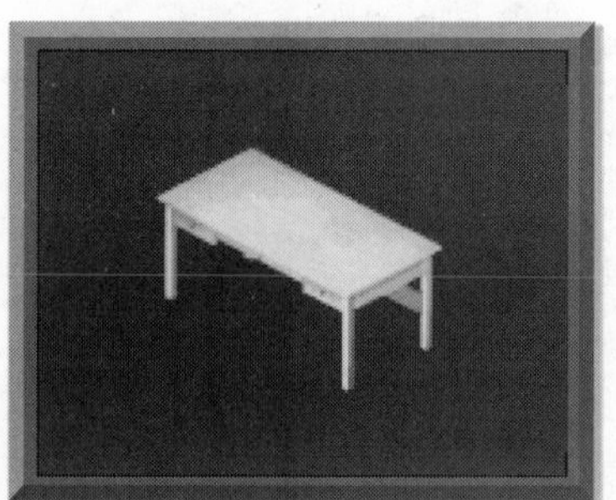

Cost: §220

Motive: None

London "Mesa" Dining Design

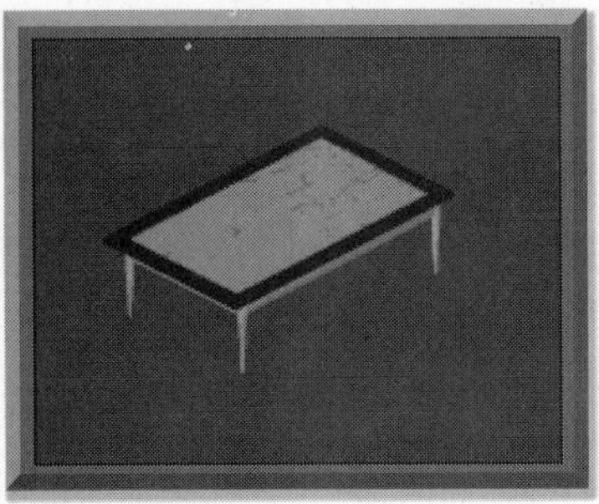

Cost: §450

Motive: Room (2)

The "Redmond" Desk/Table

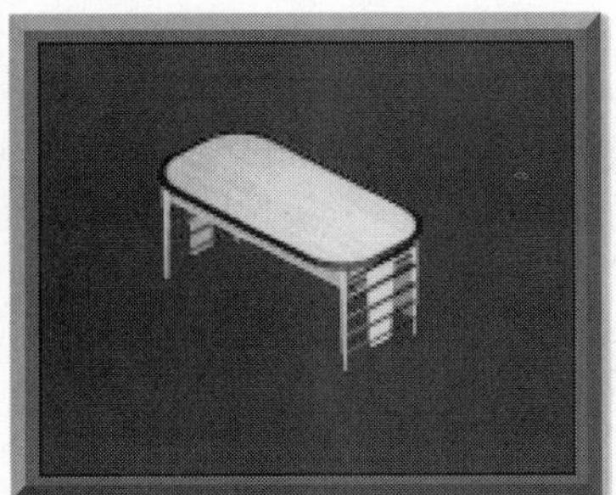

Cost: §800

Motive: Room (2)

Parisienne Dining Table

Cost: §1,200

Motive: Room (3)

Decorative

After the essential furnishings are in place, you can improve your Room score by adding decorative objects. Some items, such as the grandfather clock and aquarium, require regular maintenance, but most decorative items exist solely for your Sims' viewing pleasure. You might even get lucky and buy a painting or sculpture that increases in value. In addition to enhancing the Room score, the aquarium and fountain have Fun value.

Pink Flamingo

Cost: §12

Motive: Room (2)

African Violet

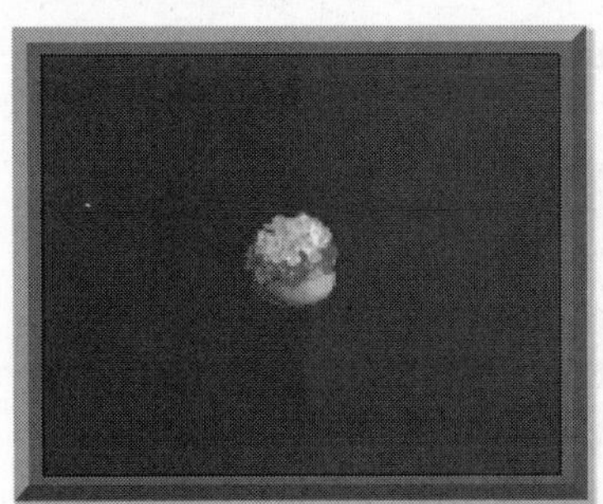

Cost: §30

Motive: Room (1)

Spider Plant

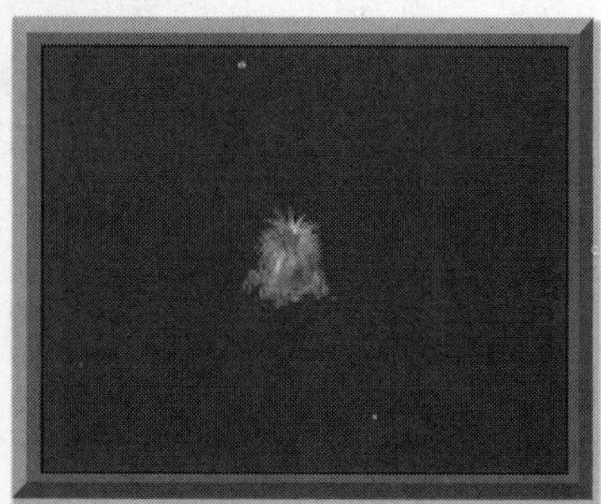

Cost: §35

Motive: Room (1)

"Roxana" Geranium

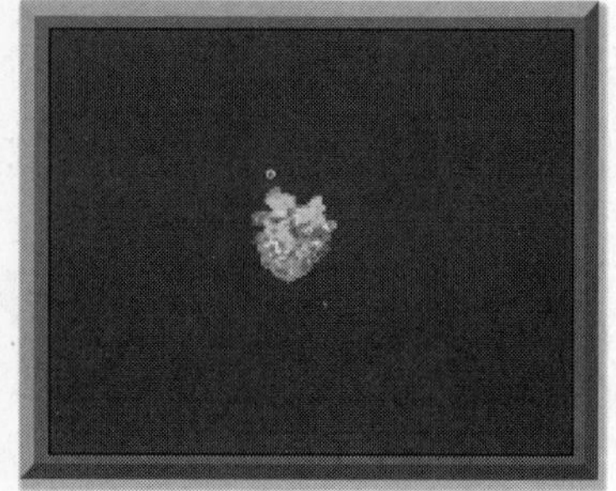

Cost: §45

Motive: Room (1)

"Tragic Clown" Painting

Cost: §45

Motive: Room (1)

Watercolor by J.M.E.

Cost: §75

Motive: Room (1)

Rubber Tree Plant

Cost: §120

Motive: Room (2)

Echinopsis maximus Cactus

Cost: §150

Motive: Room (2)

Jade Plant

Cost: §160

Motive: Room (2)

Poseidon's Adventure Aquarium

Cost: §200

Motive: Fun (1), Room (2)

"Bi-Polar" by Conner I.N.

Cost: §240

Motive: Room (2)

"Delusion de Grandeur"

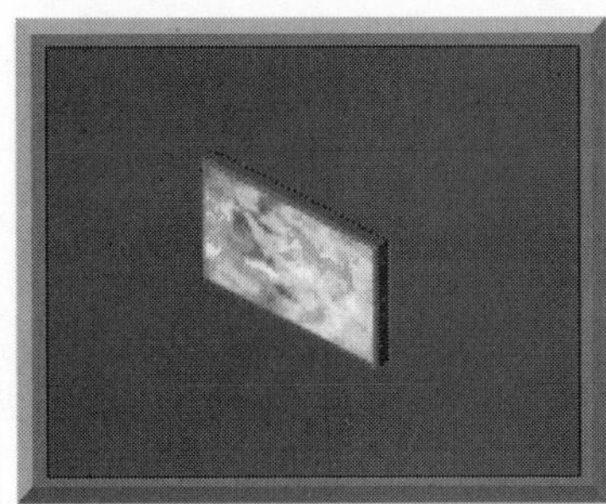

Cost: §360

Motive: Room (2)

"Fountain of Tranquility"

Cost: §700

Motives: Fun (1), Room (2)

Landscape #12,001 by Manny Kopees

Cost: §750

Motive: Room (3)

Bust of Athena by Klassick Repro. Inc.

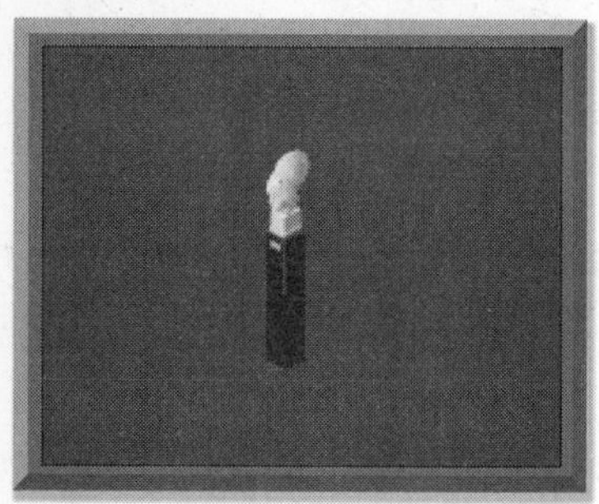

Cost: §875

Motive: Room (3)

"Scylla and Charybdis"

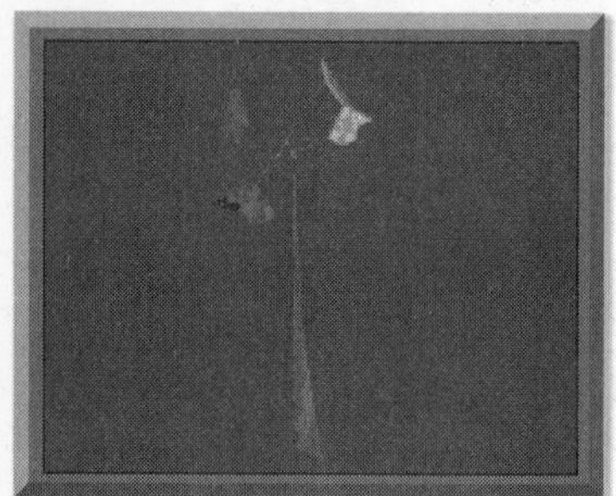

Cost: §1,450

Motive: Room (4)

Snails With Icicles in Nose

Cost: §2,140

Motive: Room (5)

Portrait Grid by Payne A. Pitcher

Cost: §3,200

Motive: Room (8)

Grandfather Clock

Cost: §3,500

Motive: Room (7)

Blue China Vase

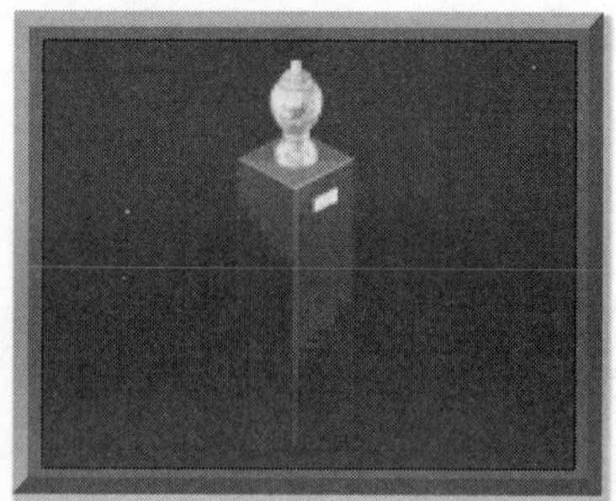

Cost: §4,260

Motive: Room (7)

"Still Life, Drapery and Crumbs"

Cost: §7,600

Motive: Room (9)

"Large Black Slab" by ChiChi Smith

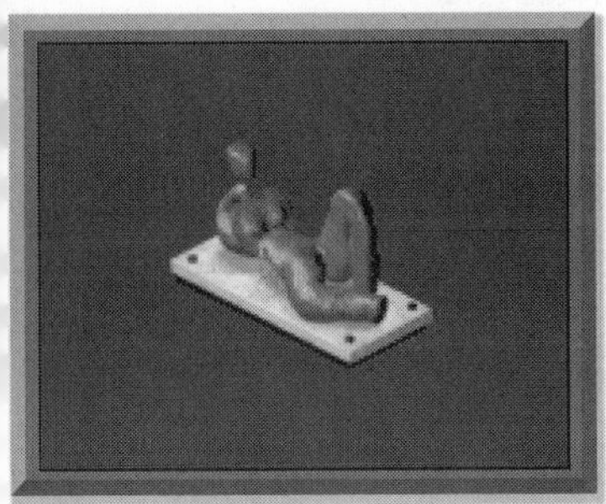

Cost: §12,648

Motive: Room (10)

Electronics

This game offers a veritable potpourri of high-tech gadgetry, ranging from potentially lifesaving items such as smoke detectors to nonessential purchases such as pinball games or virtual reality headsets. Beyond the critical electronics items—smoke detectors, telephone for receiving calls or calling services and friends, TV for cheap fun, and computer for finding a job—you should focus on items with group activity potential, especially if you like socializing and throwing parties.

> **TIP**
>
> *Electronic items can break down on a regular basis, so it is a good idea to bone up on Mechanical Skills. Until you have a qualified fix-it Sim in the house, you'll be shelling out §50 an hour for a repairman.*

FireBrand Smoke Detector

Cost: §50

Motive: None

Notes: Each detector covers one room. At the very least, place a detector in any room that has a stove or fireplace.

SimSafety IV Burglar Alarm

Cost: §250

Motive: None

Notes: An alarm unit covers one room, but an outside alarm covers an area within five tiles of the house. The police are called immediately when the alarm goes off.

SCTC BR-8 Standard Telephone

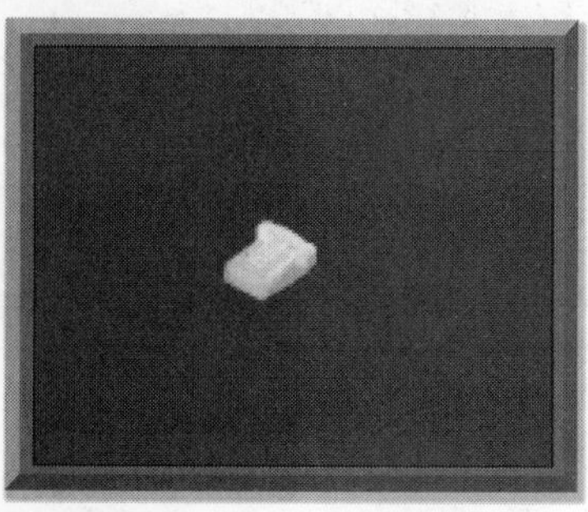

Cost: §50

Motive: None

Notes: This phone needs a surface, so it's less accessible. Best location is in the kitchen; stick with wall phones in the rest of the house.

SCTC Cordless Wall Phone

Cost: §75

Motive: None

Notes: Place these phones wherever your Sims spend a lot of time.

Urchineer Train Set by Rip Co.

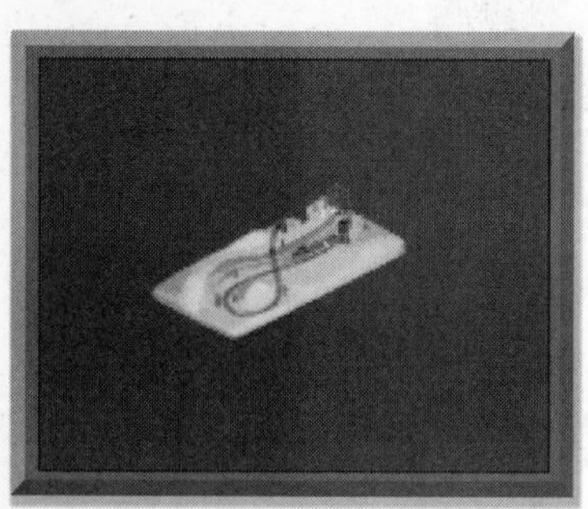

Cost: §80

Motive: Fun (2)

Notes: Group activity; can only be used by kids.

Televisions

Buying a TV is the easiest way to put a little fun into your Sims' lives, and it is a group activity. You can maximize the effect by matching the program category with your Sim's personality, as noted in the following table.

Personality	Favorite TV Show
Active	Action
Grouchy (low nice)	Horror
Outgoing	Romance
Playful	Cartoon

Your TV will eventually break down, especially if you have a family of couch potatoes. Do not attempt to repair the TV unless your Sim has at least one Mechanical Skill point (three is even better). If your Sim doesn't have the proper training, poking around inside the TV will result in electrocution.

Monochrome TV

Cost: §85

Motive: Fun (2)

Notes: Strictly for tight budgets, but it gives your Sims a little mindless fun.

Trottco 27" Color Television B94U

Cost: §500

Motive: Fun (4)

Notes: A lazy Sim's favorite activity is watching TV.

Soma Plasma TV

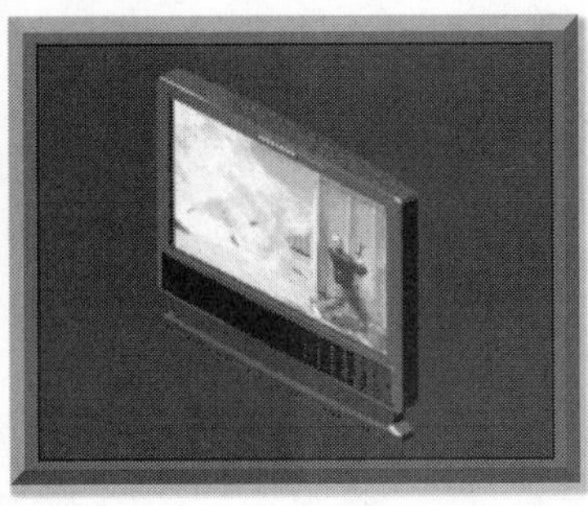

Cost: §3,500

Motive: Fun (6), Room (2)

Notes: It's expensive, but it provides instant entertainment for a full house.

Stereos

Dancing to the music is a great group activity, especially for Sims with effervescent personalities (although it is perfectly acceptable to dance alone). When a Sim dances with a houseguest, it increases both their Fun and Social ratings. You can personalize *The Sims* by placing your own MP3 files in the Music/Stations directory.

"Down Wit Dat" Boom Box

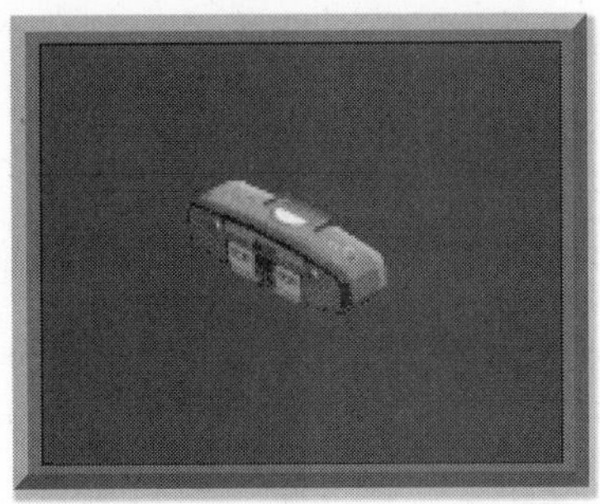

Cost: §100

Motive: Fun (2)

Notes: An inexpensive way to start a party in your front yard.

Zimantz Component Hi-Fi Stereo

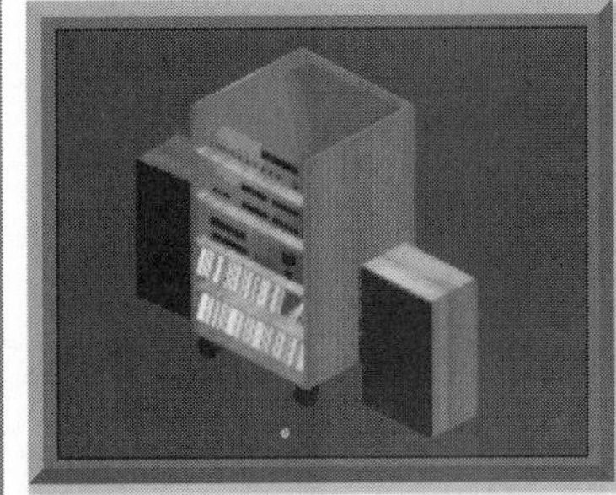

Cost: §650

Motive: Fun (3)

Notes: Perfect for your big party room.

Strings Theory Stereo

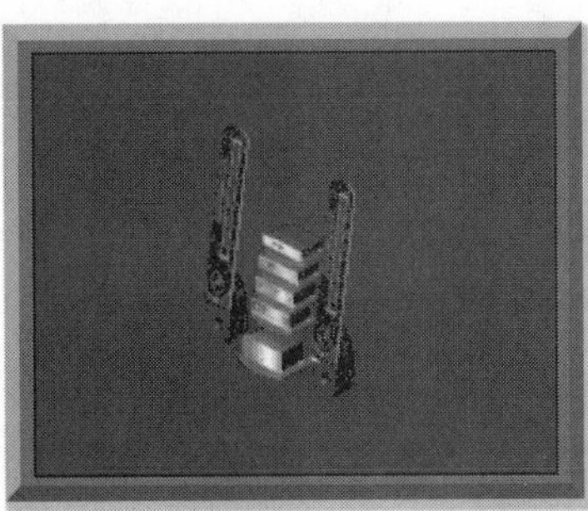

Cost: §2,550

Motives: Fun (5), Room (3)

Notes: The ultimate party machine, this is the only stereo that enhances your Room score.

Computers

A computer is a Sim's best tool for finding a job. The computer has three job postings every day, making it three times as productive as the newspaper employment ads. Aside from career search, the computer provides entertainment for the entire family, and it helps the kids keep their grades up (better chance of cash rewards from the grandparents). Playful and lazy Sims love the computer. However, if only serious Sims occupy your house, you can grab a newspaper and let the age of technology pass you by.

Moneywell Computer

Cost: §999

Motive: Fun (3), Study

Notes: All you need is a basic computer for job searching.

Microscotch Covetta Q628-1500JA

Cost: §1,800

Motive: Fun (5), Study

Notes: More power translates into better gaming.

The Brahma 2000

Cost: §2,800

Motive: Fun (7), Study

Notes: More than twice the fun of a basic computer.

Meet Marco

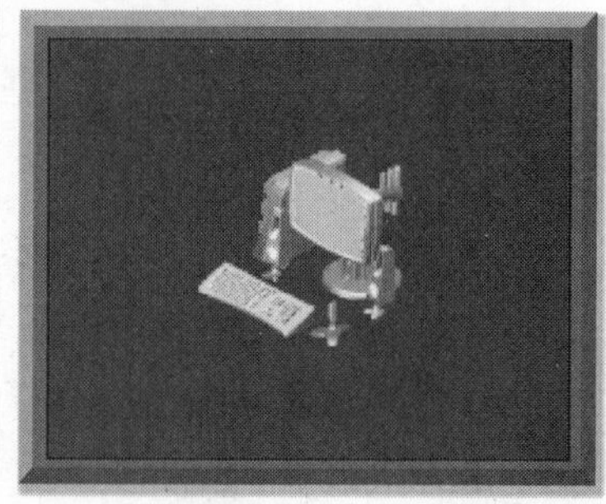

Cost: §6,500

Motive: Fun (9), Study

Notes: For Sim power users—the family will fight for playing time on this beast.

Games

OCD Systems SimRailRoad Town

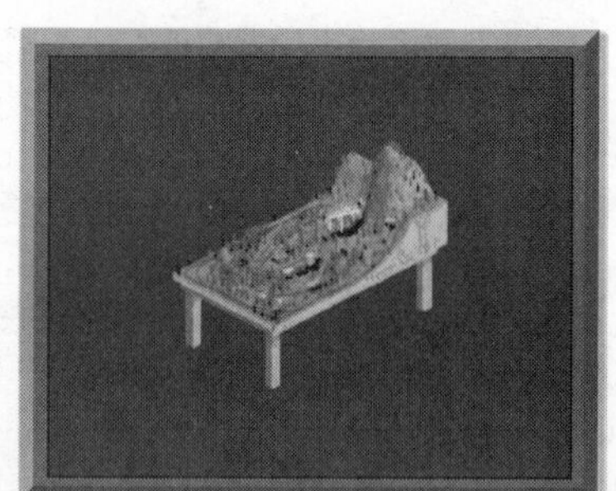

Cost: §955

Motive: Fun (4), Room (3)

Notes: You need a large area for this train table, but it is an excellent group activity and it gives a serious boost to your Room score.

"See Me, Feel Me" Pinball Machine

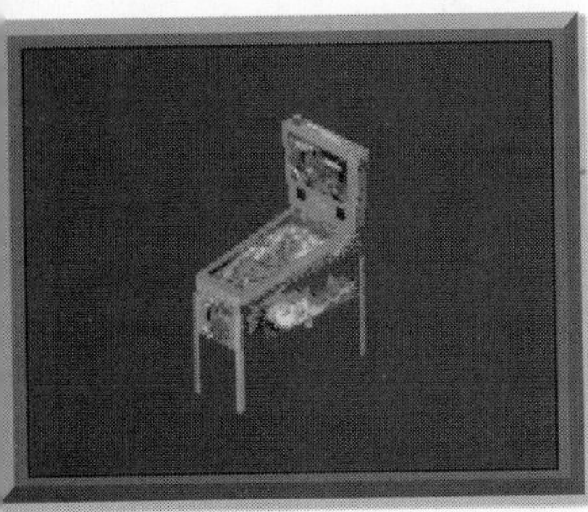

Cost: §1,800

Motive: Fun (5)

Notes: Build a big family room and add a pinball machine to keep your guests occupied for hours.

SSRI Virtual Reality Set

Cost: §2,300

Motive: Fun (7)

Notes: Playful Sims have been known to don VR glasses on their way to the bathroom (even with full bladders). For grins, wait until a Sim puts on the glasses, then immediately issue another command. The Sim head on the control panel will wear the glasses for the duration of your game.

Appliances

With the exception of the dishwasher and trash compactor, the Sim appliances are all devoted to the creation of food or java. At a bare minimum, you need refrigeration. However, if you want your Sims to eat like royalty, train at least one family member in the gentle art of cooking and provide that Sim with the latest in culinary tools.

Mr. Regular-Joe Coffee

Cost: §85

Motive: Bladder (-1), Energy (1)

Notes: Only adults can partake of the coffee rush. The effects are temporary, but sometimes it's the only way to get rolling.

Gagmia Simore Espresso Machine

Cost: §450

Motive: Bladder (-2), Energy (2), Fun (1)

Notes: If you want a morning jolt, espresso is the way to go. You'll fill your bladder twice as fast as with regular coffee, but it is a small price to pay for more energy and a splash of fun.

Brand Name Toaster Oven

Cost: §100

Motive: Hunger (1)

Notes: This little roaster is better at starting fires than cooking food. Improve your Cooking Skills and buy a real oven. Until then, use a microwave.

Positive Potential Microwave

Cost: §250

Motive: Hunger (2)

Notes: You can warm up your food without burning the house down.

Dialectric Free Standing Range

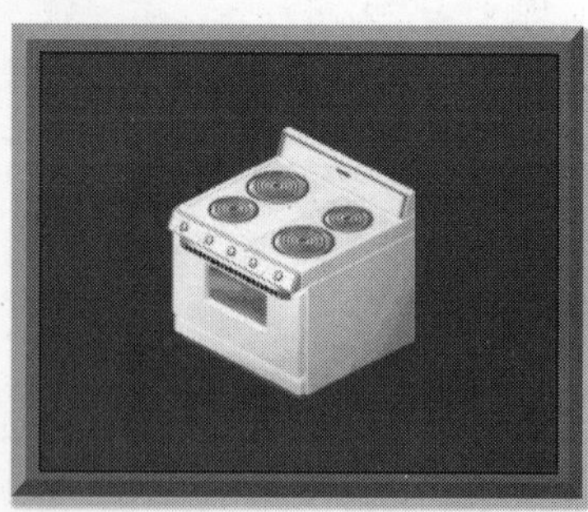

Cost: §400

Motive: Hunger (5)

Notes: After raising your Cooking Skills to three or above, you can create nutritious (and satisfying) meals on this stove.

The "Pyrotorre" Gas Range

Cost: §1,000

Motive: Hunger (7)

Notes: A skilled chef can create works of art on this stove.

NOTE

Although an expensive stove enhances your Sim meals, it is only one of three steps in the cooking process. To maximize the potential of your stove, you need an excellent refrigerator for storage, and a food processor for efficient preparation.

Wild Bill THX-451 Barbecue

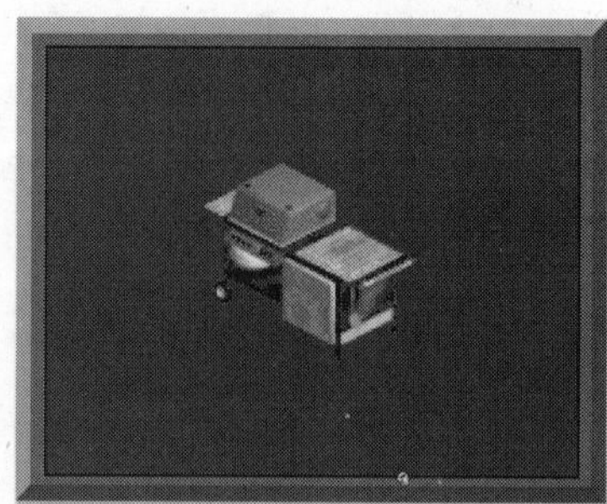

Cost: §350

Motive: Hunger (4)

Notes: Only experienced adult chefs should fire up the barbecue. Be careful not to position the grill near flammable items.

XLR8R Food Processor

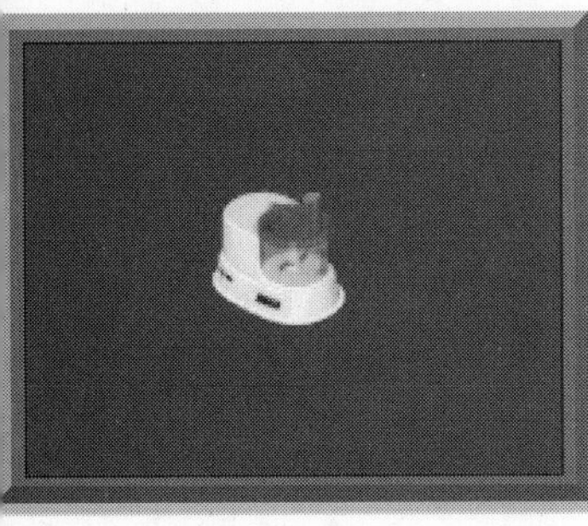

Cost: §220

Motive: Hunger (2)

Notes: A food processor speeds up meal preparation and enhances food quality.

Junk Genie Trash Compactor

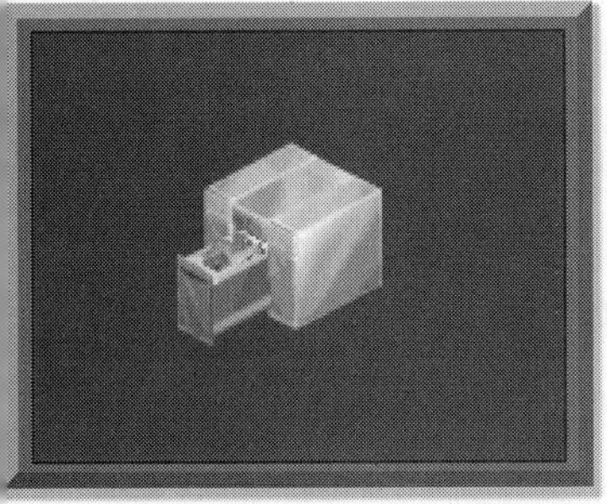

Cost: §375

Motive: None

Notes: A compactor holds more garbage than a trash can, and even when it is full, it will not degrade the Room rating because the trash is concealed.

Dish Duster Deluxe

Cost: §550

Motive: Dirty dishes lower your Room score.

Notes: Kids can't use the dishwasher, but it still cuts cleanup time considerably, and the countertop can be used for placing other items (sorry, no eating allowed).

Fuzzy Logic Dishwasher

Cost: §950

Motive: Dirty dishes lower your Room score.

Notes: The Cadillac of dishwashers cleans up kitchen messes in a snap. This model has fewer breakdowns than the Dish Duster.

Llamark Refrigerator

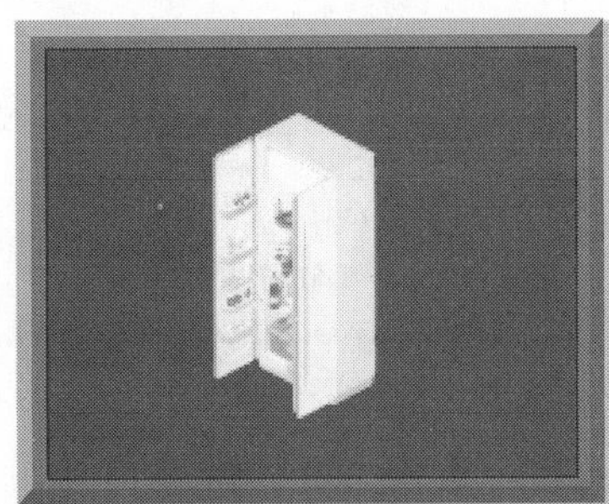

Cost: §600

Motive: Hunger (6)

Notes: This model is sufficient while your Sims are building up their Cooking Skills.

Porcina Refrigerator Model P1g-S

Cost: §1,200

Motive: Hunger (7)

Notes: This model produces more satisfying food for your Sims.

Freeze Secret Refrigerator

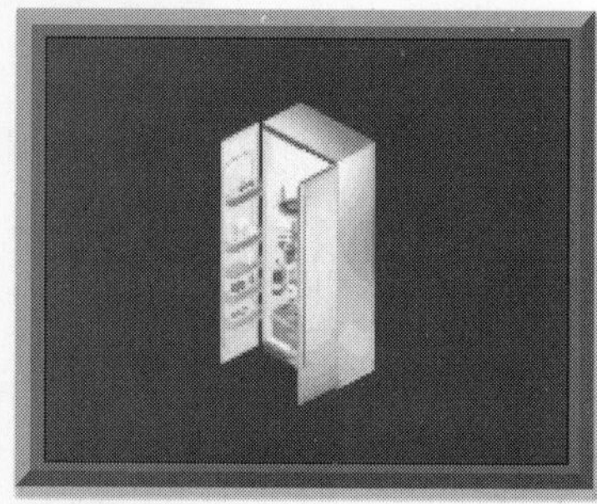

Cost: §2,500

Motive: Hunger (8)

Notes: The best place to store your food. When it's matched with a food processor, gas stove, and an experienced chef, your Sims will be licking their lips.

Plumbing

Sims can't carry buckets to the well for their weekly bath, and the outhouse hasn't worked in years, so install various plumbing objects to maintain a clean, healthy environment. Of course, not every plumbing object is essential, but you can't beat a relaxing hour in the hot tub with a few of your closest friends (or casual acquaintances).

Hydronomic Kitchen Sink

Cost: §250

Motive: Hygiene (2)

Notes: Without it the Sims would be washing dishes in the bathroom.

Epikouros Kitchen Sink

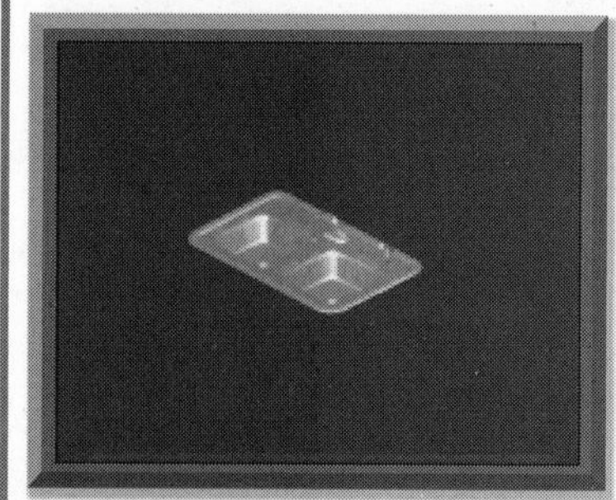

Cost: §500

Motive: Hygiene (3)

Notes: It's twice as big as the single, but a dishwasher is a better investment.

"Andersonville" Pedestal Sink

Cost: §400

Motive: Hygiene (2)

Notes: Neat Sims like to wash their hands after using the toilet.

lygeia-O-Matic Toilet

Cost: §300

Motive: Bladder (8)

lotes: Hey, your only other option is the floor.

lush Force 5 XLT

Cost: §1,200

Motives: Comfort (4), Bladder (8)

lotes: Your Sims can't go to the ballpark to get a good seat, but hey can sit in a lap of luxury in the bathroom.

SpaceMiser Shower

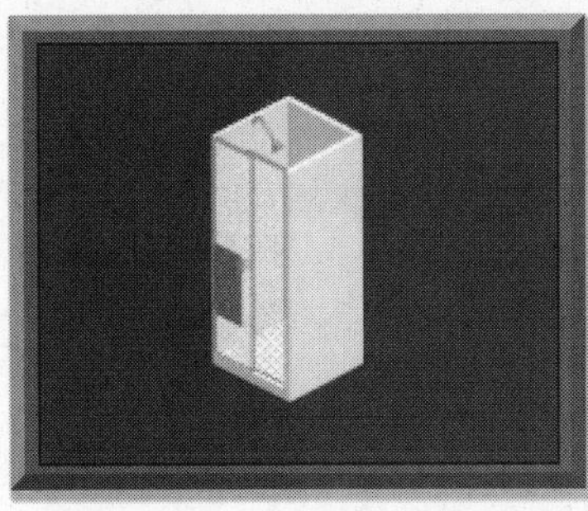

Cost: §650

Motive: Hygiene (6)

Notes: This is basic equipment in a Sims bathroom. One Sim can shower at a time, and the neat ones tend to linger longer than the sloppy ones. Sims are generally shy if they are not in love with a housemate, so you may need more than one shower (and bathroom) to prevent a traffic jam in the bathroom.

Justa Bathtub

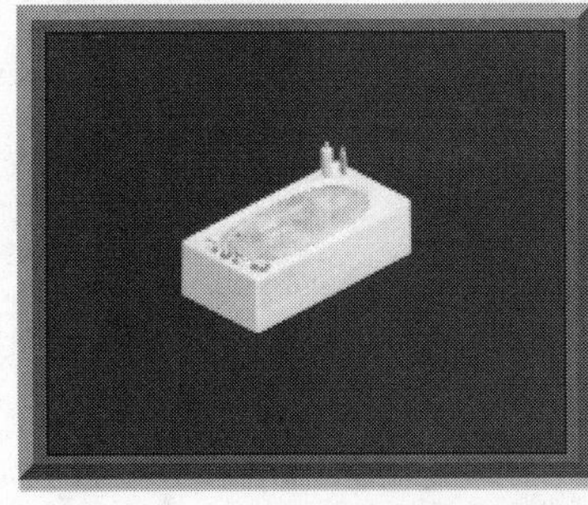

Cost: §800

Motives: Comfort (3), Hygiene (6)

Notes: Your Sims get a double benefit from a relaxing bath when they have a little extra time.

Sani-Queen Bathtub

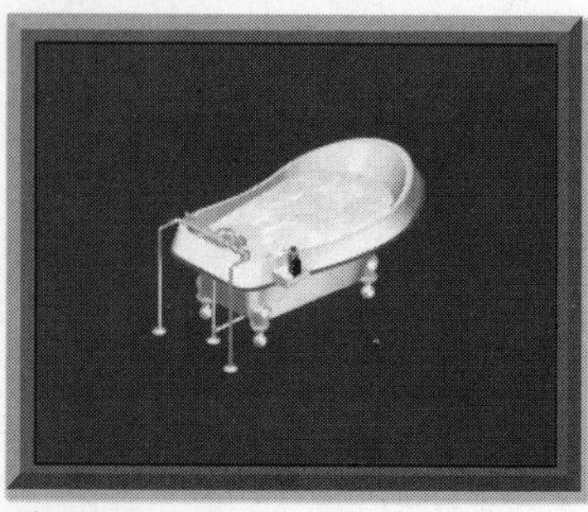

Cost: §1,500

Motives: Comfort (5), Hygiene (8)

Notes: Almost twice the price, but the added Comfort and Hygiene points are worth it.

Hydrothera Bathtub

Cost: §3,200

Motives: Comfort (8), Hygiene (10)

Notes: The most fun a Sim can have alone. Save your Simoleans, buy it, and listen to sounds of relaxation.

WhirlWizard Hot Tub

Cost: §6,500

Motives: Comfort (6), Hygiene (2), Fun (2)

Notes: Up to four adult Sims can relax, mingle, and begin lasting relationships in the hot tub.

Lighting

Sims love natural light, so make sure the sun shine through your windows from every direction. And, when the sun goes down, your Sims need plenty c lighting on the walls, floors, and tables to illuminate their world until bedtime. Although only three lamps listed below have direct impact on the Room score, all of the lamps have a collective effect when spread evenly throughout the home. Pay special attention to key activity areas in the kitchen, family room, bedrooms, and of course, the bathroom.

CAUTION

Lamp bulbs burn out with use, and they must be replaced. Sims can replace their own bulbs, but without Mechanical Skills, they run the risk of electrocution. Hiring a repairman is another option, but at §50 per hour, this can be very costly.

Table Lamps

Bottle Lamp

Cost: §25

Motive: None

ve n' Haight Lava Lamp

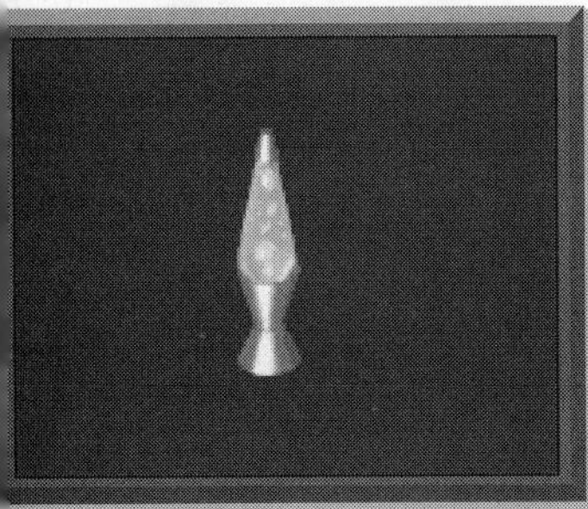

Cost: §80

Motive: Room (2)

eramiche Table Lamp

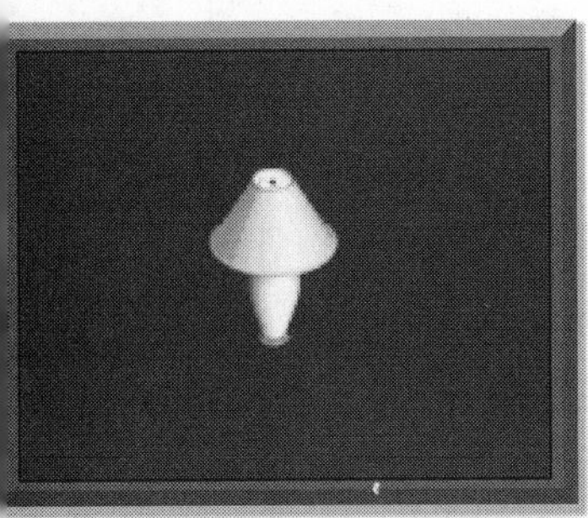

Cost: §85

Motive: None

lite Reflections Chrome Lamp

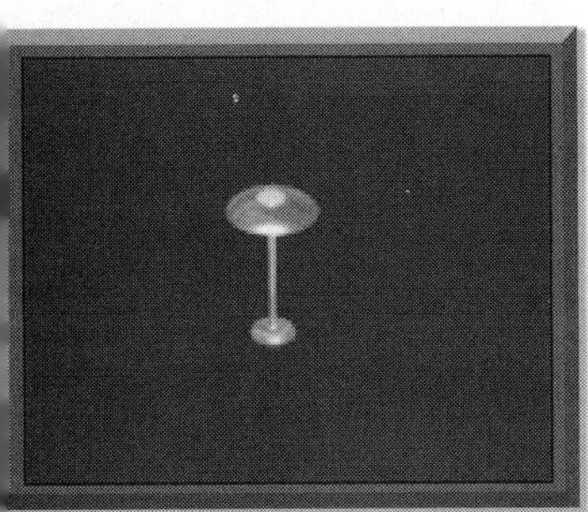

Cost: §180

Motive: None

SC Electric Co. Antique Lamp

Cost: §300

Motive: Room (1)

Floor Lamps

Halogen Heaven Lamp by Contempto

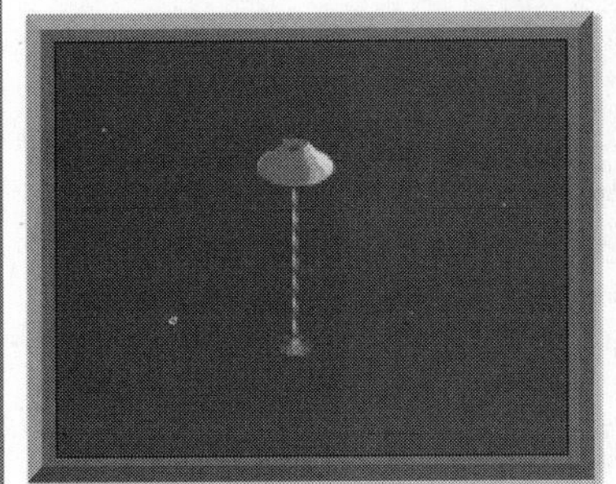

Cost: §50

Motive: None

Lumpen Lumeniat Floor Lamp

Cost: §100

Motive: None

Torchosteronne Floor Lamp

Cost: §350

Motive: Room (1)

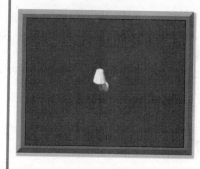

Wall Lamps

White Globe Sconce

Cost: §35

Motive: None

Oval Glass Sconce

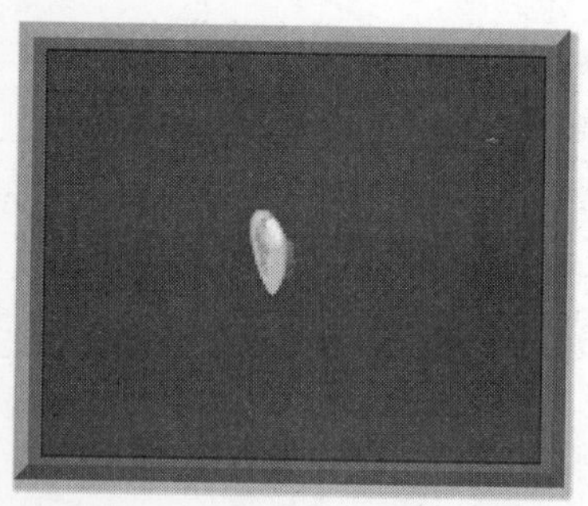

Cost: §85

Motive: None

Top Brass Sconce

Cost: §110

Motive: None

Blue Plate Special Sconce

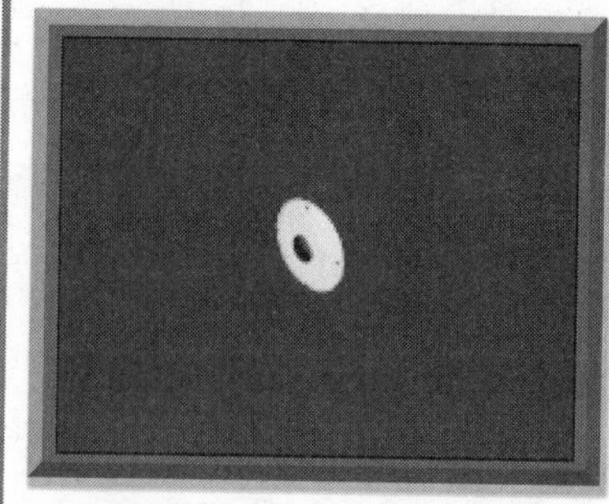

Cost: §135

Motive: None

Outside Lamp

Garden Lamp (Outdoor Use Only)

Cost: §50

Motive: None

Miscellaneous

We're down to the objects that are hard to fit into a category—everything from bookcases to beverage bars. Don't make the mistake of ignoring these items because you think they're luxuries; your Sim's life would be extremely difficult without a trash can, alarm clock, and bookcase. Plus, if you want to improve your Sim's Charisma and Body ratings, you'll need a mirror and exercise machine. So, once you install the basic objects in your house, look to the Miscellaneous category for objects that take your Sim's lifestyle to the next level.

SnoozMore Alarm Clock

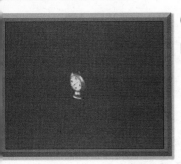

Cost: §30

Motive: None

Notes: After you set the clock, it will ring two hours before the carpool arrives for every working Sim in your house.

Trash Can

Cost: §30

Motive: None

Notes: Without a place to put trash, your Sim house will become a fly-infested hovel.

Magical Mystery Toy Box

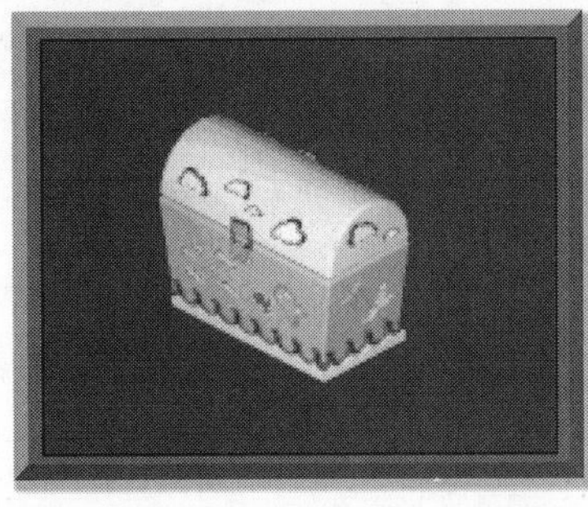

Cost: §50

Motive: Fun (2)

Notes: A good entertainment alternative if your kids are getting bleary-eyed in front of the computer.

Narcisco Wall Mirror

Cost: §100

Motive: Improves Charisma

Notes: Adults can Practice speech in front of the mirror to improve their Charisma.

Medicine Cabinet

Cost: §125

Motive: Hygiene (1), Improves Charisma

Notes: Your Sims can Practice speech in the bathroom and improve their Hygiene at the same time.

Narcisco Floor Mirror

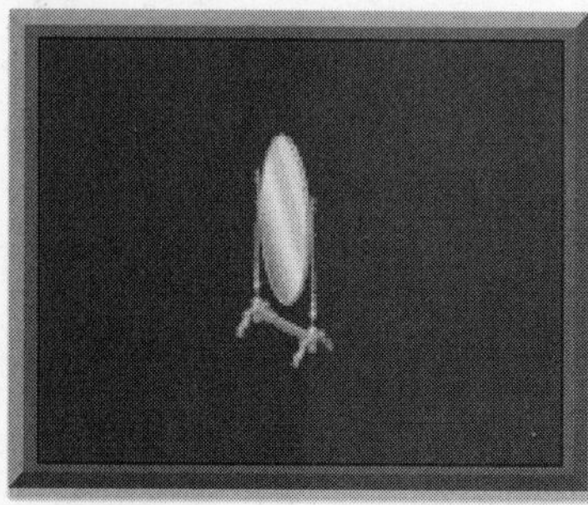

Cost: §150

Motive: Improves Charisma

Notes: Place this mirror anywhere to practice Charisma without locking other Sims out of the bathroom.

Will Lloyd Wright Doll House

Cost: §180

Motive: Fun (2)

Notes: An engaging group activity for kids and adults.

Cheap Pine Bookcase

Cost: §250

Motive: Fun (1), Improve Cooking, Mechanical, and Study Skills

Notes: Reading books is the best way to prevent premature death from fires or electrocution.

"Dimanche" Folding Easel

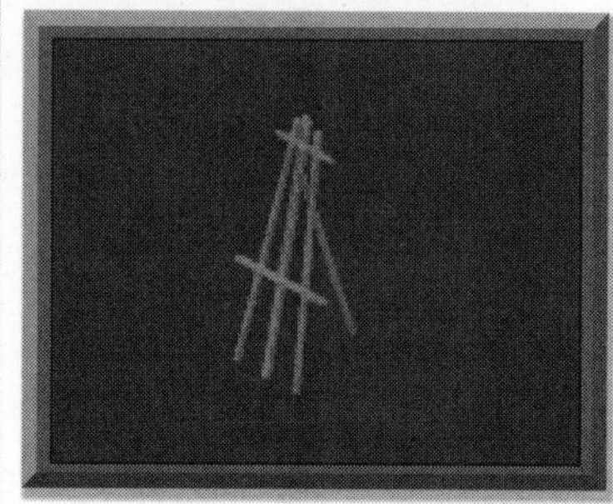

Cost: §250

Motive: Fun (2), Improve Creativity

Notes: With practice, a Sim can improve Creativity, and eventually sell a picture for up to §166.

Pinegulcher Dresser

Cost: §250

Motive: None

Notes: A Sim can change into various formal, work, and leisure outfits, and even acquire a new body type.

Kinderstuff Dresser

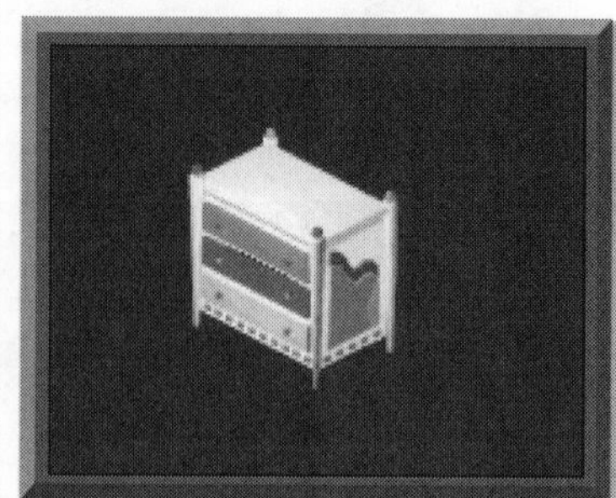

Cost: §300

Motive: None

Notes: Kids like to dress up too!

mishim Bookcase

Cost: §500

Motive: Fun (2), Improves Cooking, Mechanical, and Study Skills

otes: This expensive bookcase awards Skill points at the same ate as the cheaper one.

huck Matewell Chess Set

Cost: §500

Motive: Fun (2), Improves Logic

otes: Serious Sims gain the most Fun points by playing, and ny two Sims can improve Logic by playing each other.

raditional Oak Armoire

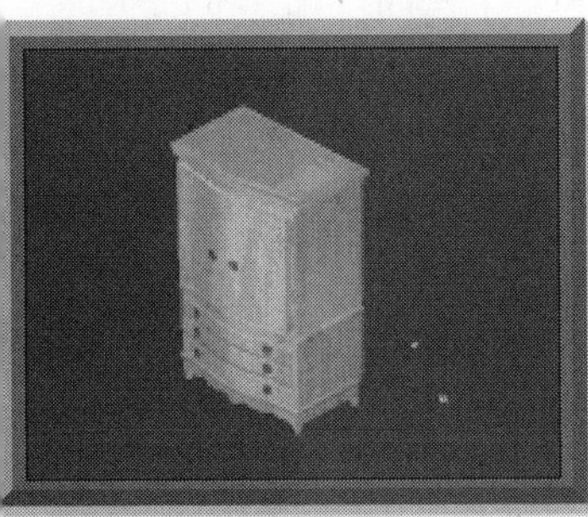

Cost: §550

Motive: Room (1)

otes: This dresser allows your Sim to change clothes (body kins). The choices vary, depending upon the Sim's current outfit.

SuperDoop Basketball Hoop

Cost: §650

Motive: Fun (4)

Notes: Active Sims love to play hoops, and any visitor is welcome to join the fun. A Sim with higher Body points performs better on the court.

"Exerto" Benchpress Exercise Machine

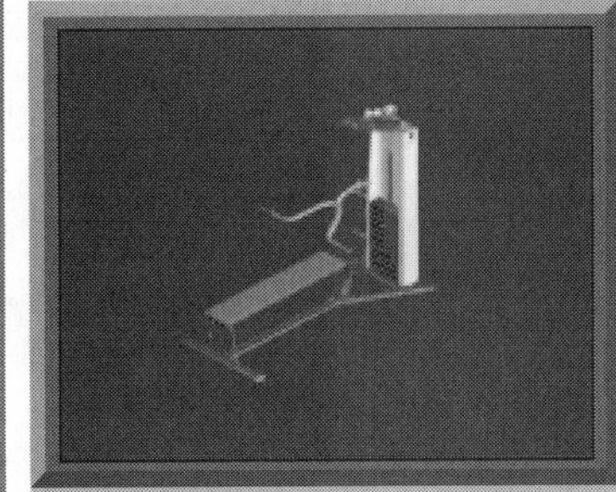

Cost: §700

Motive: Improves Body

Notes: Adult Sims can bulk up their Body points with exercise sessions.

Bachman Wood Beverage Bar

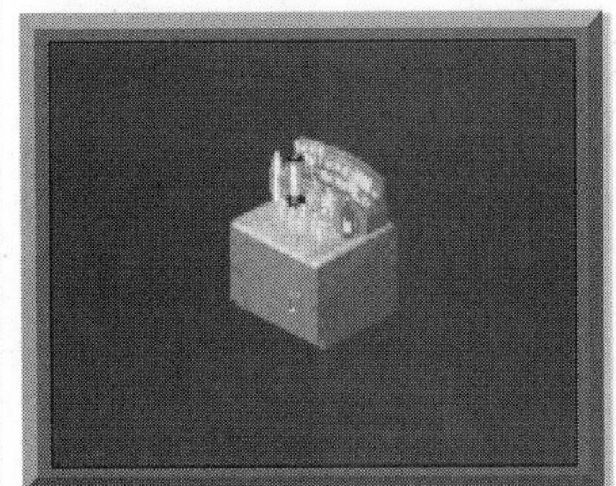

Cost: §800

Motive: Hunger (1), Fun (3), Room (2)

Notes: Every drink lowers the Bladder score, but adult Sims like to make drinks for themselves and friends. Kids can grab a soda from the fridge.

Libri di Regina Bookcase

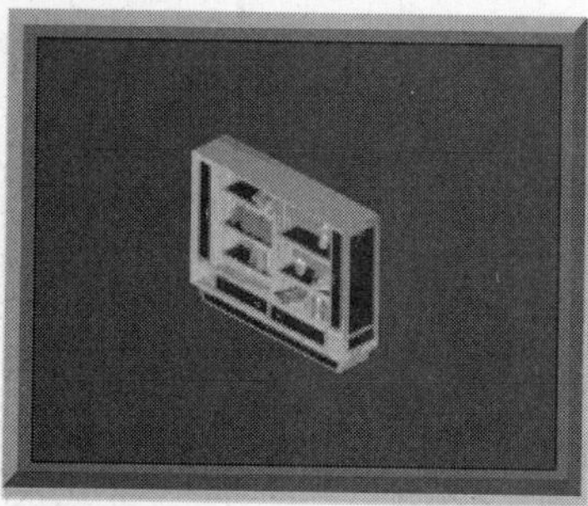

Cost: §900

Motive: Fun (3), Improves Cooking, Mechanical, and Study Skills

Notes: This stylish bookcase is perfect for a swanky Sim pad, but it still imparts Skill points at the same rate as the pine model.

Antique Armoire

Cost: §1,200

Motive: Room (2)

Notes: A more expensive version of the cheaper armoire, but it adds twice as many Room points.

The Funinator Deluxe

Cost: §1,200

Motive: Fun (5)

Notes: When the house is swarming with kids, send them outside to raise their Fun bar and burn some energy.

Chimeway & Daughters Piano

Cost: §3,500

Motive: Fun (4), Room (3) Improves Creativity

Notes: The most creative Sims will produce more beautiful music. The better the music, the greater the chance that listeners will like it. If a listener does not like the music, both Sims' Relationship scores will deteriorate.

Aristoscratch Pool Table

Cost: §4,200

Motive: Fun (6)

Notes: Up to two Sims use the table at the same time. Make sure that you allow enough room for Sims to get to the table and walk around it during play.

CHAPTER 7: ALL IN THE FAMILY

Introduction

Up to this point, we've covered the mechanics of *The Sims*. By now you should be familiar with creating families, building houses, buying objects, and getting jobs; and you should have considerable insight into how a Sim thinks and acts. Now, let's put it all together and join several Sim households in action. In this chapter we introduce you to working Sims families, ranging from one-Sim homes to larger households with kids and babies. Finally, we take an in-depth look at one of the toughest challenges in *The Sims*: building positive (and long-lasting) Relationships.

You Can Make It Alone

The biggest difficulty in being a bachelor is that you have to do everything yourself (sounds like real life, doesn't it?). You'll need to cook, clean, and improve your Skills, while at the same time keep up with a work schedule and satisfy your personal Motives. There's always time for Fun, and a good sofa or easy chair will provide a measure of Comfort. However, it's impossible to socialize while at work, and you will be frustrated watching neighbors drop by during the day and then leave when no one answers the door.

The Single Sim's Career

As a lone Sim you must choose a job that has decent hours and light friendship demands. This leaves a Military career as your only option. At most levels you work a six-hour day, and you won't need a single friend for the first five levels. A promotion to Level 6 requires one friend, but that can be established after you refine your schedule.

Designing a Bachelor Pad

There are several considerations when designing and furnishing a house for one Sim. Review the following checklist before you place your first wall stake.

Fig. 7-1. It's hardly the lap of luxury, but you have everything you need to get a job, keep your sanity, and learn how to cook.

- **Keep your house small, and place the front door close to the street. This allows you to milk a few extra minutes out of every morning before meeting the car pool.**
- **The interior should include a bedroom, bathroom, and living room. Rather than add a family room, use an outside patio area for Fun objects and an exercise machine. A Military career requires an ever-increasing number of Body Skill points.**
- **Install only enough counter space to place a food processor and prepare your meals. This leaves more space for a table and chairs. Buy at least two chairs so that you can socialize with a friend while sharing a meal.**
- **Without the space or the budget to buy expensive sofas or recliners, get a top-of-the-line bed, which enables your Sim to get by on fewer hours of sleep. Buy an inexpensive nightstand for an alarm clock, and add a few wall lights to boost your Room score.**
- **You'll need a computer for your job search, but keep in mind that you can return it within 24 Sim-hours for a full refund. Find your Military job and then pack up the PC.**

Buy an expensive refrigerator to maximize the quality of your food, but don't bother with a stove until your Sim learns how to cook.

Because of your career, there's no need to socialize until you are up for promotion to Level 6, so don't waste money on living room chairs or an expensive sofa. A cheap TV will provide enough Fun for now.

Leaving the Single Life

Eventually you will tire of the solitary lifestyle, which, thanks to the romantic tendencies of most Sims, is not a problem. The first step is friendship. After the Relationship bar tops 70, your Sim needs to lay on the romance, with plenty of kissing and hugging. Eventually, the Propose option will appear on the menu.

Fig. 7-2. The kissin' and huggin' pays off; now it's time to pop the question.

A marriage proposal can only take place in the home of the proposer, so set the mood (you know, empty your Bladder somewhere other than on the floor, clean up yesterday's dishes, and hide those overdue bills). After accepting the proposal, your new spouse moves into your place, along with a good job (a good thing) and plenty of money (a really good thing). But, proposing does not guarantee a positive response. For example, a Sim will never accept the proposal on an empty stomach, so you might want to eat dinner first.

Fig. 7-3. "We're alone, the time is perfect, and I've got grass stains on my knee."

Fig. 7-4. "Nope, sorry, I can't marry you on an empty stomach. Besides, your current lover is hiding in the bushes."

Keep in mind that you have to create potential mates, because the game won't provide them. You might as well choose compatible personalities, and it doesn't hurt to spend some time on career development. Remember that another Sim can also propose to you in his or her house; so unless you want to change residences, hold the romantic interludes at your place.

> **NOTE**
>
> *After marriage, your Sim will still share a bed with any other Sim with a high enough Friendship score (over 70), so don't be surprised if your Sim ends up on the couch when his buddy beats him to the sack.*

Fig. 7-5. When two Sims decide to get married, they change clothes and complete the ceremony within seconds.

Interestingly, if your future spouse already has children, and at least one adult still resides in his or her original house, the kids stay. So, your new spouse arrives with job and bank account intact, sans kids. What a deal!

That isn't the only unusual aspect of married life in SimsVille. Marriage is not sacred here, at least not in the legal sense. A Sim can have multiple mates all living under the same roof, as pictured in figure 7-6. The interpersonal dynamics can sometimes get a little dicey, but it's workable, and the extra income is great!

Fig. 7-6. After the wedding, our Sim bride goes to bed with her former boyfriend.

TIP

A three-way relationship makes it easier to have babies. Not only are there additional combinations for procreation, but you can also have one of the working adults take a night job, so there is a caregiver for the baby during the day. Even with staggered schedules, there will be at least one sleepless Sim until the baby matures, so don't get too complacent with this arrangement.

Married, with Children

After your Sims promise undying love and devotion to each other (or, at least until the next promotion), it's time to have a baby. Actually, your Sims can live together for years without having children, but if they do, you'll be missing one of the *The Sims*' most vexing experiences.

Conception

The exercise of making a baby is similar to the steps taken to activate the marriage Proposal option. First, get a male and female Sim together, and then concentrate on strengthening their relationship. When both Sims are obviously enjoying each other's company, lay on the hugs and kisses. Keep smooching until you receive the option to have a baby, as pictured in figure 7-7.

Fig. 7-7. A little bundle of joy is just a click away.

If you answer yes, a bassinet appears almost ıstantly, amid an explosion of dandelions. The appy couple celebrates the new arrival, then they uickly go back to their daily routine. This baby ıing is a snap. Well, not exactly.

Fig. 7-8. Yippee! It's a boy!

In short order, the little bundle of joy starts :reaming. A Sim will eventually respond to the ries, but rather than wait, get someone to the aby immediately. Clicking on the bassinet reveals ıree options: Feed, Play, or Sing. When in doubt, eed the baby, but be prepared to come right ack with Play or Sing when the baby starts ailing again.

Fig. 7-9. Kids do a great job entertaining the baby during one of its frequent crying sessions.

This mayhem continues for three Sim days, during which time the household will be in an uproar. Forget about getting eight hours of beauty sleep. Designate one Sim as primary caregiver, preferably one who does not work, because the baby's cries wake any Sim in the room. The first day is nonstop crying. By the second day, the baby sleeps for a few hours at a time; take advantage of the break and send the caregiver to bed. As long as you stay responsive, the baby evolves into a runny-nosed kid, and the family can get back to normal. However, if you spend too much time in the hot tub and not enough time with the baby, a social service worker will march into your house and take the baby, as pictured in figure 7-10. You'll only receive one warning, so don't take this responsibility lightly.

Fig. 7-10. We hardly knew the little tyke!

NOTE

The bassinet appears near the spot where your Sims made the decision to have a baby. Although the Sims cannot move the bassinet, you can use the Hand Tool to move it. Pick a location that is isolated from other sleeping areas, so the disturbance is kept to a minimum.

Building and Maintaining Healthy Relationships

Gathering an ever-increasing number of friends is critical for career advancement, especially at the higher levels. It is also your Sims' only way to build up their Social scores and fend off frequent bouts of depression. In this section we outline the steps required for finding potential friends, building up positive feelings, and then maintaining healthy relationships.

Talk Is Cheap

The easiest way to make friends is often overlooked, because it is uneventful compared to other social events. However, you can almost always initiate a conversation between Sims (regardless of their Friendship scores), and keep it going for a very long time. During this benign exchange of thought balloons, you can usually nudge the Friendship score in a positive direction. When starting from 0 it takes a few encounters to get over 50 (true friendship), but once you reach this threshold, the action picks up considerably. Our newly married Sims went from a score of 64 to a marriage proposal in one evening. Although the woman eventually declined because her stomach was growling, she proposed the next day and the marriage was consummated.

Fig. 7-11. Keep talking and your Friendship score will grow.

Finding Time to Socialize

After your Sim starts working, it's difficult to find time to call other Sims and arrange meetings. Mornings are worst, although you have more options if your neighborhood has several non-working Sims. Your best bet is to start socializing right after coming home from work. Take care of personal needs first—Hygiene and Bladder—and then "Serve Dinner." Don't let a bad chef get near the stove; you can't afford to waste time putting out a fire or your guests will leave. With a counter full of food, your friends head straight for the kitchen, where you can chat over a plate of Sim-grub and then plan the rest of your evening.

Positive Social Events

After everyone is finished eating, take a little time for pleasant conversation. In the case of the female Sims pictured in figure 7-11, there is a lot of fence mending to accomplish, because one just stole the other's love interest. But, Sims are generally forgiving, and a quarrel can be mended with a few drinks, a game of pool, or a long soak in the hot tub.

Ideally, your house has an entertainment room with group activity items such as a pool table, stereo, or beverage bar. After you get everyone into the room, keep them busy with a string of activities. Even our former lovers can't resist a dance when the music starts playing, as pictured in figure 7-12.

Fig. 7-12. Our Sim guy is enjoying this dance with his former girlfriend, although his current wife will probably slap him when the music stops playing (if she can stay awake long enough).

CAUTION

Avoid close activities such as dancing, hugging, etc. when the current spouse or love interest is in the room. When the dance was over (figure 7-12), our Sim wife did indeed slap her new husband, causing her recently mended Relationship score with the other woman to drop from +14 to –7.

One of the most difficult aspects of ntertaining in the evening is keeping the host rom falling asleep on the floor. After a hard day's vork, most Sims begin nodding out around 10:00 .m. You can squeeze a little extra time out of the vening if they take a short nap after coming ome from work. Be prepared for a grouchy Sim n the morning (figure 7-13) if the evening's estivities stretch too far into the night.

Fig. 7-13. Our tired party girl hurries off to the car pool without a shower—not a good way to impress her superiors.

TIP

After your guests arrive, you need to micromanage your Sims so they don't go off and take care of their own needs. Obviously, you must pay attention to a full Bladder, but you can delay other actions by redirecting your Sims to group activities. Break up the party when your Sims are teetering on the edge of exhaustion or they'll fall asleep on the floor.

CAUTION

Visiting Sims generally hang around until 1:00 a.m. or later, which is undoubtedly past your bedtime. Direct your Sims to bed at the appropriate time, or they may feel compelled to hang out with their guests until well past midnight, as pictured in figure 7-14.

Fig. 7-14. Our host Sim is still cleaning up dishes when he should be asleep.

Stockpiling Potential Friends

When your career advances to the top promotion level, you need more than 10 friends in every career except the Military. Hence, it's a good idea to create a few additional families early in the game, and you might want to fill one house with the maximum of eight Sims to dramatically increase your pool.

Visitors Coming and Going

The following tables include important information on how and why visitors do the things they do. You may not be able to directly control your guests' actions, but at least you won't take it personally when they decide to split.

Visitors' Starting Motives

MOTIVE	STARTING VALUE
Bladder	0 to 30
Comfort	30 to 70
Energy	35
Fun	-20 to 20
Hunger	-30 to -20
Hygiene	90
Social	-50 to -40

In a perfect Sim-world, visitors leave your house just past 1:00 a.m. However if one of their Motives falls into the danger zone, they will depart earlier. When this happens, the Sim's thought balloon reveals a reason for the early exit.

Visitors' Leaving Motives

MOTIVE	DROPS BELOW THIS VALUE
Bladder	-90
Comfort	-70
Energy	-80
Fun	-55
Hunger	-50
Hygiene	-70
Mood	-75
Room	-100
Social	-85

Guest Activities

There are three types of visitor activities: those initiated by a family member, shared activities, and autonomous activities where guests are on their own. The following sections and tables describe each type.

Activities Initiated by Family Member

One of the Sims under your control must prepare food or turn on the TV before visitors can join in. Turning on the TV takes a second, but you need a little prep time for a meal. It's a good idea to begin meal preparation immediately after inviting friends over.

Shared Activities

A Sim can start any of the following activities and then invite the participation of a guest.

OBJECT	VISITORS' INVOLVEMENT
Basketball Hoop	Join
Chess	Join
Dollhouse	Watch
Hot Tub	Join
Pinball Machine	Join
Play Structure	Join
Piano	Watch
Pool Table	Join
Stereo	Join, Dance
Train Set	Watch

Autonomous Activities

Visiting Sims can begin any of the following activities on their own.

Visitors' Autonomous Activities

OBJECT	AUTONOMOUS ACTION
Aquarium	Watch Fish
Baby	Play
Bar	Have a Drink
Chair	Sit
Chair (Recliner)	Sit
Coffee (Espresso Machine)	Drink Espresso
Coffeemaker	Drink Coffee
Fire	Panic
Flamingo	View
Fountain	Play
Lava Lamp	View
Painting	View
Pool	Swim
Pool Diving Board	Dive In
Pool Ladder	Get In/Out
Sculpture	View
Sink	Wash Hands
Sofa	Sit
Toilet	Use, Flush
Tombstone/Urn	Mourn
Toy Box	Play
Trash Can (Inside)	Dispose

Social Interactions

The results of various interactions are best learned by experience because of the individual personality traits that come into play. However, it helps to have an idea what each action may produce. The following table offers notes on each interaction.

INTERACTION	DESCRIPTION
Back Rub	When well-received, it is a good transition into kissing and hugging, but the Relationship score should already be over 50.
Brag	This is what mean Sims do to your Sim. Don't use it, unless you want to ruin a good friendship.
Compliment	Generally positive, but you should withhold compliments until your Relationship score is above 15.
Dance	Great activity between friends (40+), but it almost always causes a jealous reaction from a jilted lover.
Entertain	A somewhat goofy activity, but it usually works well with other Playful Sims.
Fight	Don't do it (unless you know you can take the other Sim!).
Flirt	A great way to boost a strong Relationship (70+) into the serious zone, but watch your back. Flirting usually triggers a jealous reaction from significant others.
Give Gift	A benign way to say you like the other Sim, or that you're sorry for acting like an idiot at the last party; best used with 40+ Relationship scores.
Hug	This one's always fun if the hug-ee's Relationship score is +60; a good transition to kisses, and then a marriage proposal.
Joke	Good between casual friends (+15) who are both Playful.
Kiss	The relationship is heating up, but if a jealous ex or current lover is in the vicinity, someone could get slapped.
Talk	The starting point of every friendship.
Tease	Why bother, unless you don't like the other Sim.
Tickle	Not as positive as it might seem, but Playful Sims are definitely more receptive.

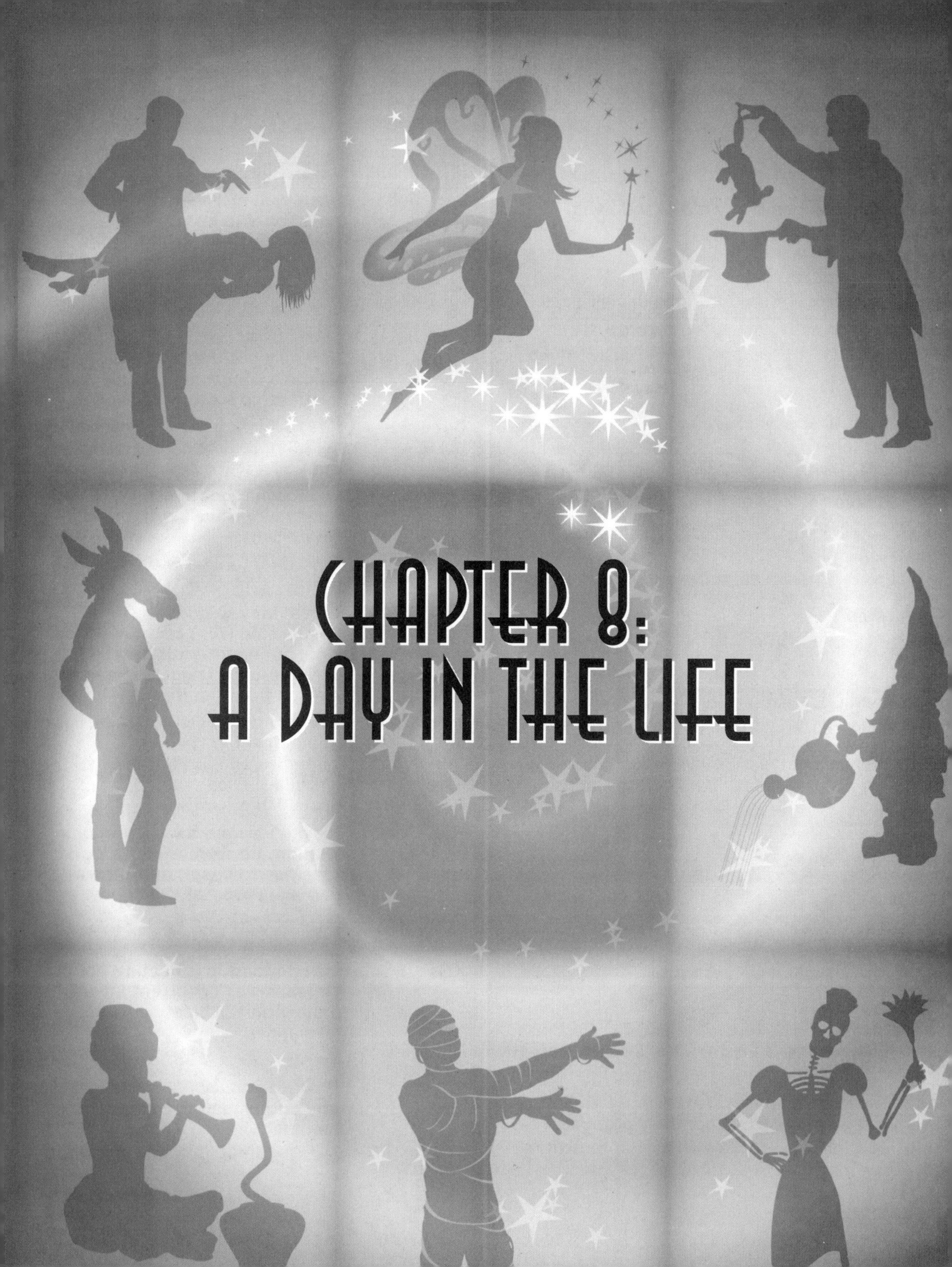

CHAPTER 8: A DAY IN THE LIFE

ntroduction

ow, it's time to turn on our Sim-Cam and follow few of our families as they handle the ups and owns of Sim life. In this chapter we switch to a crapbook format, with screenshots of our Sims n interesting—and sometimes compromising—ituations. Admittedly, we coaxed our Sims into ome of these dilemmas. But it's all in fun, and we hink it's the best way for you to get a feel for this mazing game.

As the Sim Turns

Five o'clock wake-up call is not pretty. Even with full Energy bars, your Sims can be a little cranky, but don't give them any slack. Get the best chef into the kitchen pronto, to serve breakfast for everyone in the house.

Switching to Zoomed Out view is a good way to manage the household early in the morning. This way you can quickly target important tasks for completion before the car pool arrives.

Our third adult roommate, Mortimer, just returned home from his night shift, so for now, his needs are secondary. We put him to work mopping the kitchen floor (the dishwasher broke last night, but everyone was falling asleep, so we figured it would keep until morning).

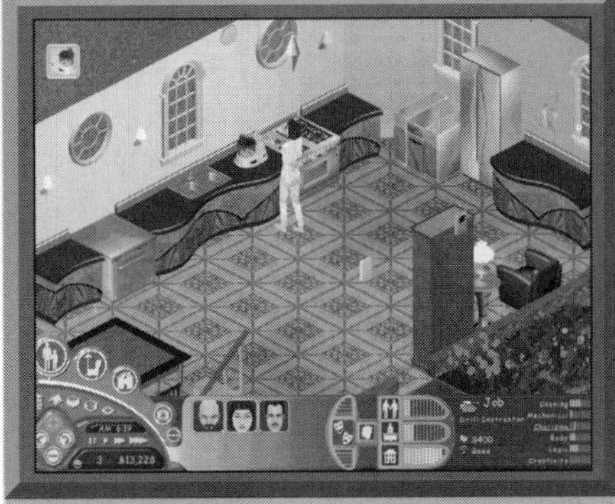

Before we are accused of being sexist, we should explain that the only reason Bella is cooking for everyone is that she is the most experienced chef. If Mark turns on the stove, chances are the kitchen will burn down. We promise to boost his Cooking Skills at the first opportunity.

Mark is, well, busy at the moment. It's too bad he doesn't gain Energy points for sitting on the toilet, because he stayed up much too late last night. A good breakfast helps, but getting through the day won't be easy, and he can forget about any promotions thanks to his sub-par mood.

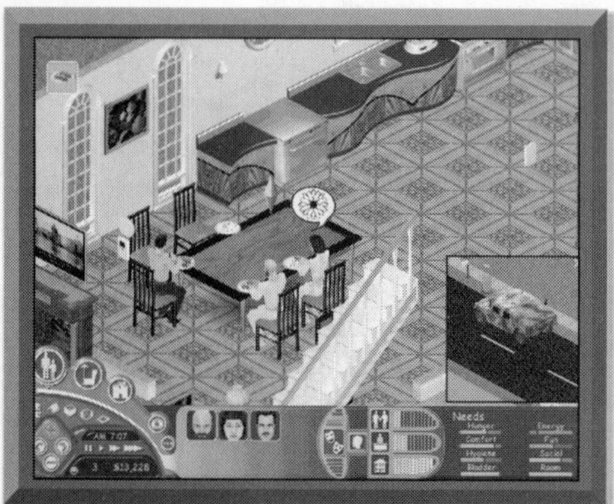

It's a nice family breakfast with husband Mortimer on the left, wife Bella on the right, and Bella's ex-boyfriend Mark in the middle. However, there isn't much time for chitchat, because the car pool has arrived, and it will leave at a few minutes past nine.

Bella is on her way to the car pool and we have about a half hour to get Mark in gear, which may be a problem due to his low Energy rating. Unfortunately, Bella's Hygiene leaves much to be desired. We make a mental note to get her into the shower before bedtime tonight so she'll be fresh as a daisy in the morning).

Uh-oh, big time problem with Mark. He's standing in the kitchen in his pajamas, in a catatonic state. With only a half hour to get to the car pool, we need to shake him up a little and point him to the door.

After canceling his thoughts about sleeping, we click on Mark's car pool. He changes clothes faster than Superman and sprints to his ride in the nick of time. Have a nice day, Mark!

Poor Mortimer! We've been so focused on getting Bella and Mark to work, we didn't notice that the poor slob is asleep on his feet! We need to wake him up (he'll be so happy), and send him to bed.

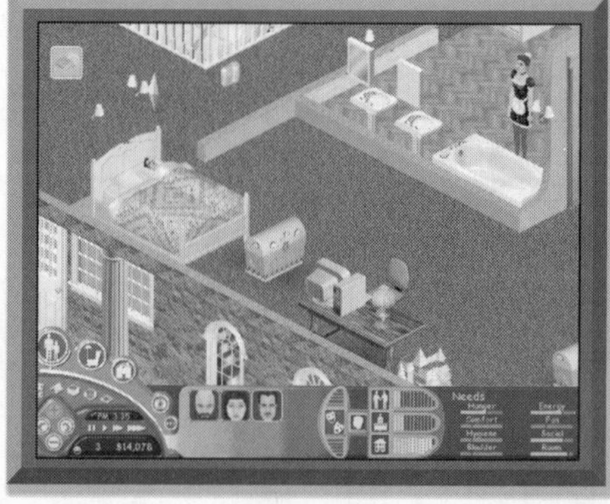

We receive a reminder that Mortimer's car pool arrives at 4:00 p.m. Unfortunately we forgot to set his alarm, and his Hygiene and Bladder bars have gone south, so we need to wake him up soon. Fortunately, he ate before bedtime, so he can probably get by without a big meal.

Mortimer is up and he's not happy. With the amount of time remaining before his car pool shows up, he can empty his bladder and get in half a shower before racing out the door.

With Mortimer out of the house, we can concentrate on Bella and Mark, who have both arrived home from work. Mark socialized a little too much the night before, so he went straight to bed without any prompting.

Mortimer arrives home at 1:00 a.m.. After a bathroom break and quick shower, we send him straight to bed so he can party with Bella tomorrow, who has decided to take the day off.

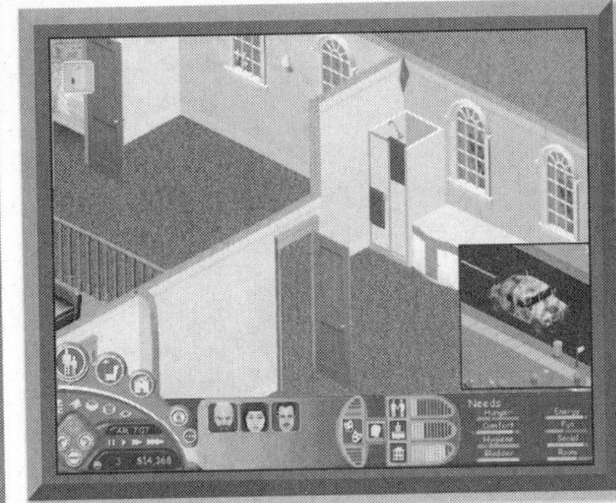

Mark is well rested, so he can fend for himself this morning. He steps into the shower as the car pool arrives, so he has almost one hour to get ready. But, while in the shower, he decides to take the day off and join Bella.

The three housemates share a pleasant breakfast together. Perhaps they have finally buried the hatchet after the Mortimer-Bella-Mark thing. We can only hope.

Mark grabs the phone to invite a friend over, but before he can dial, a local radio station calls with great news. He just won §550 in a promotion!

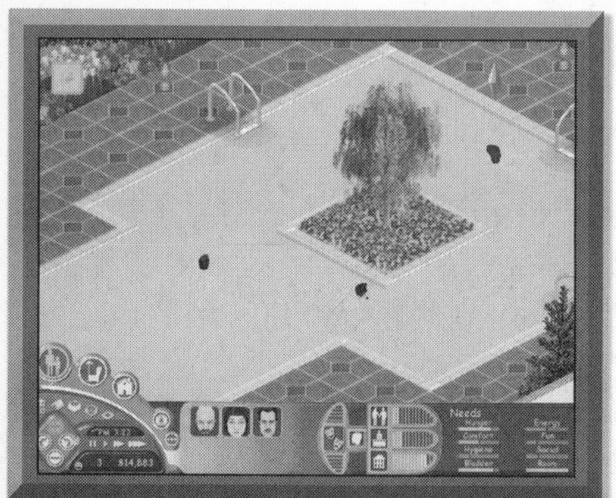

Mark calls a friend, who says he'll be right over. While Mark changes into his Speedo, Mortimer, Jeff, and Bella enjoy a dip in the pool. That's right, Mortimer missed his car pool, too. It's a day off (without pay) for the entire house!

It's on to the hot tub for a long, relaxing soak. Comfort, Hygiene, Social, and Fun scores are soaring. It's too bad we have to eat and empty our Bladders or we'd never leave!

Everyone will be hungry after the swim and soak, so Bella hops out to make dinner. Soon, everyone grabs a plate and starts discussing what life will be like when they are all unemployed. Everyone, that is, except Mortimer, who prefers standing.

After dinner, Jeff heads for home. Bella and Mark retreat to the den, where Bella rubs Mark's back.

One good rub deserves a hug, as things suddenly heat up between the former lovers.

Mortimer takes one look at the lip-locked Sims and heads straight for the bar.

After a couple of adult beverages, Mortimer follows the lovers into the hallway where they are still groping each other like teenagers on prom night.

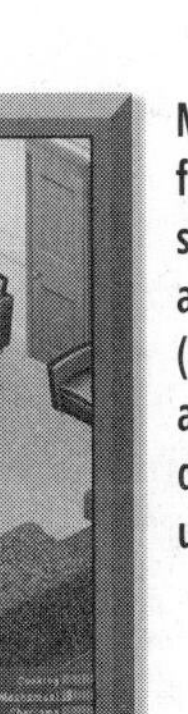

Mortimer shows his frustration by slapping Mark across the cheek (he's such an animal). Bella is disgusted and goes upstairs to bed.

One slap turns to another and seven hours later, Mortimer and Mark are still duking it out.

Bella drives off to work while our two Sim-Neanderthals take their fight to the bathroom.

What will become of our star-crossed lovers?

Will Bella leave Mortimer and go back to Mark?

Will Mark feel guilty about wrecking Mortimer's marriage, and move in with the Newbies?

Will Bella reveal what she and Jeff were really doing in the hot tub?

Who will clean up the bathroom?

For the answers to these burning questions, stay tuned for the next episode of...*As the Sim Turns.*

Life with the Pleasants

Jeff experiences the joys of working a night shift—cleaning up his family's dinner dishes...

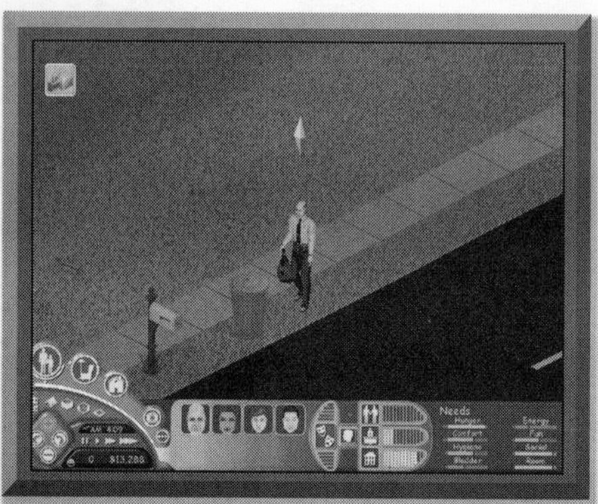

...and taking out the trash at four in the morning.

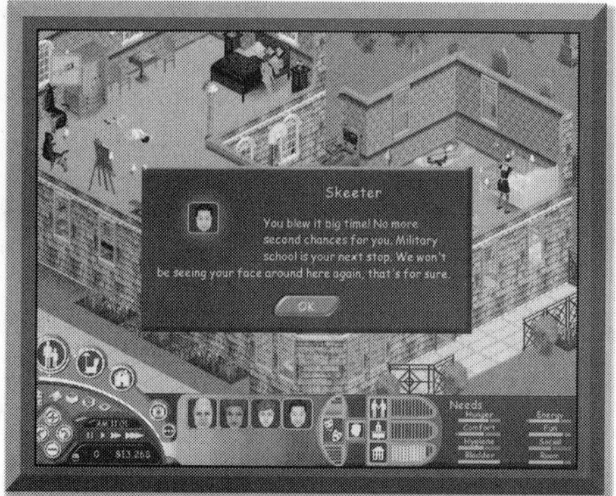

Skeeter misses one too many days of school and gets the bad news—he's on his way to military school, never to be seen again.

Everyone is asleep, so Jeff takes an opportunity to practice his Charisma in front of the bathroom mirror. Unfortunately for Jeff, the walking dead also take this opportunity to float through the mirror and scare the •&$%$# out of him.

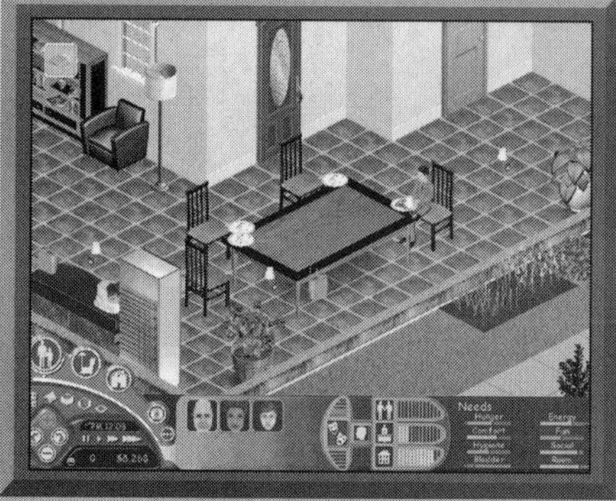

Although his icon has already disappeared from the control panel, Skeeter enjoys one last breakfast before he is exiled from the game.

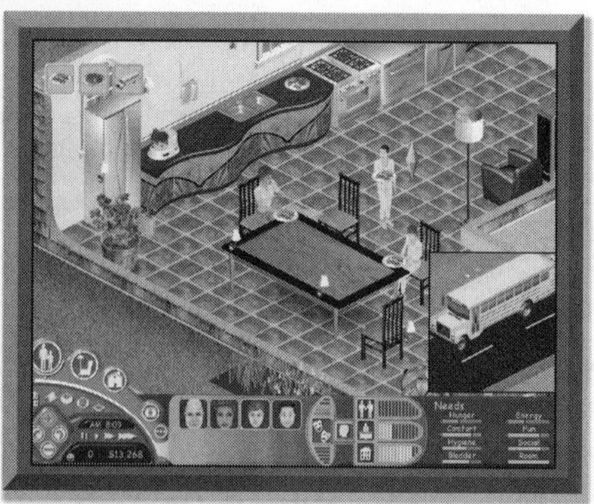

Like all kids, Daniel and Skeeter can only make snacks on their own, so someone must serve their breakfast before school.

Not wanting to follow in his brother's footsteps, Daniel hits the books and improves his grades.

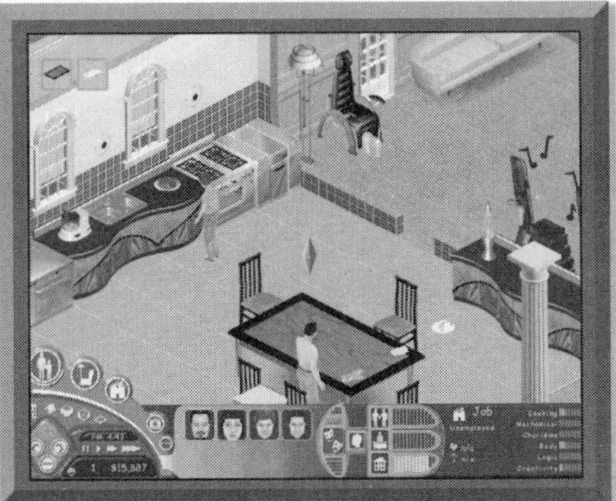

Hmmm. Which pile should I pay first, the red one or the yellow one? Get a clue, Jeff—if you don't pay the red ones, they'll repossess your furniture!

The Maid should get riot pay for all the garbage this family leaves on the floor!

Maids are limited to cleaning up Sim-messes, but that frees up the family to take care of other important needs, like advancing their skills. Diane Pleasant takes a break to bone up on her Mechanical Skills. Perhaps she can fix the dishwasher and save §50-an-hour repair bills.

Pity the Poor Bachelor

With garbage a foot thick on the floor of his house, our bachelor decides to stay outside and entertain a new lady friend with his juggling act.

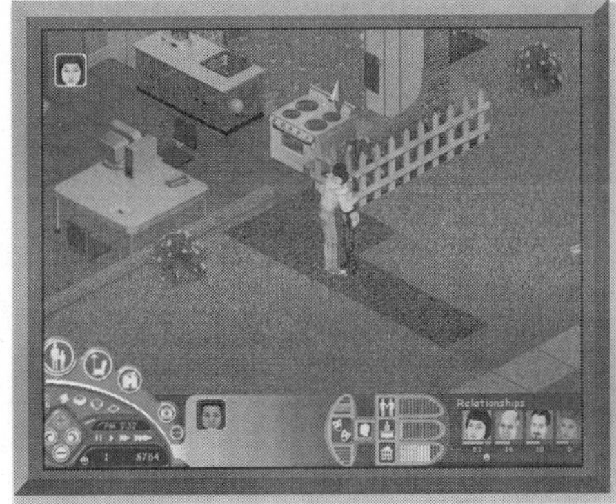

"Wow, she really likes me! Maybe she won't notice the garbage if I invite her inside."

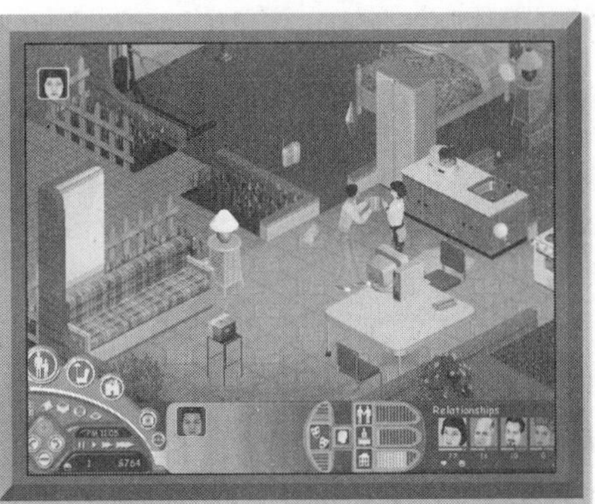

"I really like you Bella, so I got you a pair of basketball shoes!"

Bachelors on a fixed budget can have a difficult time having fun. A basketball hoop in the back yard is a good investment, and if you can find a Playful friend, it's a cheap date, too.

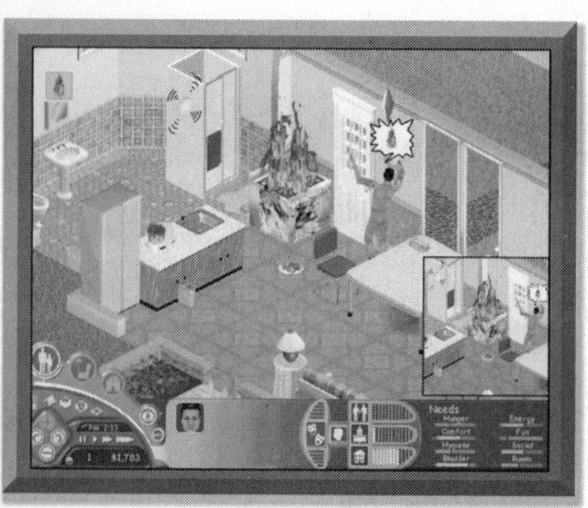

Armed with a new gas stove and absolutely no cooking ability, this bachelor decides to flame-broil the kitchen.

Whew, the fireman is here to put out the fire. There's only one problem: he can't get into the house because our hero is standing in front of the stove, which happens to be next to the door. We understand that the bachelor's quarters are tight, but it's probably not a good idea to put the stove next to the front door. By the time the fireman makes his way to the back door, your bachelor could be toast.

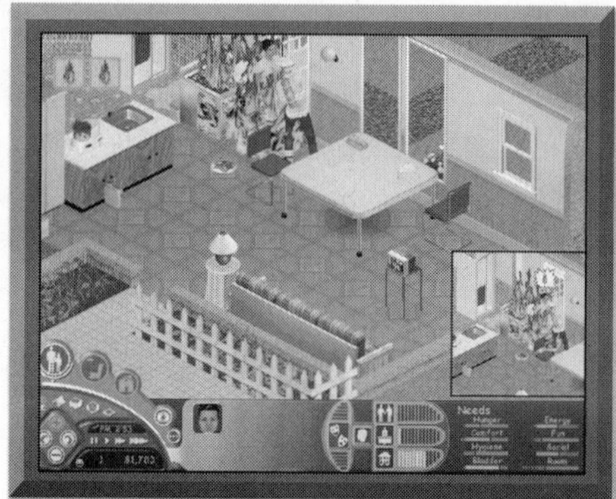

"Excuse me, son, could you please move out of the fire so I can extinguish it?"

Kids Are People, Too

Toy boxes are small and relatively inexpensive. If they are placed in the bedroom, your kids can sneak in a little Fun time before school.

Children have fewer inhibitions, but they still don't like to use the bathroom in front of the Maid or their siblings.

Skeeter and Matthew enjoy a little Social and Fun time playing with their railroad town.

Left to their own devices, kids often stay up long past the time their parents hit the sack. In fact, even with Free Will activated, parents feel no responsibility for getting their children to bed early. So, if you forget to send the kids to bed, get ready for some serious tantrums in the morning.

Unlike the railroad, the pinball machine is a solo activity.

Skillful Sims

An exercise machine is the obvious choice for improving a Sim's Body Skill, but if you can keep your Sims in the pool, they'll increase Body scores even faster, and boost Fun at the same time.

Unlike adults, who need toys for their playtime, kids can play with each other.

Sometimes it can be hard to get your Sims to slow down long enough for serious Skill enhancement, especially if it means sitting down to read. The solution is simple: Place two comfortable chairs close to the bookcase, and give each Sim different Skill assignments. Remember that you only need one Cooking expert and one Mechanical expert in the same house. Divide reading assignments appropriately to bring their Skills quickly up to speed.

You might be concerned about an adult male who stands for hours in front of a full-length mirror in his Speedo. However, it makes sense to place a mirror in the family room for easier access. This way, your Sims won't tie up the bathroom practicing Charisma in the mirror over the sink.

Increasing the Creativity Skill through painting has an added bonus—the ability to sell your painting. But, don't get too excited; a bad painting fetches only §1 on the open market.

With minimal Mechanical Skill, repairing this shower seems to take forever, and all the while, Mark's Comfort and Energy scores are dropping. Maybe a Repairman is worth the price until Mark earns a few more Mechanical points.

As the Sim Turns: Part Two

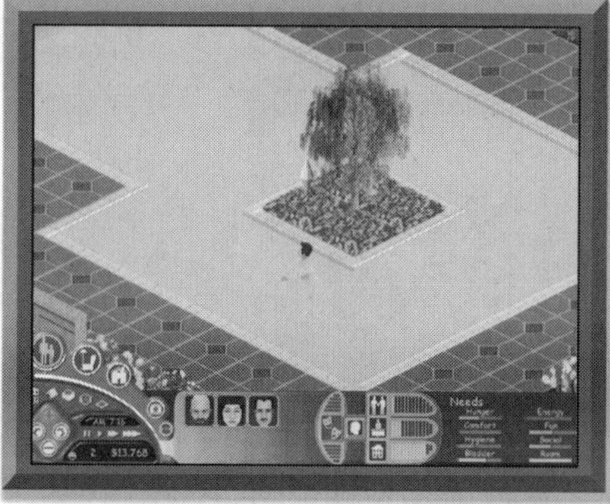

As we return to our Sim soap, Mortimer has just returned from another night shift, and after a light snack, he decides to take an early morning swim, thinking that Mark and Bella are busy getting ready for work. After swimming a few laps, he is ready to go to bed, but wait…where is the ladder? "I can't get out of the pool!" says Mortimer, frantically. "I'll just tread water for a while until Mark or Bella come out. If I can just…keep… going…getting tired… so tired…."

Mark and Bella finally come outside, but it's too late. Poor Mortimer, exhausted and confused, has already dropped like a stone to the bottom of the pool.

After Mortimer's body is removed from the pool, a tombstone is erected on the spot where the ladder used to be. If Mortimer were still here, he would have appreciated the humor…maybe not.

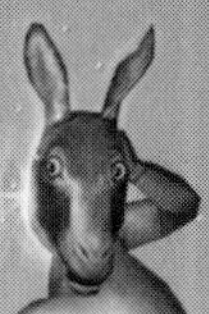

After getting over the initial shock, Mark and Bella grieve at the site where their "friend" died.

"O.K., enough grieving," says Bella, as she tells Mark a real knee-slapper.

After some welcome comic relief, the two mourners console each other with a supportive hug. Right.

Then, they console each other further...with a dance?

Thinking the time is right (and that they have carried on the charade long enough), Mark pulls Bella close for a kiss. But, much to Mark's surprise, Bella suddenly cools and pushes him away.

What is this strange turn of events?

Did Bella entice Mark into helping her solve the "Mortimer" problem, only to leave him in the lurch?

Find the answers on the next episode of *As the Sim Turns*, on a computer near you!

Sims in the Kitchen

In the Motives chapter, we provided a basic explanation of how Sims satisfy their Hunger score. As you know by now, food is readily available in the refrigerator, 24 hours a Sim-day. The supply is endless, and you never have to go to the market. However, the difference between what is in the refrigerator and what a Sim actually eats lies in the preparation. The following screens take you through the various options available to a Sim chef, and the table at the end of this chapter explains how the different appliances and countertops modify the quality of each meal.

The snack, a §5 bag of chips, is the lowest item on the Sim food chain. It's better than nothing when your Sim is racing around getting ready for the car pool, but it barely nudges the Hunger bar.

For a much more satisfying meal, direct the best chef in the house to Prepare a Meal. In this screen, Bella is getting ready to throw the raw ingredients into the food processor (a positive modifier, as noted in the table). While one Sim prepares breakfast, you can assign the other Sims to menial labor, such as mopping or picking up garbage.

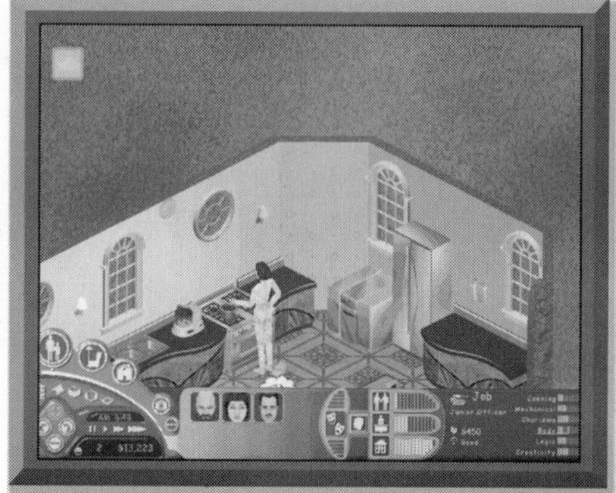

After processing the food, Bella throws it in a pot and works her magic. Two more modifiers are at work here: Bella's Cooking Skill and the special features of the Pyrotorre Gas Range.

When the meal is finished, Bella places a stack of plates on the counter.

Thrilled that he doesn't have to eat his own tasteless slop, Mark grabs a plate from the counter.

Another option for preparing multiple portions is to call out for a pizza. This is a good choice for a Sim who has a low Cooking Skill. Rather than using the stove and setting the kitchen on fire, a telephone call and §40 will buy a hot pie, delivered to the door in an hour.

The Sims love their pizza, and they can't wait to set it down and grab a slice. So, don't be surprised if your Sim plops the carton down on the first available counter—even in the bathroom—and starts grazing.

How Appliances and Surfaces Affect Hunger Score

APPLIANCE/SURFACE	HUNGER POINTS ADDED TO MEAL
Dishwasher	5
Trash Compactor	5
Fridge (Llamark)	9
Toaster Oven	9 (plus Cooking Skill)
Fridge (Porcina)	12
Counter (Barcelona)	16
Counter (NuMica)	16
Counter (Tiled)	16
Fridge (Freeze Secret)	16
Microwave	16 (plus Cooking Skill)
Food Processor	32
Stove (Dialectric)	32 (plus 1.5 x Cooking Skill)
Stove (Pyrotorre)	48 (plus 1.5 x Cooking Skill)

CHAPTER 9: SURVIVAL TIPS

Introduction

The beauty of playing *The Sims* is that everyone's experience is different. When you take a serious approach to shaping your family, the game can mirror your own life. However, if you mismanage your Sims, they can sink into despair, waving their little arms in the air over failed relationships, poor career decisions, or even a bad mattress. You can always delete your family and start over. But then you would never get that warm, fuzzy feeling that comes from turning your pitiful Sims' world into Shangri La.

This chapter is devoted to the *Sims* player who wants to go the distance and fight the good fight. Because most Sim problems can be traced back to one or more deficient Motive scores, we have arranged the following tips into separate Motive sections. Although some of the information is covered in other chapters, this is meant to be a quick-reference guide for times of crisis. Simply turn to the appropriate Motive and save your Sim's life with one of our game-tested tips.

Of course, you can also take a more devious approach to satisfying or altering your Sim's needs. Our Cheats section gives you a bundle of unofficial commands to rock your Sim's world. We take no responsibility for the results. (In other words, don't come crying to us if you stick your Sim in a room with no doors and he or she drops dead!).

Hunger

Maximize Food Quality and Preparation Time

For the best food quality, upgrade *all* appliances and countertops. Anything short of the most expensive refrigerator, countertop, stove, etc., reduces the potential Hunger value of your meals. Preparing a meal quickly is all about kitchen design. Align your objects in the order of preparation, beginning with the refrigerator, followed by the food processor (figure 9-1), and then ending with the stove (figure 9-2).

Fig. 9-1. The food goes from the refrigerator directly to the food processor.

Fig. 9-2. Next stop is the stove, right next door.

Have an open countertop next to the stove on the other side so the food preparer can set the plates down (figure 9-3). Although it has nothing to do with preparation, position the kitchen table and chairs close to the stove so that your Sims can grab their food, sit down together, and boost their Social scores (figure 9-4).

Fig. 9-3. From the stove, the chef moves just a couple steps to the counter and sets down the plates.

Fig. 9-4. If your Sims are prompted to eat, they'll be ready to grab a plate as soon as it hits the counter, and with the table nearby, they can eat, chat, and make it to work on time.

Designate one Sim as your chef. Make sure that Sim has easy access to a chair and bookcase, and then set aside time each day to Study Cooking. When the resident chef's Cooking Skill reaches 10, you have achieved the pinnacle of food preparation.

Make Breakfast the Night Before

Sim food lasts for at least seven hours before the flies arrive and the food is officially inedible. If you have one Sim in the house who doesn't work, have him or her prepare breakfast for everyone at around midnight, as pictured in figure 9-5.

Fig. 9-5. After making dinner, our hard-working Sim can go to bed and sleep late in the morning.

After the food is on the counter, immediately send the Sim to bed. Most Sims should get up by 5, or the very latest, 6 a.m. to be on time for their morning jobs (the chef can sleep in). When everyone comes downstairs, breakfast (it's really dinner, but Sims don't care what you call it, as long as it doesn't have flies) will be on the counter (figure 9-6), fresh and ready to go. You'll save at least 20 Sim-minutes of morning prep time.

Fig. 9-6. It's only 5:30 a.m., but our Sim kid is already eating breakfast. After taking care of his Hygiene, he'll still have time for studying or boosting his Fun score before the school bus arrives.

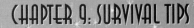

Comfort

When You Gotta Go, Go in Style

A toilet is often overlooked as a source of Comfort. The basic Hygeia-O-Matic Toilet costs only §300, but it provides zero Comfort. Spend the extra §900 and buy the Flush Force 5 XLT (figure 9-7). Your Sims have to use the bathroom anyway, so they might as well enjoy the +4 Comfort rating every time they take a seat.

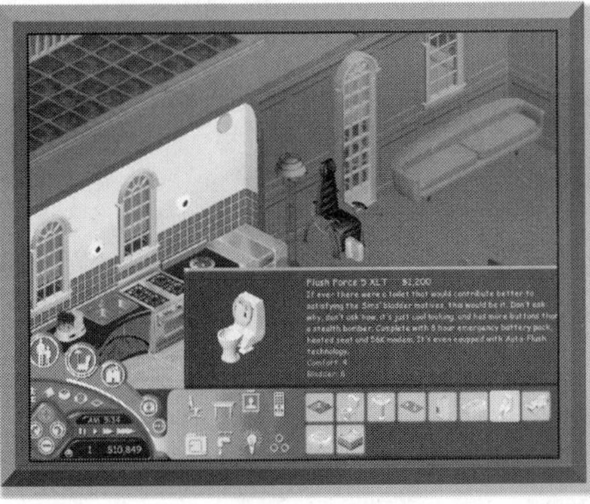

Fig. 9-7. You can live with a black-and-white TV for a while, but it doesn't make sense to do without the added comfort of the Flush Force.

Rub Your Sim the Right Way

Giving another Sim a Back Rub is a great way to increase your chances of seeing Hug, and eventually Kiss on the social interaction menu. However, don't forget that it also raises the recipient's Comfort level. If your Sim's Comfort level is down, even after a long night's sleep, try a few Back Rubs. It will send your Sim to work in a better mood, which might be just enough to earn the next promotion.

Fig. 9-8. Our Sim is hungry, but he always has time to receive a nice Back Rub.

Hygiene

Your Mother Was Right

One of the biggest contributors to declining Hygiene is the lack of hand washing after using the bathroom (in the Sims and in real life). If your Sim does not have a Neat personality, you may need to initiate this action. If you keep it up throughout the day, your Sim will be in better shape in the morning, when a shorter shower can be the difference between making the car pool or missing a day of work.

Fig. 9-9. This Sim has an average Neat rating, which means she won't always wash her hands after using the bathroom. A few gentle reminders are in order.

Flush Your Troubles Away

Sad but true, sloppy Sims don't flush (figure 9-10). It's easy to overlook this nasty habit during a busy day, but it could lead to trouble. A clogged toilet may not affect Hygiene directly, but if your Sim is forced to pee on the floor because the toilet is not working, the Hygiene score drops dramatically.

Fig. 9-10. Second time tonight for this soldier, and we're still waiting for the first flush.

Bladder

Sorry, there's no magic formula for relieving a full Bladder. However, to guard against emergencies and the resulting puddles on the floor, try building two semi-private stalls in your bathroom. This allows two Sims to use the facilities without infringing on each other's privacy, as pictured in figure 9-11.

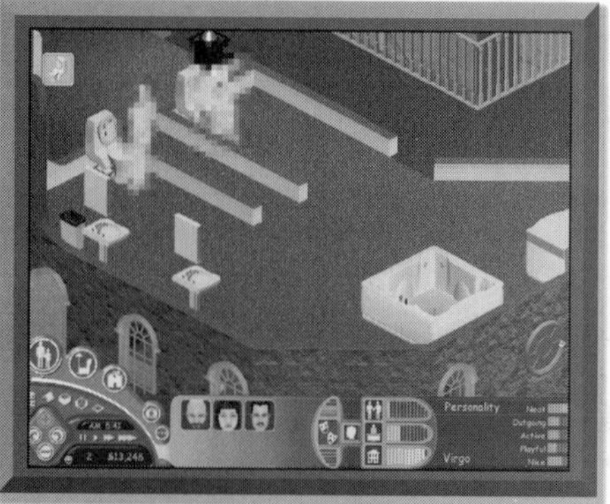

Fig. 9-11. Dual stalls improve the traffic flow (and other flows) in the bathroom.

Energy

Getting Enough Sleep with Baby

Nothing drains a Sim's Energy bar faster than having a baby in the house (figure 9-12). If you want to survive the three-day baby period without everyone losing their jobs, you must sleep when the baby sleeps. Most likely, this will be in the middle of the day, because Sim babies, like their real counterparts, couldn't care less about their parents' sleep schedules. The baby will not sleep for a full eight hours; however, if you get five or six hours of sleep with the baby, you'll have enough Energy to carry out other important household tasks.

Fig. 9-12. This Sim mom is at the end of her rope, and the baby is just getting warmed up.

Kids Make Great Babysitters

It does nothing for their Fun or Social levels, but Sim kids will dutifully care for their baby siblings. When they come home from school, feed them, allow a short play period, and then lock them in the room with the baby (if you're feeling particularly sadistic, you can go into Build mode and wall them in). They usually respond on their own, but you can always direct them to the crib, as pictured in figure 9-13, (unless they are too exhausted and need sleep). Take advantage of this time by sending the regular caregiver to bed for some much-needed sleep.

Fig. 9-13. Big brother makes a great nanny.

Fun

Finding the Right Activity for Your Sim

Unless your Sims live in a monastery, you should have plenty of Fun objects in your house. The trick is matching the right kind of activity with a Sim's personality. In the frenzy of daily schedules and maintaining Relationships, it's easy to lose touch with your Sim's personality traits. Visit the Personality menu often (click on the "head" icon) to review the five traits. Make sure you have at least one of the following objects readily available to your Sim (the bedroom is a good spot).

NOTE

A Sim should have at least six points (bars) in one of the following traits to maximize the recommended activity. Of course, an even higher number produces faster Fun rewards. To qualify for the opposite trait (e.g., Active/Lazy, Playful/Serious) a Sim should have no more than three points in the trait).

Favorite Fun Activities

TRAIT	BEST ACTIVITIES
Neat	N/A
Outgoing	TV (Romance), Hot Tub, Pool (if Playful is also high)
Active	Basketball, Stereo (dance), Pool, TV (Action)
Lazy	TV (as long as it's on, they're happy!), Computer, Book
Playful	Any fun object, including Computer, Dollhouse, Train Set, VR Glasses, Pinball, etc. If also Active, shift to Basketball, Dance, and Pool.
Serious	Chess, Newspaper, Book, Paintings (just let them stare)
Nice	Usually up for anything
Mean	TV (Horror)

When in Doubt, Entertain Someone

If your Sim does not have access to a Fun activity, simply Entertain someone for an instant Fun (and Social) boost, as pictured in figure 9-14. You can usually repeat this activity several times, and it doesn't take much time (great for kids on busy school mornings).

Fig. 9-14. When a good toy is not around, Sim kids love to Entertain each other.

Social

Satisfying Social requirements can be very frustrating, especially when Sims are on different work or sleep schedules. Socializing is a group effort, so plan small parties on a regular basis. Keep a notepad with all of your Sims' work schedules, so you know whom to invite at any time of the day.

- **It's O.K. to ask your guests to leave. After you shmooze a little and boost your Relationship score, send the Sim packing, and call up a different one. Use this round-robin approach to maintain all of your friendships.**
- **Don't let Mean Sims abuse you. This can be tough to control if you're not paying attention. When you're socializing with a Mean Sim, keep an eye on the activity queue in the screen's upper-left corner. If that Sim's head pops up (without you initiating it), it probably says "Be Teased by...," or "Be Insulted by...." Simply click on the icon to cancel the negative event and maintain your Relationship score. Once you diffuse the threat, engage the Sim in simple talking, or move your Sim into a group activity (pool table, hot tub, pool, etc.)**
- **Unless you like being the bad guy, don't advertise your advances toward one Sim if you already have a Relationship with another. Sims are extremely jealous, but you can still maintain multiple love Relationships as long as you don't flaunt them in public.**

Room

A Room score crisis is easy to remedy. If you have the money, simply add more lights and paintings. Also check the quality of objects in the room, and upgrade whenever possible. If your room is jammed with expensive objects, lights, and paintings and your Room score is still low, there must be a mess somewhere. A normally maxed out Room score can slip with so much as a puddle on the floor (as pictured in figure 9-15). Clean up the mess to restore the Room score to its normal level.

Fig. 9-15. It looks like someone fell short of the toilet. A mop will take care of the mess and raise the Room score.

Scan your house on a regular basis for the following negative Room factors:

- **Dead plants**
- **Cheap objects (especially furniture)**
- **Puddles (they can also indicate a bad appliance; when in doubt, click on the item to see if Repair comes up as an option)**
- **Dark areas**
- **If you have the money, replace items taken by the Repo guy.**

Cheats

Activate the cheat command line at any time during a game by pressing Ctrl + Shift + C. An input box appears in the screen's upper left corner. Type in one of the codes listed below. You must re-activate the command line after each cheat is entered. The following cheats work only with Version 1.1 or later of *The Sims* and its expansions.

CODE INPUT	DESCRIPTION
autonomy <1-100>	Set free thinking level
bubble_tweak z-offset	Input random large numbers to cause the think bubble to move
draw_all_frames off	Draw all animation disabled
draw_all_frames on	Draw all animation enabled
draw_floorable off	Floorable grid disabled
draw_floorable on	Floorable grid enabled
draw_routes off	Selected person's path hidden
draw_routes on	Selected person's path displayed
genable default	Resets objects to default status
genable objects on/off	Makes stuff invisible
genable status	Checks the status of genable objects in the house
history	Save family history file
interests	Display personality and interests
log_mask	Set event logging mask
map_edit off	Map editor disabled
map_edit on	Map editor enabled
move_objects off	Move any object (off)
move_objects on	Move any object (on)
prepare_lot	Rotates the house and zooms according to your original orientation on the lot
rosebud	1,000 Simoleans
rotation <0-3>	Rotate camera
sim_log begin	Start sim logging
sim_log end	End sim logging
sim_speed <-1000-1000>	Set game speed
sweep off	Ticks disabled
sweep on	Ticks enabled
tile_info off	Tile information hidden
tile_info on	Tile information displayed

PART II:

The Sims™ Makin' Magic

CHAPTER 10: WELCOME TO MAGIC TOWN

Introduction

When the MagiCo Mystery Man drops a Magic Starter Kit on your Sims' front lawn, it marks the beginning of a wild and wacky foray into the world of spells, castings, and supernatural minions. With a collection of "starter" ingredients, you can begin practicing basic spells at home. But, you can't pull rabbits out of your hat forever. To develop your magical powers to their fullest, visit Magic Town, where you can view and perform strange and unusual sideshows, barter with mysterious vendors, and take part in magical quests. You also have a chance to meet, and even duel, other Magical Sims. In this chapter, we offer a preview of Magic Town, introducing the vendors and activities you find at each of the six commercial lots.

A Spooktacular Spot: 93 Calamity Forest

Surrounded by gnarled wood fencing, 93 Calamity Forest is one of the smaller lots in Magic Town. But, the cozy surroundings still attract a steady stream of Magical Sims who arrive via balloon taxi or through one of several magic portals.

Stop at All Things Draconic to buy Dragon Strength products, including Dragon Chew Toys, Nests, Treats, Tears, and Scales. Vicki Vampiress is your friendly neighborhood vendor, and she is always willing to talk or barter if you have a Magic Wand in your pocket.

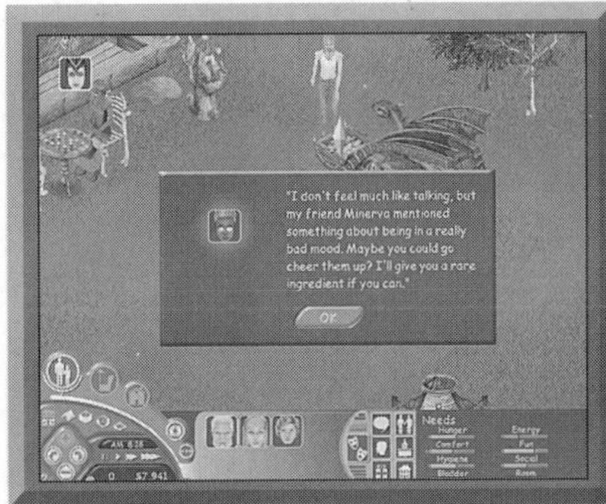

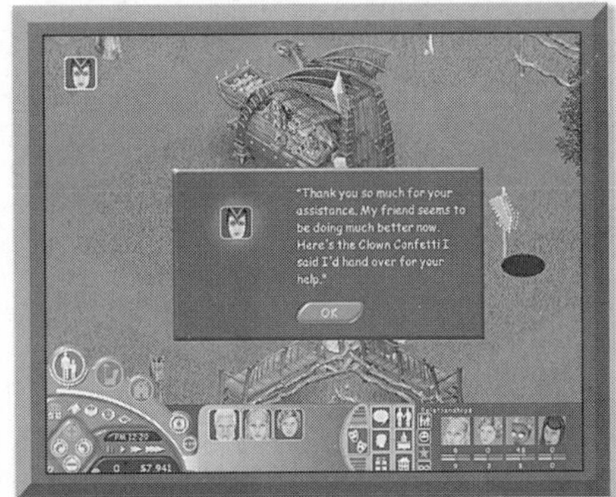

Vicki may offer to give you a rare ingredient if you perform a simple task, such as cheering up a friend. After a little conversation, a few compliments, and perhaps a brief puppet show, you can return to Vicki and receive your reward.

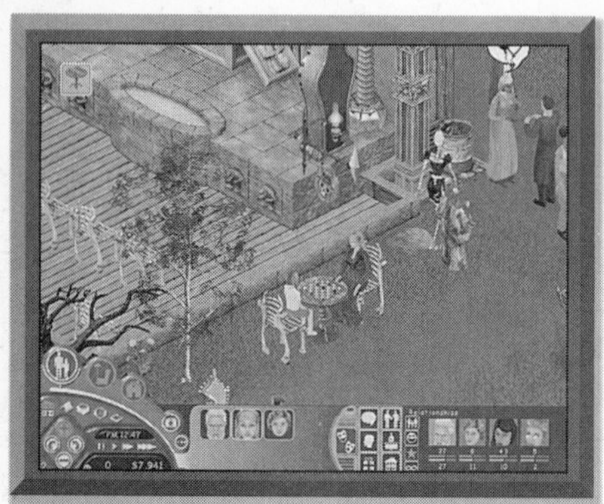

Relax and play chess when you need a break from the crowd.

Electro's Spooky Laboratory offers magicians of all skill levels the opportunity to perform in front of a live audience. However, it's a good idea to practice your magic at home (and build up your Logic skills) before taking the stage, or the trick may not go as planned.

When your Sim's tummy starts growling, stop at Madame Magyar's Gulyas Goulash for a cup of hot Goulash.

If you have some extra simoleans, visit the Creepy Classics Painting Display to buy a portrait that randomly comes to life when a Sim chooses to "view" it. These paintings will scare non-magical Sims, and you don't even have to use a spell!

When you feel like going mano a mano, find a willing victim and enter the Diametric Dueling Device. But, don't expect to win with brawn alone. It takes supreme Logic and the ability to analyze your opponent's weaknesses to leave the platform with a victory.

Vernon's Vault: 94 Calamity Forest

Leave your dueling spells behind and ride the haunted roller coaster at this spacious Magic Town lot.

After your Sim's stomach settles down, wander over to the Ghoulish Graveyard Gumbo stand for a bowl of lime-green gumbo. Don't ask what's in it, just eat up and refill your Hunger motive.

There's more fun at Hole of Harmony Mini-Gold, where your Sim can putt golf balls into the hole.

Find a variety of spell ingredients at the Wagon O'Wares stand. Spend your MagiCoins freely to beef up your inventory.

Vicki the Vampiress runs the All Things Draconic shop in the far corner of the lot, near the pond. If you'd rather not raise a dragon, you can buy Dragon Scales and Dragon Tears, or if you're ready to be a parent to a scaly child, take home a Nest.

Electro's Spooky Laboratory offers more opportunities for perfecting your magic.

Before calling the balloon taxi or jumping into the nearest portal, stop at the Wishing Well and maybe your magical wish will come true.

Coldwind Meadow: 95 Calamity Forest

Balloons, fortunetellers, and sideshows transform Coldwind Meadow into a bustling midway of wonders. Grab some cotton candy for a quick sugar-rush and stroll the grounds.

Mea Fortuna looks into your future for a couple simoleans. Some of her visions are meaningful, but her goal in life is to make enough money to retire on a beach in Jamaica, so don't take everything she says seriously.

If you're not quite sure what to do next, the Mystery Man can give you hints about what you need to know in ***Makin' Magic***.

If you're not ready to take the stage, stop at one of the magic stands and practice your parlor tricks. (You won't be able to learn a new skill here though.)

The Berry Stand offers many of the ingredients needed to grow vines and make nectar.

If your Fun motive needs a boost, waste some simoleans on the Cyclops Game.

The mini-golf tent has four challenging holes for your putting enjoyment.

How are your Mechanical skills? If they are up to par, take the stage and try your hand at Levitation, Metamorphosis, or the Segmented Woman. Just don't blow the trick or your lovely assistant might get upset.

Do you have a duel-personality? Try your hand at magical fisticuffs at the Diametric Dueling Device. You can also duel vendors here.

Clowntastic Land: 96 Calamity Forest

Fun and games are the priorities at Clowntastic Land. Get your visit off to a wild start with a trip on the three-part roller coaster that includes a dunking, plenty of shakes and twists, and a tumble into a head full of balls (or was that a ball full of heads?).

Food service is limited to popcorn and cotton candy, so make sure your Sim has a full belly before journeying to Clowntastic Land.

Nagganaste and His Pet Cobra Cyril are good for a few laughs, and you can try your hand at snake charming. The snake charmer also deals in rare Snake Venom on the side, if you have the commodity he desires.

The focus is on entertainment at Clowntastic Land, so the shopping outlets are limited to a single Wagon O'Wares where you can replenish your supply of Llama Spit, Toad Sweat, and other pleasantries.

When it's time to head for home, stroll between the two giant clown heads and continue across a star-studded walkway to reach the portal.

Serra Glen: 97 Calamity Forest

After the bright lights of Clowntastic Land, Serra Glen is a welcome diversion. You won't find any sideshows or duels here. Instead, you can linger in a large market area in the center of the meadow, spending your simoleans on a variety of groceries and berries, or add to your art collection at the painting kiosk.

For the pause that refreshes, take a break from shopping and enjoy a steaming bowl of goulash.

Redeem your MagiCoins at the Wagon O'Wares for more exotic ingredients to add to your Wand Charger.

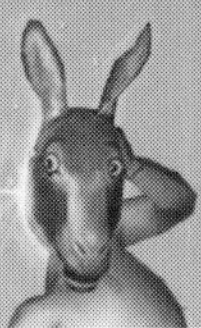

If you have enough MagiCoins in your inventory, visit Faerie Mara to purchase Pixie Dust, Sands of Time, or the very exotic and expensive Diamond Dust.

The goulash chef is always ready to dive under her cart in search of secret ingredients.

orest Edge Camp: 98 Calamity Forest

Our journey through Magic Town ends at Forest Edge Camp, a peaceful but often busy marketplace and gathering spot. You'll find *Makin' Magic* outhouses here, but they are enclosed in a private building, with adjacent sinks. Sorry, this is about as luxurious as personal hygiene gets in Magic Town.

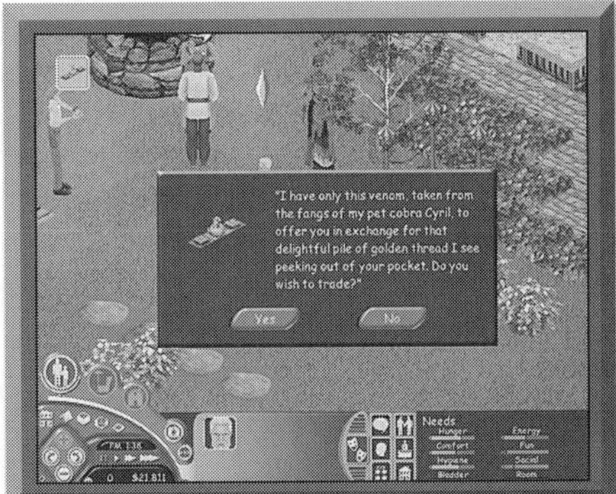

Don't forget to barter with the snake charmer if you have a supply of Golden Thread in your inventory.

Buy berries in the market building, or climb to the rooftop checkers parlor for some fun and games.

Flowers, trees, and a thriving garden surround Faerie Mara's Odds and Ends wagon in the corner of the lot.

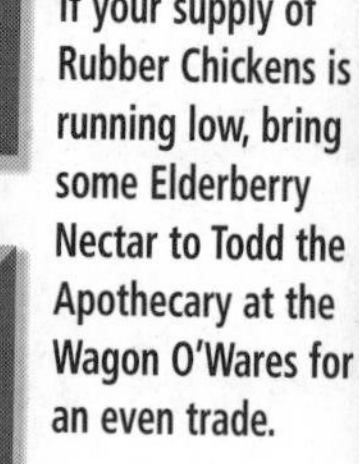

If your supply of Rubber Chickens is running low, bring some Elderberry Nectar to Todd the Apothecary at the Wagon O'Wares for an even trade.

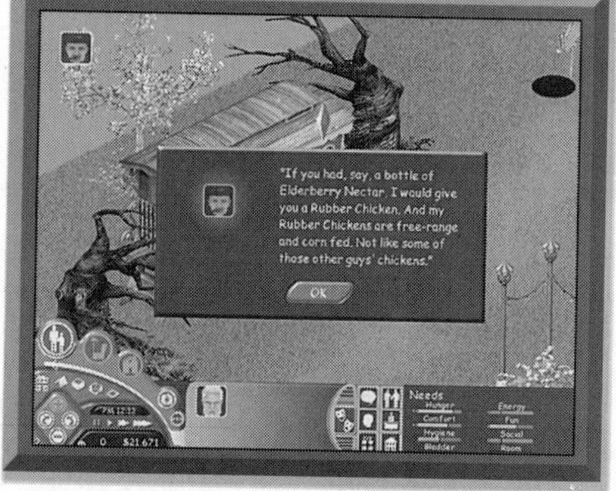

Residential Lots

There are three residential lots in Magic Town: 90, 91, and 92 Creepy Hollow. The lots are similar to other residential properties, with one important exception. Aside from carrying a price tag in simoleans, each lot requires a substantial amount of MagiCoins (minimum of 1000). Hence, at the beginning of the game, you must move into a regular neighborhood, then perform magic tricks in Magic Town to earn enough MagiCoins for your mystical dream home. Living in Magic Town has other advantages, as explained in the list below.

- **Only 10 casts required for a Magic Growth object (15 on a regular neighborhood lot).**
- **Magic Growth objects grow faster in Magic Town.**
- **Magic Crystals have 5 uses (3 on a regular neighborhood lot).**

CHAPTER 11:
YOUR FIRST SPELL

Introduction

When your Sims move into their house, it seems like just another day in the neighborhood...until the MagiCo Mystery Man drops a mysterious package on the front lawn. In this chapter, we take you through those first few magical moments when your Sim waves a wand and strange things begin to happen.

Opening the Box

The MagiCo Mystery Man rings the doorbell, but he doesn't wait around for idle conversation. Open the box to reveal the following items: Spellbound Wand Charger (atop a Truly Charming End Table), The Start Here Spell Book, Version 2.0, and A Hole in the Ground (magic portal). The box also contains one Magic Wand. Any adult Sim on the lot can remove it and add it to his or her inventory, but children cannot take the wand from the box. Items left inside the box include Toadstools, Toad Sweat, Butter, and 35 MagiCoins.

The large items are left in a cluster nea[r] the box. Go into Bu[y] Mode and use the hand tool to select each item and relocate it. The Wand Charger contains a Magic Wand, but you must add it to your inventory before your Sim is officially deemed "magical." Don't forget to add the items inside the bo[x] to your inventory.

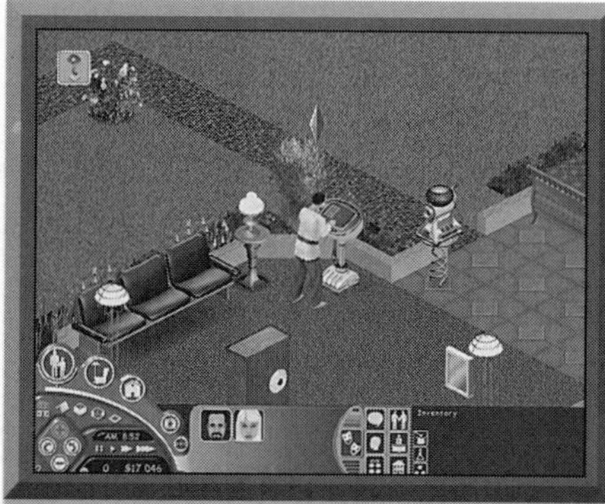

Aside from holding the Magic Wand, the Wand Charger is your vehicle for recharging your wand with new spells. A magic spell requires a combination of three ingredients. The Spell Book contains five pages of spells, with each ingredient noted. You can create a handful of ingredients at home, but most of these ingredients can be purchased in Magic Town, either with simoleans or MagiCoins. However, the most powerful ingredients are more difficult to obtain, requiring you to barter, go on Quests, or perform magic.

NOTE

A Sim requires Logic (a rating of 6 will guarantee a good result) to earn MagiCoins for successfully performing simple parlor tricks at Magic Town. Later, you'll also need Mechanical skill to perform more advanced magic on stage (and earn even more MagiCoins). So, it is a good idea to spend quality time at home playing chess (Logic) or studying at your bookcase (Mechanical), before visiting Magic Town (see the Quests, Duels, and Performances chapter for more information).

You can use the opening ingredients (Toadstools, Toad Sweat, Butter) to perform Toadification. However, we'll take you through the motions of earning MagiCoins, bartering, performing Quests and buying the necessary ingredients for a different spell.

It doesn't take long to boost your Logic skills, especially if you sit down at the checker table after a good night's sleep and a hearty meal. Playing with a friend also satisfies the Social motive.

Our First Trip to Magic Town

After pumping up our Logic skill, we leap into the magic portal for a quick trip to Magic Town (you can also call the balloon taxi, but because we don't have a phone, we'll take the direct route). From the Magic Town neighborhood screen, we select Coldwind Meadow, where our Sim tries out his magic skills. Each successful trick earns 11 MagiCoins.

Our Sim has just enough energy to perform three tricks, earning 33 MagiCoins. After a delicious bag of popcorn, we jump into the portal for the trip home. After a meal and a good night's sleep, we'll return to Magic Town.

Our encore performances at Coldwind Meadow increases our MagiCoins inventor to 66, more than enough to buy the necessary ingredients for the Smiley Face spell.

Creating Our First Spell

The magic portal also allows you to move from one lot to another in Magic Town, so we pop over to Vernon's Vault, where Todd the Apothecary peddles his strange and unusual concoctions at Wagon O'Wares. We fork over §21 for Toad Sweat. We'll need to go elsewhere for Honey and Garlic, but our Fun motive is dropping like a stone, so we take a spin on the haunted rollercoaster.

After buying Honey at the grocery display in Serra Glen, we take the Magic Portal to Vernon's Vault, where we trade Beeswax to Vicki the Vampiress for a little Garlic. Now, we have all the ingredients necessary for Smiley Face.

We add all of the ingredients to the Wand Charger, then charge the wand to transfer the spell to our Magic Items inventory.

NOTE

Having all the ingredients for a spell does not guarantee a successful outcome. See the Complete Book of Magic chapter for detailed information on the requirements, results, and possible backfires for all Makin' Magic *spells.*

Casting the Spell

With our wand all charged up, we jump in the Magic Portal and drop into Forest Edge Camp. We can try our Smiley Face on the first Sim we see, but to guarantee a positive outcome we need to find a Sim who lacks a Magic Wand (and therefore cannot block our spell).

Who better to unleash Smiley Fac[e] on then grumpy ol[d] Mortimer Goth. We catch up with him just as he is about to settle into a game of checkers. After a little small talk, where he tells us how much he hates magic (does this guy need Smile[y] Face, or what?), we cast the spell. Instantly, Mortimer is surrounded by happy faces, and in a moment, he is in love with the world. As the spell settles in, Mortimer becomes a new family friend.

NOTE

Every spell has a predetermined number of "charges," or casts, displayed as a small number in the corner of the spell's inventory icon. After you exhaust the final charge, the spell is removed from your inventory. Your Sim's Cooking skill influences the number of Spell charges, while Mechanical skill affects the number of Charm charges.

CHAPTER 12: THE COMPLETE BOOK OF MAGIC

Introduction

In the previous chapter, we introduced the process of finding ingredients, blending them in the Wand Charger, then charging the wand. A good start, but there is more to *Makin' Magic* than snapping your wand. In this chapter, we look at the range of ingredients, spells, and charms at your disposable, with tips on how to make them, when to use them, and what to do when things go wrong.

Magical Recipes

We'll get into casting spells and charms in a moment, but first let's examine the Family Spellbook and Cookbook. These books contain spells, charms, and baking recipes from *Makin' Magic*. In the Spellbook, all of the ingredients are listed, but the spells and charms are not revealed until you add the correct trio of ingredients to the Wand Charger or EverAfter (Charm) Crafter. So, check your inventory, make a shopping list, then go to Magic Town to buy, barter, or earn the necessary ingredients.

We've made your task even easier by listing all of the ingredients and their corresponding spells and charms. You'll also find a separate list of ingredients, with their corresponding locations in Magic Town. Spell interactions, including backfires, are listed in the Spell Interactions Table later in this chapter.

Family Spellbook

After a charm is finished, your Sim carries it to the closest surface, or places it on the floor.

NOTE

The spells and charms are listed in their order of appearance in the Family Spellbook.

Sims Unleashed and Sims Superstar Bonus Spells

If you have these expansion packs installed, you have access to an additional spell and charm. They require ingredients that can only be found in *Unleashed* and *Superstar*.

NAME	TYPE	INGREDIENT #1	INGREDIENT #2	INGREDIENT #3
A Friend Indeed	Spell	Butter	Pet Treats	Clown Confetti
Make Me Famous	Charm	Beeswax	Diamond Dust	Black Roses (delivered by the Obsessed Fan)

amily Spellbook

NAME	TYPE	INGREDIENT #1	INGREDIENT #2	INGREDIENT #3
Toadification	Spell	Butter	Toadstools	Toad Sweat
Beauty or Beast	Charm	Beeswax	Beeswax	Beeswax
Relationship Boost	Spell	Honey	Honey	Pixie Dust
Horn of Plenty	Charm	Golden Thread	Magic Beans	Magic Beans
Enchant	Spell	Butter	Toadstools	Pixie Dust
Dish Wish	Charm	Golden Thread	Golden Thread	Llama Spit
Get Happy	Spell	Honey	Grapes	Pixie Dust
Rain of Riches	Charm	Beeswax	Rubber Chicken	Diamond Dust
Shed Your Skin	Charm	Beeswax	Beeswax	Sands of Time
Smiley Face	Spell	Honey	Garlic	Toad Sweat
Polar Attraction	Charm	Beeswax	Dragon Scales	Llama Spit
Banish	Spell	Butter	Snake Venom	Garlic
Clone Drone	Charm	Beeswax	Sands of Time	Pegasus Feather
Perfect Garden	Charm	Golden Thread	Magic Beans	Four Leaf Clover
Magic Mood	Charm	Beeswax	Magic Beans	Glacial Glass
Love Struck	Spell	Honey	Dragon Tears	Pixie Dust
Hypnotize	Spell	Butter	Toad Sweat	Clown Confetti
Of House and Home	Charm	Golden Thread	Glacial Glass	Pegasus Feather
The Big Question	Spell	Honey	Clown Confetti	Wizard Eyelashes

Family Cookbook

In addition to fashioning spells and charms, your magical Sim can prepare special foods in the Standard-Plus Brick Oven for Bakers and the Nectar Press. The following sections describe the procedures for baking breads, cakes, and pies; and making your favorite beverages.

Gathering ingredients for baking is easier than finding ingredients for spells and charms. Purchase such food items as Butter, Honey, and Baking Mix at the Grocery Stand. Find Berries and Grapes in the same vicinity on Berry Stands.

Standard-Plus Brick Oven for Bakers

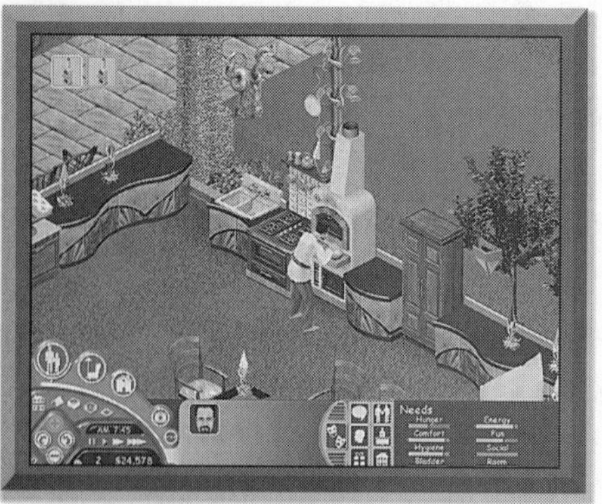

At first glance, this looks like a regular oven. However, it operates like the Wand Charger, in that you must first prime it with the proper ingredients before beginning the baking process. The recipes can be found in the Family Cookbook (see table on page 148).

NOTE

Honey, Sugar, and other such ingredients do not cost MagiCoins for those non-magically inclined players.

If you are more of a naturalist, you can grow your own Berries and Grapes by purchasing Sprigs at the Berry Stand. With regular watering, you can harvest your own crop and save a few simoleans.

Buy an Old-Fashioned Butter Churn and give your Sim that down home feeling while producing your own Butter.

You can also make your own Honey and Beeswax (an ingredient for spells and charms) by purchasing a Wax n' Honey Maker. If you're in a bad mood, be prepared for a few stings in exchange for a free supply of Beeswax and Honey.

Productivity with the Old-Fashioned Butter Churn and Wax n' Honey Maker is influenced by your Sim's Cooking skill.

After checking the Family Cookbook for the recipe, add the ingredients to the oven, then bake. If your Sim's cooking skills are adequate, you will enjoy a freshly baked pie, cake, or loaf of bread.

However, sometimes the best intentions of the worst bakers turn into flaming disasters, such as the one pictured here. Make sure you have a Smoke Detector in your kitchen, or wherever you locate the oven.

Nectar Press

Find the necessary ingredients for making nectar at the Grocery and Berry Stands. After adding the ingredients to the Nectar Press, complete the process by making nectar; your Sim will leap into the press and stomp the fruit into liquid. Store your finished product in the Taste of the Vine Nectar Bar.

NOTE

A good supply of Elderberry Nectar enables you to barter with Todd the Apothecary for a Rubber Chicken.

Where to Find Ingredients

Collecting a Quest reward from Mara at the Faerie Stand

The table on the following page includes every ingredient in *Makin' Magic*, along with the supplier and location(s) in Magic Town. When a Quest is listed as a possible source, you must "Talk" to the vendor, at which time he or she makes the offer. See the Quests, Duels, and Performances chapter for more information.

Family Cookbook

NAME	TYPE	INGREDIENT #1	INGREDIENT #2	INGREDIENT #3
Grape Nectar	Nectar Press	Grapes	Grapes	Sugar
Elderberry Nectar	Nectar Press	Sugar	Elderberries	Elderberries
Honey Nectar	Nectar Press	Honey	Grapes	Sugar
Freshly Baked Bread	Oven	Baking Mix	Baking Mix	Baking Mix
Homemade Cake	Oven	Butter	Sugar	Baking Mix
Elderberry Pie	Oven	Sugar	Elderberries	BakingMix
Magic Nectar	Nectar Press	Grapes	Grapes	Toad Sweat
Magic Tart	Oven	Baking Mix	Butter	Pixie Dust

Ingredient Sources

INGREDIENT	SOURCE	MAGIC TOWN LOCATIONS	COST
Dragon Tears	Dragon Stand	Spooktacular Spot, Vernon's Vault	24 MagiCoins (or, tickle your dragon)
Dragon Scales	Dragon Stand	Spooktacular Spot, Vernon's Vault	21 MagiCoins (or, groom your dragon)
Garlic	Dragon Stand	Spooktacular Spot, Vernon's Vault	Barter with Vicki (Beeswax)
Llama Spit	Wagon O'Wares	Vernon's Vault, Clowntastic Land, Serra Glen, Forest Edge	25 MagiCoins
Magic Beans	Wagon O'Wares	Vernon's Vault, Clowntastic Land, Serra Glen, Forest Edge	27 MagiCoins
Toadstools	Wagon O'Wares	Vernon's Vault, Clowntastic Land, Serra Glen, Forest Edge	9 MagiCoins (or from Champignon Toadstool Chair)
Beeswax	Wagon O'Wares, Wax n' Honey maker	Vernon's Vault, Clowntastic Land, Serra Glen, Forest Edge	17 MagiCoins
Rubber Chicken	Wagon O'Wares	Vernon's Vault, Clowntastic Land, Serra Glen, Forest Edge	Barter with Todd (Elderberry Nectar)
Toad Sweat	Wagon O'Wares	Vernon's Vault, Clowntastic Land, Serra Glen, Forest Edge	21 MagiCoins
Diamond Dust	Faerie Stand	Serra Glen, Forest Edge Camp	199 MagiCoins
Golden Thread	Faerie Stand	Serra Glen, Forest Edge Camp	14 MagiCoins, or from Prick-Me-Not Spinning Wheel
Sands of Time	Faerie Stand	Serra Glen, Forest Edge Camp	25 MagiCoins
Pixie Dust	Faerie Stand	Serra Glen, Forest Edge Camp	31 MagiCoins
Glacial Glass	Faerie Stand	Serra Glen, Forest Edge Camp	Quest for Mara (Faerie Stand) or Todd (Wagon O'Wares)
Four Leaf Clover	Faerie Stand	Serra Glen, Forest Edge Camp	Barter Honey with Mara (Faerie Stand)
Sugar	Grocery Stand	Serra Glen	§8
Honey	Grocery Stand	Serra Glen	§20, or from Wax n' Honey Maker
Butter	Grocery Stand	Serra Glen	§20, or from Old-Fashioned Butter Churn
Baking Mix	Grocery Stand	Serra Glen	§10
Grape Vine Sprig	Berry Stand	Coldwind Meadow, Serra Glen, Forest Edge Camp	§60
Grapes	Berry Stand	Coldwind Meadow, Serra Glen, Forest Edge Camp	§30, or from garden plot

Ingredient Sources, continued

INGREDIENT	SOURCE	MAGIC TOWN LOCATIONS	COST
Elderberry Sprig	Berry Stand	Coldwind Meadow, Serra Glen, Forest Edge Camp	§30
Elderberries	Berry Stand	Coldwind Meadow, Serra Glen, Forest Edge Camp	§15, or from garden plot
Snake Venom	Snake Charmer	Clowntastic Land, Forest Edge Camp	Barter Gold Thread with Nagganaste (Snake Charmer)
Clown Confetti	Wagon O'Wares	Vernon's Vault, Clowntastic Land, Serra Glen, Forest Edge Camp	Complete any quest
Glacial Glass	Wagon O'Wares, Faerie Stand, Dragon Stand	Spooktacular Spot, Vernon's Vault, Clowntastic Land, Serra Glen, Forest Edge Camp	Complete any quest
Wizard Eyelashes	Dragon Stand	Spooktacular Spot, Vernon's Vault	Complete any quest
Pegasus Feather	Dragon Stand, Faerie Stand	Spooktacular Spot, Vernon's Vault, Serra Glen, Forest Edge Camp	Complete any quest

NOTE

The Clown Confetti, Glacial Glass, Wizard Eyelashes, and Pegasus Feather are all rare rewards, randomly chosen at the beginning of each of the quests. Each NPC favors a particular item, giving you a better chance of receiving that particular item, but it's not a guarantee. Vicki tends to reward Wizard Eyelashes, Faerie Mara gives out the Pegasus Feather most often, and Apothecary Todd rewards with the Clown Confetti. Each one has the same chance to choose to reward Glacial Glass also.

Casting Spells and Charms

The following tables provide guidelines for when to use spells and charms for maximum results. Each casting has a potential backfire, and although some of the bad results are random, you can improve your success rate by studying the backfire conditions.

NOTE

The number of available castings for a charm or spell is based on Mechanical skill (charms) and Cooking skill (spells). A charm keeps spinning and becomes illuminated when it has castings remaining. When it stops spinning, it is no longer active.

The number of available spells appears on the Spell icon in your Magic inventory.

A Gallery of Charms and Spells

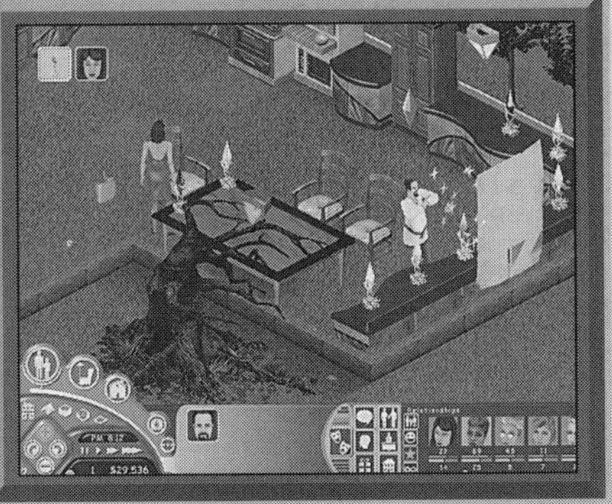

As your Sim recites the proper incantation, the charm begins to sparkle.

Clone Drone creates a mirror image of your Sim.

This Beauty or Beast charm didn't quite go as expected.

Enchant backfires and ignites a Gnome instead of bringing him to life.

Enchant a Flamingo to produce an exotic Faerie dancer who will entertain you...

...and converse with Flamingos during her break.

After casting Lovestruck, our Sim is humiliated when the spell is turned against him.

For a good laugh, use the Hypnotize spell to manipulate another Sim.

After falling asleep, Bella Goth is directed to lay a passionate kiss on our Sim.

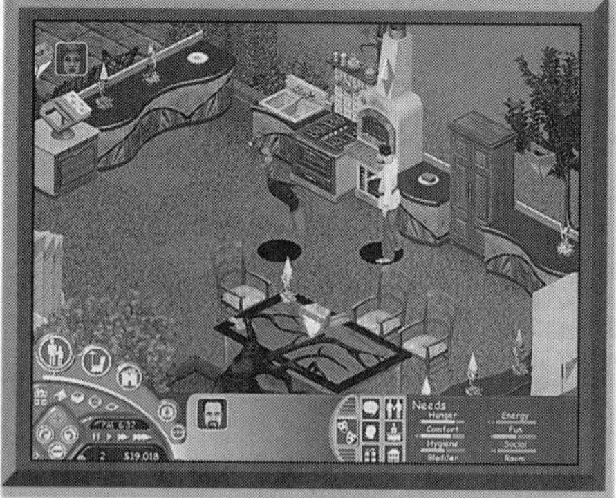

After casting Banish against another Sim with a Magic Wand, our Sim is surprised to see a portal appear under his feet when the spell is blocked. Banish is about to work, but against the caster!

With a wave of your wand, the Smiley Face spell makes an instant friend.

The Toadification spell is fun...

...unless someone does it to you.

Of House and Home charm dispatches Wally O' Wisp to your house, where he gives your bathtub a spit shine.

Adult Charms

Charm	Success	Failure	Backfire Condition
Polar Attraction	Positive Social responses from other Sims	Sims tend to react negatively to your Social advances	Caster's Body < 2
Dish Wish	Scrubbing bubbles clean up all dirty dishes	Dirty dishes spawn around the lot	0 or 1 dirty dish on the lot
Make Me Famous	Increases your Sim's Fame level to 4 stars, with plenty of Fame points for your next promotion	Your Sim takes a Fame hit and Obsessed Fan shows up	Caster's Fame ≥ 8
Shed Your Skin	Your Sim briefly turns into a ghost	Snakes appear all over your lot	Cast during the daytime
Horn of Plenty	Creates five plates of food (turkey and bread)	Spawns a bunch of toads around your Sim	Caster's Hunger ≥ 80
Mood Up All	Increases all of your Sim's Motives	Either hits all of your Motives for 50, drops Bladder to -100, or drops Energy to -100	Caster's Mood < 70
Perfect Garden	Rain clouds pour on all plants inside and outside	Gnome harasses your Sim for doing his work	Gnome is on the lot
Of House and Home	Wally O' Wisp cleans and fixes things	Wally's sister Molly breaks things	Caster's Neat > 3, Mood < 60
Rain of Riches	Coins rain down on the lot, leaving Treasure Chests, piles of gold, and gold sculptures	Rains on the lot, leaving floods inside and out	Caster's Mood < 0
Clone Drone	Clone goes to work for you when car comes (one day)	Clone stays home, waters the mailbox, and then erupts into flame	Caster's Hunger < -20
Beauty or Beast	Sim dons special costume	Everyone gets a donkey head	Someone else is in the room when your Sim transforms

In the following table, Mood Up, Smiley Face, and Enchant are also kid spells, with the same results and conditions.

dult Spells

Spell	Success	Failure	Backfire Condition
Magic Mood	Increases all of target's Motives	Hits all of your motives for 50, drops Bladder to -100, or drops Energy to -100	If target's Nice < 5 and Mood < 70
Banish	Removes target Sim from lot; if family member, target is moved out of world for a short time	Caster is rebuffed and sent out of world for a short time	Target has Magic Wand
Hypnotize	Forces target to interact with your Sim in some way	Target makes you dance like a chicken and bark like a dog	Target has Magic Wand
Toadification	Turns target into a toad for a period of time	Caster is turned into toad	Target has Magic Wand
Relationship Boost	Increases your Relationship with target	Decreases your Relationship with target	Target's Mood < -20
LoveStruck	Increases your Relationship with target Sim to love level	Your Sim gets rebuffed and struck with lightning	Target has Magic Wand
The Big Question	Boosted to love Relationship and Motives fixed an accept on marriage proposal	Caster becomes small and green	Target has Magic Wand
Smiley Face	Promoted to friend level with target	Relationship with target is reduced	If target is already a friend
Enchant	Target Gnome or Flamingo come to life for a period of time	Target is set on fire	Low Mechanical skill; as Mechanical skill rises, backfires decrease in frequency
Friend Indeed	Turns target pet into an adult Sim (cannot be undone)	Dog will attack you and cat will hide	Pet is in a bad mood, or not a member of family

Kid Magic

A Sim child becomes magical after charging a wand in the NeoMagical Newt. Children do not have simoleans or MagiCoins, and therefore cannot buy anything in Magic Town, so kid's spells and charms use only ingredients that are readily available (after related objects are purchased for the house). These ingredients and sources are listed in the table on page 156.

Cassandra plays with her NeoMagical Newt while Bella and Mortimer wonder where they went wrong.

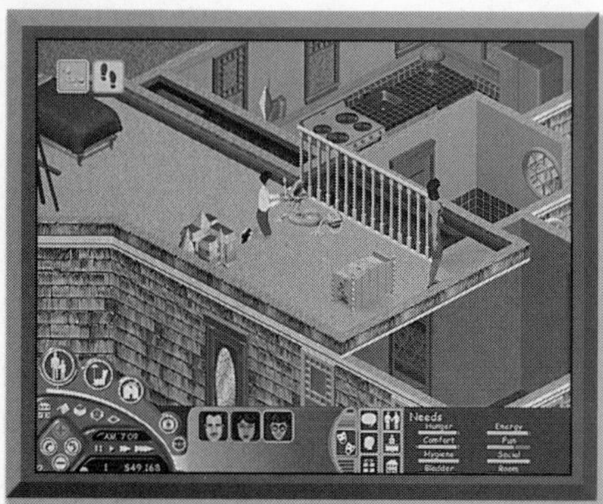
After adding a wand to her inventory, Cassandra is primed and ready for magic.

When a child plays with the Visions of Sugarplums Faerie Toy Box there is a chance she will play with Faeries.

When the play session is over, the Faeries leave a bag of Faerie Dust.

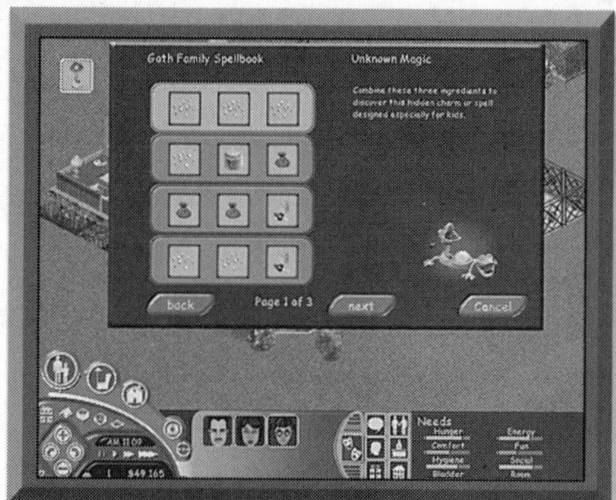
When Cassandra looks in the Goth Family Spellbook she sees only the kid spells.

Kid Magic Ingredients

INGREDIENT	SOURCE
Toadstools	Sit on a Champignon Toadstool Chair
Dragon Scales	Groom a dragon
Faerie Dust	Play with the Visions of Sugarplums Faerie Toy Box
Dragon Tears	Tickle a dragon

Cassandra harvests Toadstools after sitting on the Champignon Toadstool Chair several times.

After adding ingredients to the NeoMagical Newt, she produces her first charm, Beauty or Beast Jr.

Unfortunately for Cassandra, the charm is invoked with another Sim in the room, and instead of Cassandra wearing a costume, the entire family (even the sleeping Bella) sport donkey heads!

Kid Charms

Charm	Success	Failure	Backfire Condition
Beauty or Beast Jr.	Changes kid's costume for a short time	All Sims get donkey heads	Someone else in the room when casting
No More Puddles	Cleans up the child	Messes up child's Motives	Random chance to fail if caster's Hygiene is > 70
Make Cakes	Generates sweet stuff around the lot	Creates toads everywhere	Caster's Hunger motive > 80
Invisible Friend	Invisible friend wanders around and plays with child	Invisible enemy annoys the child	10% random chance to summon enemy
Clone Drone Jr.	Summons child that goes to school for the Sim	Clone waters the mailbox and erupts into flame	Caster's Hunger < -20
Age of Instant	Turns child into adult Sim (cannot be undone)	Turns kid back into baby	If grades are < A- and Hunger < 0

Magic Growth

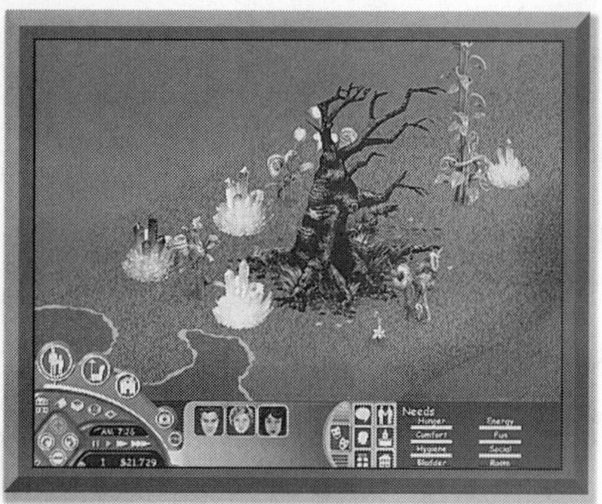

Introduction

Aside from the self-satisfaction of altering other Sims' lives, the biggest reward for spell casting is the arrival of Magic Growth objects. Every six hours, the game checks to see if your family has logged enough spell casts (spells or charms) to qualify for a Magic Growth object. If you live in a regular neighborhood, you must hit 15 casts before qualifying for Magic Growth. However, if you reside in one of the three Magic Town residential lots, your requirement is only 10 (for more information on residential lots, see page 136). In addition, Magic Growth objects grow faster in Magic Town, and Magic Crystals have five uses each, as compared to three on a regular lot. The following sections describe each type of Magic Growth.

> **NOTE**
>
> *The Magic Growth objects appear on your lot randomly, but they don't duplicate until you have received one of each type.*

Crystals

The Red Crystal includes the Hotfoot ability.

Simply select "Learn Ability" to acquire the magical properties of the crystals.

There are seven Magic Crystals, and each offers a new ability to magical Sims. Along with their special abilities, the crystals provide light, at a level similar to a lamp.

Magic Crystal Abilities

- **Red: Hot Foot**
- **Black: Extinguish**
- **White: Levitate**
- **Blue: Shock**
- **Green: Spook**
- **Purple: Teleport**
- **Yellow: Magic Trick**

> **NOTE**
>
> *A child with a Magic Wand can use the Yellow, Purple, and Red Stone.*

Root and Flower

The Root and Flower have three growth states (small, medium, and large). It takes between 18–48 hours for them to reach maturity.

Beanstalks

A Beanstalk grows like a Root or Flower; however, it has 8–17 additional growth segments. When the beanstalk reaches maximum height, it gains a "Climb" interaction. If you send your Sim to the top, you see a sleeping giant and super-size can of Magic Beans.

CHAPTER 13: QUESTS, DUELS, AND PERFORMANCES

Introduction

Although shopping for spell ingredients is an important reason for visiting Magic Town, you should also spend time perfecting your craft. In addition to performing on stage and entering the Diametric Dueling Device, you also can take on personal Quests from the vendors. In this chapter, we take you through the most demanding activities at Magic Town. They can be exhausting, so fill your Motives before jumping down your magic portal.

Quests

Magic Town offers seven different Quests, and each successful completion earns you a rare ingredient for your spells and charms. The following sections explain the Quests, with tips on how to complete them.

Tombstone Puzzle

After accepting a challenge to clean up the graveyard, your Quest is to either raise all the tombstones, or lower them to the ground. Each time you select a tombstone it changes state, as do all the tombstones that are touching the one you selected. Your quest is to get all of the tombstones raised. You have an infinite number of chances to solve the puzzle, but after every six moves it gets easier until it only needs one move to finish, as reflected in the list below.

Toadstool Race

Talk to one of the vendors (Faerie Mara, Todd the Apothecary, or Vicki the Vampiress). He or she challenges you to a race, wherein you must touch as many of nine Toadstools as possible, changing their colors to blue. The vendor does the same, changing the Toadstools to red. Finish with more blue Toadstools and you win the challenge. Return to the vendor to collect your reward.

Toadstool Race Tips

- Faerie Mara is the fastest because she teleports around the lot to reach the Toadstools.
- Todd runs to the Toadstools.
- Vicki walks, so she is easiest to defeat.
- Non-magic family members can also touch the Toadstools.

MODE	TOTAL # OF MOVES ALLOWED	MINIMUM # OF MOVES NEEDED TO SOLVE
Hard	6	3
Medium	6	2
Easy	6	1

Stop the Sleeping Cloud

After talking to a vendor, you find out that a strange cloud formation is spreading across Magic Town, putting its patrons to sleep. You must use your wand to disperse the clouds. This requires repeatedly touching the clouds with your wand until they are gone. Be patient. At first, it might seem as though the clouds are spawning faster than you can disperse them. Keep touching the clouds and eventually you'll gain the upper hand. When the clouds are gone, return to the vendor to reap your reward.

Barter

A vendor requests that your Sim find one of three items: Red Banana of Doom, Golden Apple, or Heavy Brick. Find it by approaching other Sims and asking about the item. The easiest way to find the right Sim is to zoom out, then select every Sim you see. Your Sim works through the crowd until the item is revealed. Cancel the remaining instructions, then return to the vendor to receive your reward.

Help Another

A vendor may ask you to cheer up a friend who is feeling down. If you don't want to risk a spell for an instant boost, simply find your target and talk his or her ears off. When your friend's Mood and Relationship scores have improved sufficiently, go back to the vendor and receive praise and reward.

Delivery Mission

Like Help Another, you must find a specific Sim, but instead of bringing smiles and good cheer, you deliver a package. Zoom out, pick your target out of the crowd, then make your approach. The Sim thanks you for the item, and complains a little about the lazy vendors. After dropping off the goods, return to the vendor for your reward.

CAUTION

Giving the delivery item to the wrong Sim doesn't always mean you lose; there's a small chance they will take it. You can also replace the lost item if the proper vendor is on the lot, or if you already have a bunch of those ingredients. There is also no penalty if you want to keep the ingredient, but you have to leave the lot in order to get a new Quest.

Challenge Duel

If there is a Diametric Dueling Device on the lot, a vendor may challenge you to a Duel. Vicki the Vampiress is the toughest opponent and Mara the Faerie Queen is the easiest. For complete dueling tips and strategies, see the next section.

Duels

When you want to get up close and personal with another magician, step onto the Diametric Dueling Device and choose your opponent. Each Sim stands atop a platform. At first glance, it looks like a guessing game as you try to select the right spell to overcome your opponent. But, if you look closely at the five colored orbs, you will understand the path to victory.

Blue Tornado overcomes the Red Wave.

Watch your opponent's orbs before selecting a spell. When you see one light up, check the table below to see which spell to select. However, don't wait for too long or your opponent will beat you to the draw. MagiCoins are awarded based on your number of successful spells, modified by your opponent's Logic skill. Payouts are as follows:

- **Small Loss: 1 x Opponent's Logic (0–10)**
- **Tie: 2 x Opponent's Logic (0–10)**
- **Small Win: 3 x Opponent's Logic (0–10)**
- **Big Win: 4 x Opponent's Logic (0–10)**

Everybody loves a winner.

Dueling Spell Matchups

Spell (Color)	Beats	Loses To
White Lightning	Red, Blue	Black, Yellow
Red Wave	Blue, Black	Yellow, White
Blue Tornado	Black, Yellow	White, Red
Black Blizzard	Yellow, White	Red, Blue
Yellow Brimstone	White, Red	Blue, Black

NOTE

Dueling Notes:

- *Each player is randomly assigned four of the five spells.*
- *The winner's orb grays out while the loser's orb disappears.*
- *If two spells cancel each other out, both Sims lose one spell and continue.*
- *Symbols on the ground in front of platform correspond to spells being cast.*

Magic Performances

Depending on the Magic Town lot you are visiting, you have a choice of four different performance venues: Magic Trick Table, Side Show, Spook Show, and Snake Charmer. Each choice is explained and pictured below.

Magic Trick Table

Performing basic magic tricks is the best way to get your feet wet in front of a live audience. Actually, you still earn MagiCoins playing to yourself, so the size of the audience does not matter. It is more important to prepare your skills at home before taking the stage. You need a Logic rating of at least six to guarantee a good result every time. If your skills are between three and six, results can vary. Finally, if you have less than three Logic, expect to light your hair on fire or lose the rabbit. Either way, the trick fails, but you still earn a few MagiCoins. Here is the payout schedule:

- **Good Trick: 11 MagiCoins**
- **Average Trick: 9 MagiCoins**
- **Bad Trick: 5 MagiCoins**

Side Show

Success in the Side Show depends on your Mechanical skill. A rating of less than three guarantees a bad result, while more than seven produces a successful performance. Here are the payouts:

- **Good Trick: 20 MagiCoins**
- **Average Trick: 11 MagiCoins**
- **Bad Trick: 4 MagiCoins**

NOTE

You can improve your Sim's Mechanical Skill in the following ways:

- *Studying Mechanical at the Bookcase*
- *Making Gnomes (requires KraftKing Woodworking Table)*
- *Making Gargoyles (requires Craft A Gargoyle)*
- *Making Golden Thread (requires Prick-Me-Not Spinning Wheel)*

Spook Show

One way to build up your Logic skill for the Spook Show is to play chess.

In the Spook Show, your Sim has a choice of bringing a pool of water to life, putting on a dance show with undead spouses, or bringing a mummy to life. Success requires an enhanced Logic skill. A rating of less than four guarantees a bad result, while more than seven produces a successful performance. Here are the payouts:

- **Good Trick: 25 MagiCoins**
- **Average Trick: 15 MagiCoins**
- **Bad Trick: 4 MagiCoins**

Snake Charmer

Nagganaste the Snake Charmer inspires his pet cobra from the comfort of his mat at Clowntastic Land and Calamity Forest. Aside from providing entertainment to Magic Town guests, he is the only source for Snake Venom, a rare ingredient for the Banish spell. Don't flash MagiCoins or simoleans when you visit Nagganaste. He will only part with Snake Venom if you offer Golden Thread for barter.

Advanced Creativity skill is required to be a good snake charmer. If a Sim with less than a 4 Creativity rating grabs the flute, the resulting music is bad enough to keep the snake in his basket. And, Nagganaste will give the Sim a piece of his mind as he shoos the non-musical Sim away from his mat.

A Sim with the minimum required Creativity skill may not make beautiful music, but it will be enough to get the snake to show his head.

The cobra will rise up and sway happily to the music for a Sim with a Creativity rating of 7 or more.

CHAPTER 14: DRAGONS

Introduction

You can now add cute pets to your Sim family. You can train them, enter them in pet shows, and even breed them for profit. Of course, there is a down side to having dogs and cats living in your house. They poop and pee, need regular baths, and crave your attention, sometimes in the middle of the night. Fortunately, a magical Sim has an alternative, and it doesn't poop, pee, require a bath, or demand social interaction. However, it does like to burn things...lots of things. In this chapter, we introduce the magician's best friend, a dragon. We show you how to acquire and care for one, and more importantly, how to keep it from burning down your house.

The Dragon Nest

Your dragon saga begins at All Things Draconic, a stand managed by Vicki the Vampiress. Vicki peddles her wares only at A Spooktacular Spot (93 Calamity Forest). Dragons can also be purchased from lot 94. Don't worry about meeting any stringent requirements for buying a Dragon Nest. As long as you have 44 MagiCoins, she'll send you home with a little fire-breather.

TIP

If you have enough MagiCoins, pick up a Dragon Chew Toy and some Dragon Treats when you buy the Dragon Nest. Even a good dragon needs diversions, and an investment here may keep your new pet from incinerating your favorite things.

When you return home, the Dragon Nest gets deposited on your lawn. You can leave it there, or move it inside the house where it's easier to manage during the incubation period.

How you treat the egg during the next 36–48 hours determines your dragon's personality. The egg shakes, and you hear grumbling noises, every 2–4 hours. You do not have to respond immediately, and there is no penalty for ignoring the egg. However, the number of times you interact with the egg during incubation is critical.

Your choices for interaction are Cradle, Rotate, and Play Music. Use all three activities, and interact at least six times before the egg hatches.

It's a Dragon!

If you interacted at least six times (but not more than 14), your new dragon will be Pyritie, a cute, golden, well-adjusted fire-breather. All dragons love to set things on fire, but Pyritie is usually unsuccessful, so don't worry too much if he wanders around the house shooting flames.

CAUTION

Even a good dragon can go bad, which increases the chances that it will ignite your belongings. So, don't forget to spend some time with the little guy, as explained on page 169. Chew Toys always help, too.

SIX THINGS YOU CAN DO WITH A DRAGON

Give it a Dragon Chew Toy. Your dragon plays with this little doll, then looks for it later when bored (an excellent deterrent to fire breathing).

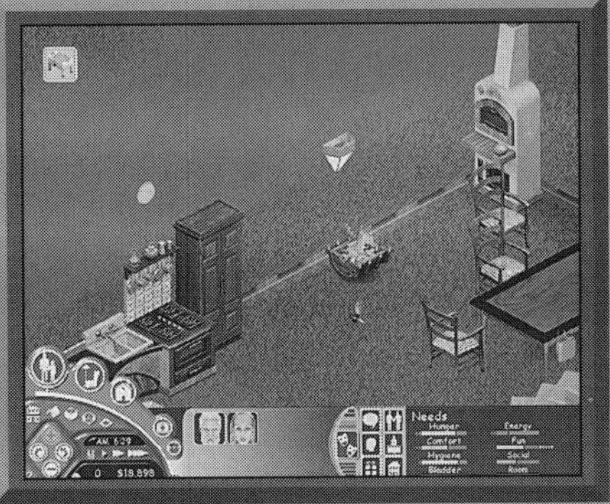

Tickle your dragon and it may leave you Dragon Tears of happiness (1 in 10 chance).

A dragon loves to be Groomed, and it pays back your kindness with Dragon Scales (1 in 10 chance).

If your dragon is trying to burn your house down with regularity, it might be a good idea to Set It Free. You can delete (sniff, sniff) the empty Dragon Nest.

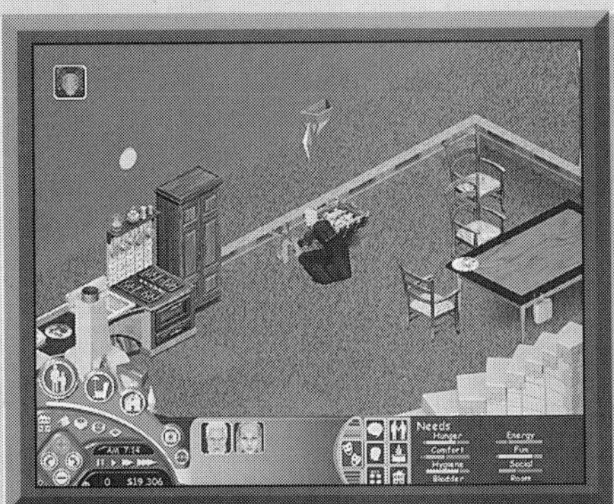

A good pet on the head keeps your dragon happy.

All pets love treats, and dragons are no exception. Replenish your supply at All Things Draconic.

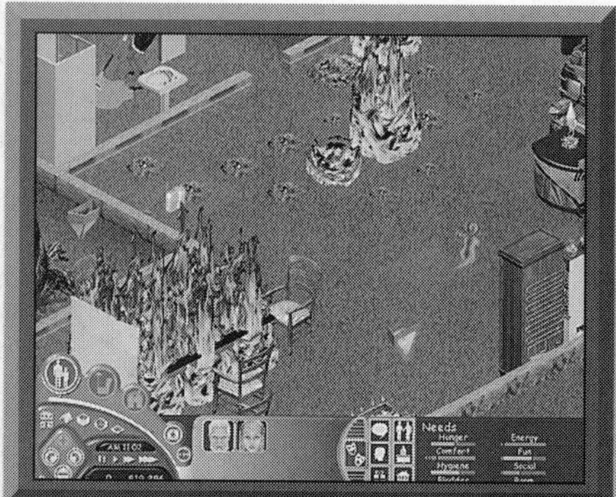

If you interacted fewer than six times, your new bundle of fire will be Burnie, a nasty little red dragon that would rather breathe fire than just breathe. This little hellion can reduce your house to ashes in no time. Keeping Burnie occupied is a full-time job, so after you have a few laughs watching him burn up the house, Set It Free, or you'll need a second income just to replace everything he destroys.

There is such a thing as too much love. If you coddle your dragon egg (more than 14 interactions), you produce Torch, a purple slacker dragon. Torch is fairly benign, and fortunately, his lack of motivation keeps him from being too destructive. Find him wandering aimlessly around your property. But, don't ignore him completely, or he will eventually set something on fire. There is very little difference between the purple and gold dragons.

Dragon Notes

- Dragons do not pee, poop, or otherwise mess up the house.
- Dragons love treats, but they also eat garbage, pet food, flowers (dead or alive), and toads. Be careful if you cast a Toadification Spell around the dragon; your Sim may accidentally lose a family member!
- When a dragon is tired, it sleeps in its bed (formerly the Dragon Nest).
- Dragon motives are limited to Fun, Hunger, and Energy. They display thought balloons when any of these motives are lacking.
- Dragons do not grow.
- There is no limit to the number of dragons you can own.
- Dragons will play with animated Gnomes.
- Dragons will play tag with other dragons, and they will also play with family pets (dogs and cats). These interactions satisfy the dragon's Fun motive.

CHAPTER 15: FUN HOUSE DESIGN

Introduction

A ride on a roller coaster is just the ticket when your Sim needs a break from all the spells, charms, and duels of *Makin' Magic*. In this chapter, we introduce the Fun House and Haunted House objects with tips on designing a properly functioning ride.

Construction 101

Correct placement

Incorrect placement

There is only one rule in designing and placing ride objects: Keep the connecting arrows going in the same direction. Each Fun House or Haunted House object (except for the tracks) is a self-contained ride, with entrance and exit stairs. When you correctly attach a section of track, the stairs transform into a track connector. When the track is incorrectly attached, the stairs remain, and the track does not function.

NOTE

Fun House and Haunted House rides can be built only on Magic Town commercial lots. The rides take up quite a bit of real estate, so you may need to delete some existing items, or bulldoze the lot and start from scratch.

A thrill ride can be a single Fun House or Haunted House, or a series of connected structures and tracks. The only limit is available space. Just make sure you have an entrance and an exit, or your Sims can't get on and off the ride. The ride pictured above incorporates five different Fun Houses, but because it is a continuous loop, it will never see a passenger.

The Haunted House ride pictured above has all the ingredients of a popular ride.

NOTE

You can mix and match Haunted House and Fun House ride objects, just as long as you have an entrance and exit.

Happy Sims and Scared Sims

A Sim responds to a ride based on personality traits. On a Fun House ride, a "Playful" Sim (rating of 6 or higher), raises his arms in glee, as pictured above.

With a Playful rating of less than 6, this Sim sees nothing funny about this Fun House ride.

On a Haunted House ride, a Sim with a Nice rating of 4 or less will be happily terrified.

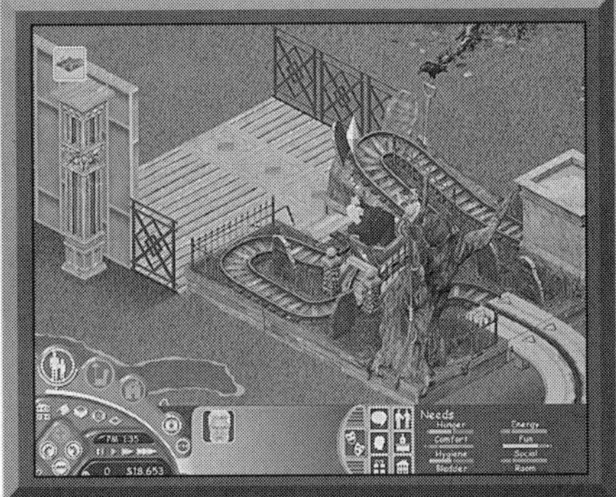

If your Sim is too Nice, a Haunted House ride causes abject fear and loathing.

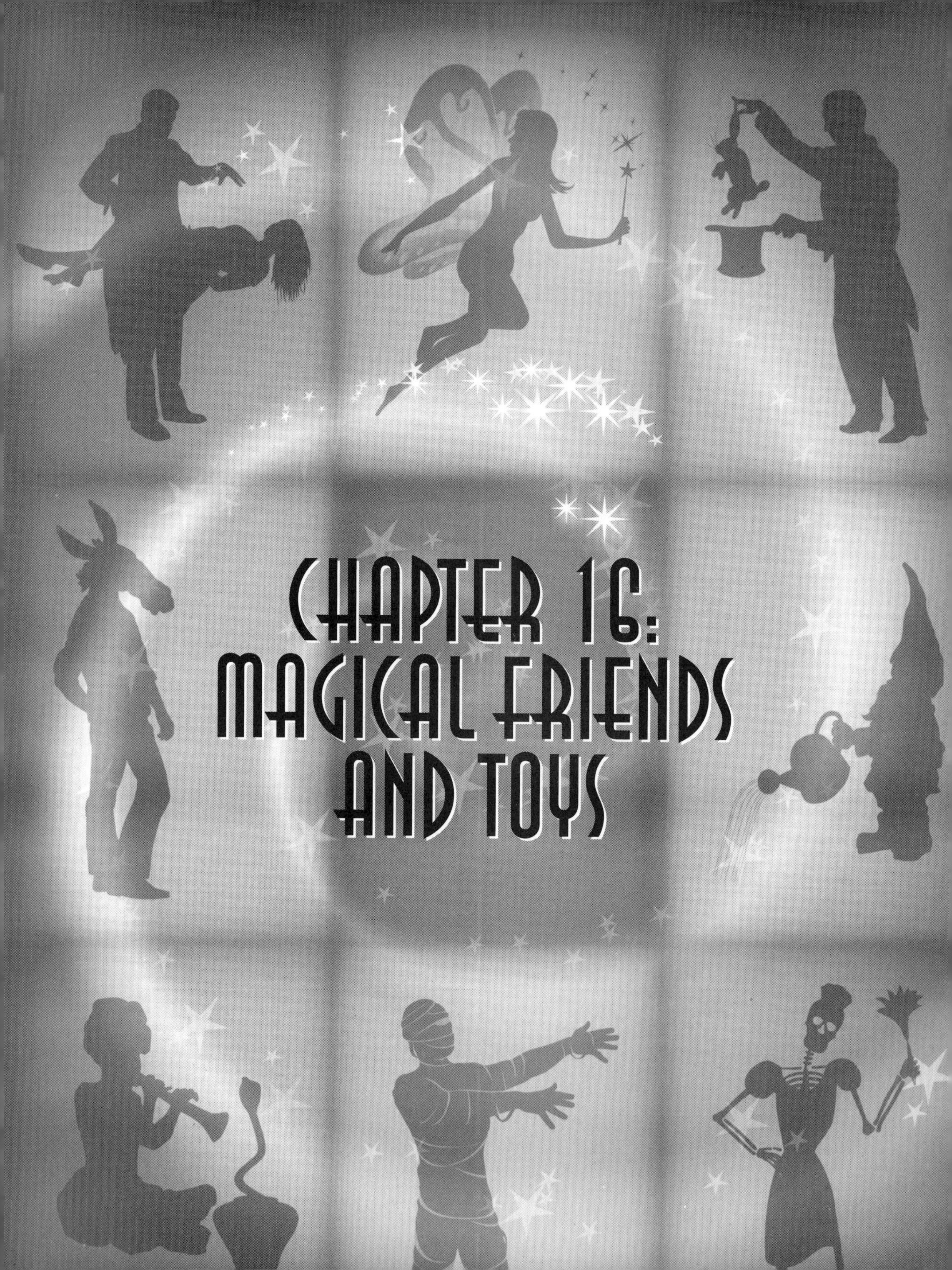

CHAPTER 16: MAGICAL FRIENDS AND TOYS

Introduction

Thanks to the Enchant spell, Flamingos and Gnomes have been elevated beyond lawn ornaments to living (albeit for a short time) characters. They are entertaining and sometimes unpredictable, as you'll see in the pictures below. Rounding out this chapter are the Skeleton Maid and the Visions of Sugarplums Faerie Toy Box.

Animated Gnomes

These guys win our prize for the funniest characters in *Makin' Magic*. Immediately upon coming to life, Gnomes take their gardening responsibilities very seriously. They weed, water, and otherwise coddle all vegetation inside and outside the house.

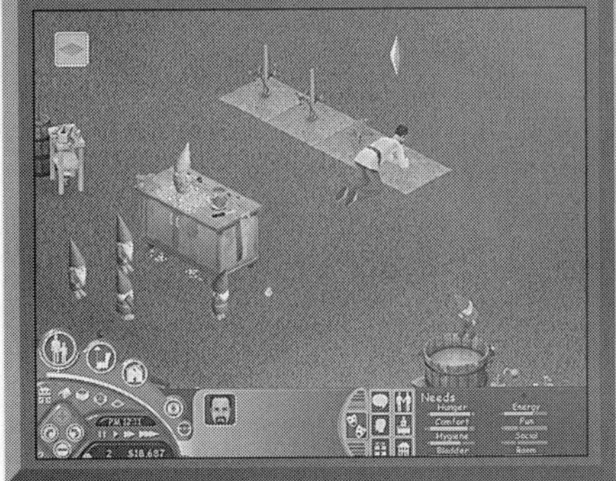

However, all bets are off when there is a Nectar Press in the vicinity. Gnomes still take care of the gardening, but they spend the rest of the day swimming in the press and drinking as much nectar as they can hold. After some time in the tank, they totter around the grounds looking for their sea legs (which they never find).

Despite their propensity for the nectar, Gnomes take great offense if you hire a Gardener, or even worse, invoke the Perfect Garden charm. This not only infuriates your Gnome, but it immediately animates any other Gnomes on the lot. They all get together and storm your Sim, berating him and kicking him in the shins.

Then, when they've had their fill of abusing you, they trash your garden. Needless to say, you should think hard before casting Perfect Garden when you have an animated Gnome on the lot.

These gentle creatures boost your Social motive with an assortment of warm and fuzzy interactions, including cheering you up, hugging you, and even blowing kisses. They are so attentive to your needs that you don't even need to call your friends to keep your Social motive solidly in the green.

Animated Flamingos

Unlike Gnomes, these gentle creatures are a joy when you animate them. They turn into beautiful dancers who frolic around your house, entertaining you and your guests. They even stop to give your Sim a warm embrace. They have no interest in nectar, and if they encounter other Flamingos on the lot, they stop and talk to them.

Skeleton Maid

She wears the same cute uniform that your regular maid wears, but somehow the Skeleton Maid doesn't quite fill it out. But, don't let her bony legs scare you off. The Skeleton Maid is a lean, mean, undead cleaning machine.

If you unleash the Skeleton Maid while your regular Maid is still employed, you'll soon be down one employee. When the regular Maid sees her bony counterpart, she flips out and storms away, never to work for you again. That's fine, because the Skeleton Maid is there when you need her, at any hour of the day. All you need to do is knock on her coffin and she'll come rattling.

NOTE

The Skeleton Maid will wave at tombstones when leaving. She even asks the Grim Reaper for his autograph if you have Living Large *and* Superstar *installed.*

Visions of Sugarplums Faerie Toy Box

The Visions of Sugarplums Fairie Toy Box is a wonderful source of entertainment for the children in your house. When your magical child opens the box, there is a chance that the mini-fairies will come out to play. After whirling around at hyper speed, they leave a neat bundle of Pixie Dust for your child's spells and charms.

CHAPTER 17: NEW OBJECTS

Introduction

The Sims Makin' Magic includes more than 200 new objects available in Buy Mode and Build Mode when you are occupying a house. The objects are arranged by category, as they appear on the Buy Mode menus (Seating, Surfaces, Decorative, etc.) with pictures, prices, and ratings (if applicable). The Efficiency Value (1–10) indicates how well an item satisfies its related Motive, with a higher number being worth more to your Sims.

> **NOTE**
>
> *The Magic Town Only section at the end of this chapter includes objects available only when you are on a community lot in Magic Town.*

Seating

Dining Chairs

Kathedra Dining Chair

Cost: §199

Motive: Comfort (3)

Ode to a Haunted Chair

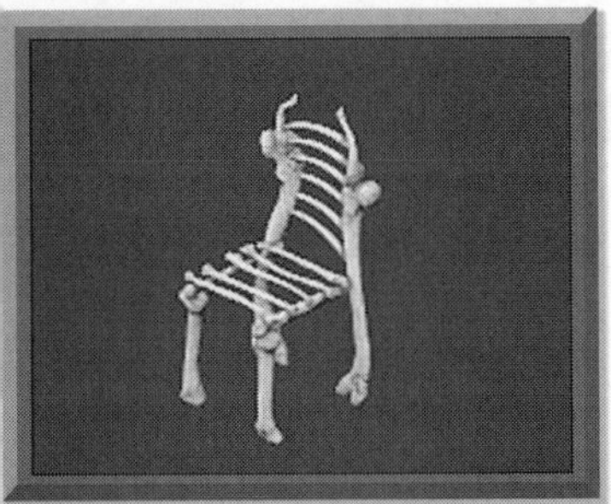

Cost: §499

Motive: Comfort (4), Room (1)

Papa's Chair

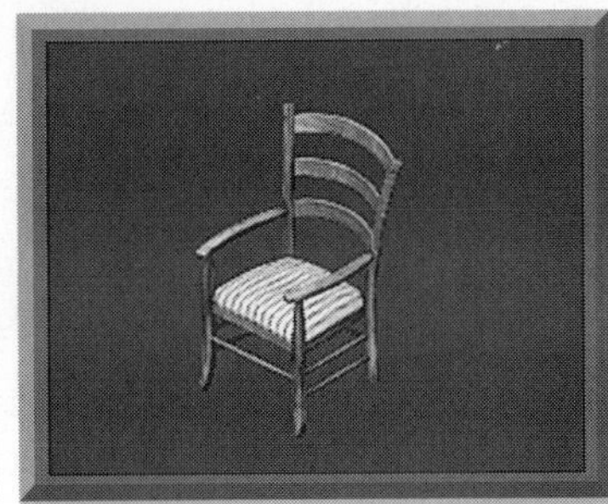

Cost: §1,100

Motive: Comfort (8), Room (3)

Beds

Midnight Mystery Canopy Bed

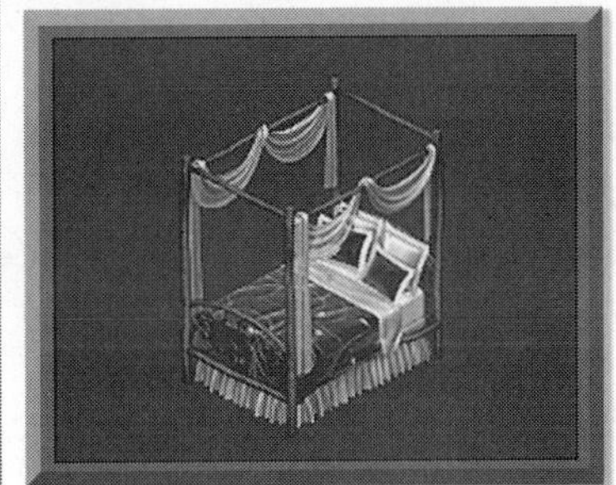

Cost: §4,999

Motive: Comfort (10), Energy (10), Room (5)

Other

Champignon Toad Stool Chair

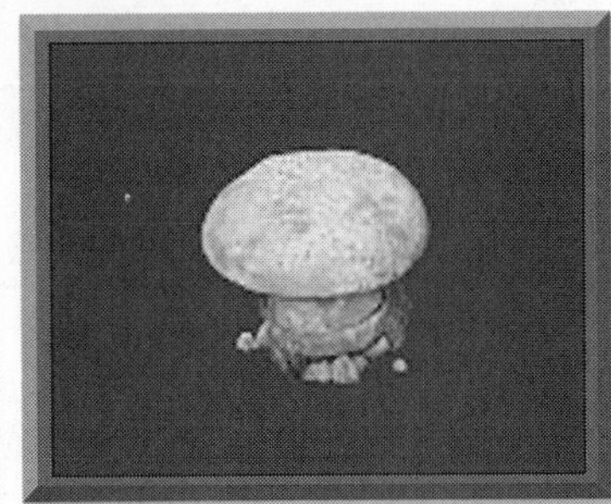

Cost: §121

Motive: Comfort (2)

Notes: Spawns mini-toadstools

Suffah Collacare Bench

Cost: §239

Motive: Comfort (2)

Surfaces

Counters

DellaGiorno Kitchen Counter

Cost: §599

Motive: N/A

Tables

Mama's Table

Cost: §419

Motive: Room (2)

End Tables

Authentic Barrel by Amos T.R. Cooper Inc.

Cost: §45

Motives: N/A

Tragic Magic Basket

Cost: §92

Motives: N/A

Truly Charming End Table

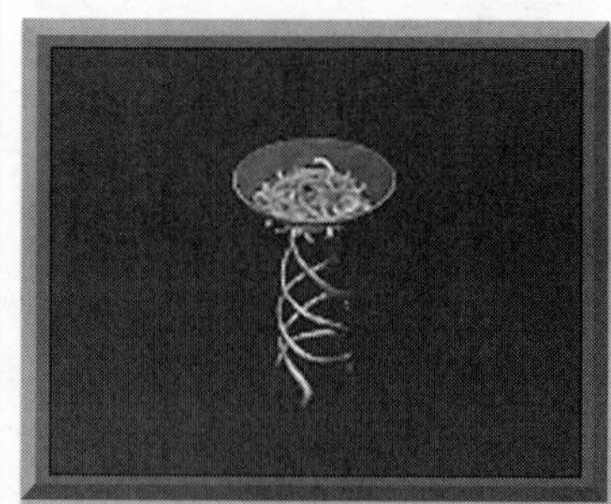

Cost: §205

Motives: Room (1)

Decorative

Paintings

"Swami Slicer and the Box of Mystery"

Cost: §39

Motive: Room (1)

"The Basket Case"

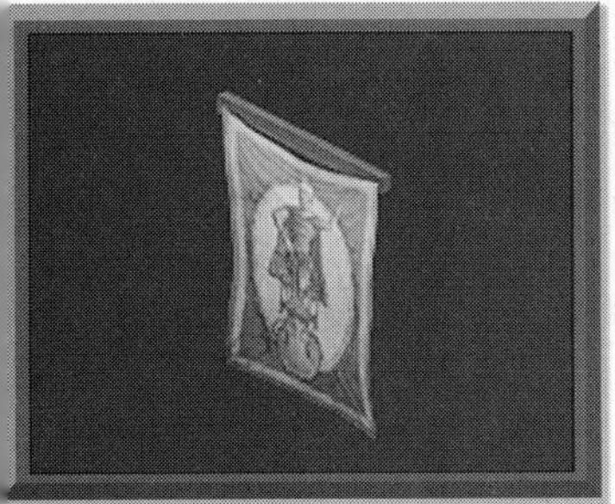

Cost: §39

Motive: Room (1)

"Code of the Carny"

Cost: §135

Motive: Room (1)

"Mr. Bones Does Broadway"

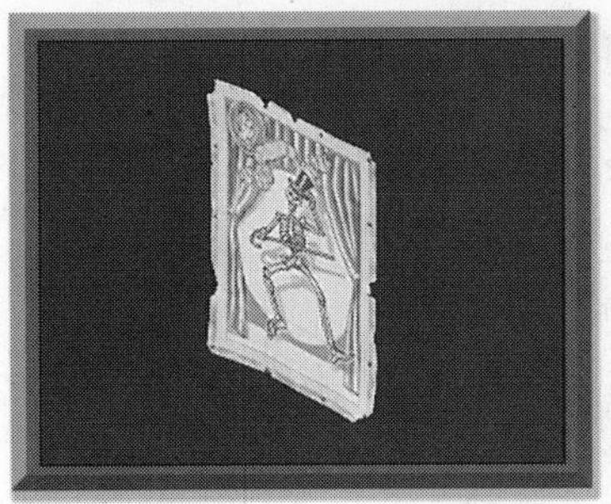

Cost: §155

Motive: Room (1)

"Zombo the Effervescent"

Cost: §208

Motive: Room (2)

Solar Stitches Tapestry

Cost: §684

Motive: Room (3)

Sculptures

"Sleight of Mind" Sandwichboard Sign

Cost: §99

Motives: Room (1)

The Bothersome Blades

Cost: §439

Motives: Room (3)

The Tomb of Sometimes Why

Cost: §1,555

Motives: Room (4)

Maniacal Melvin Maquette

Cost: §5,449

Motives: Room (7)

Rugs

Rug by Erin M. Designer

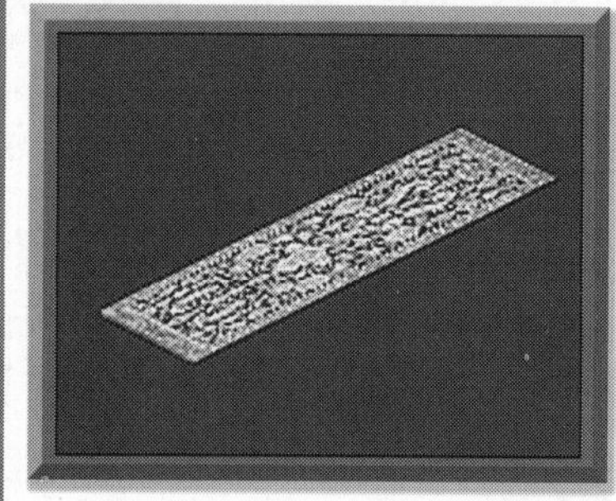

Cost: §537

Motives: Room (3)

Plants

Domesticated Grape Leaf Ivy

Cost: §111

Motives: Room (2)

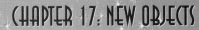

eonies in White

Cost: §333

Motives: Room (3)

ther

aid in the Shade

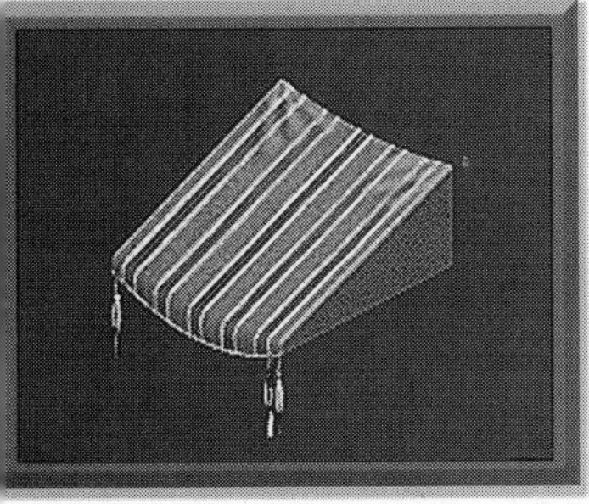

Cost: §71

Motives: N/A

"Winner Ev'ry Time" Awning

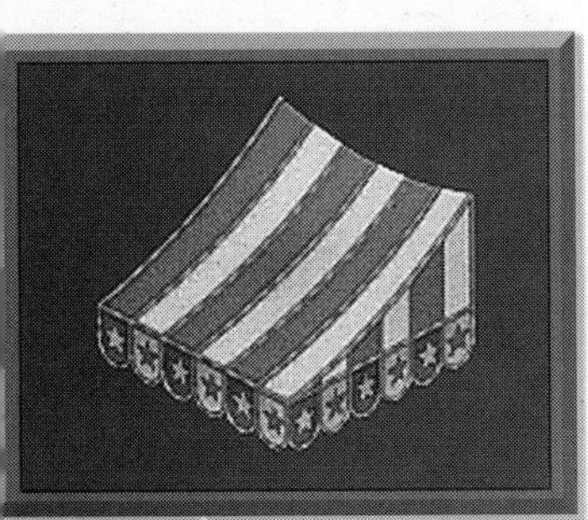

Cost: §72

Motives: N/A

Celestial Ceiling Awning

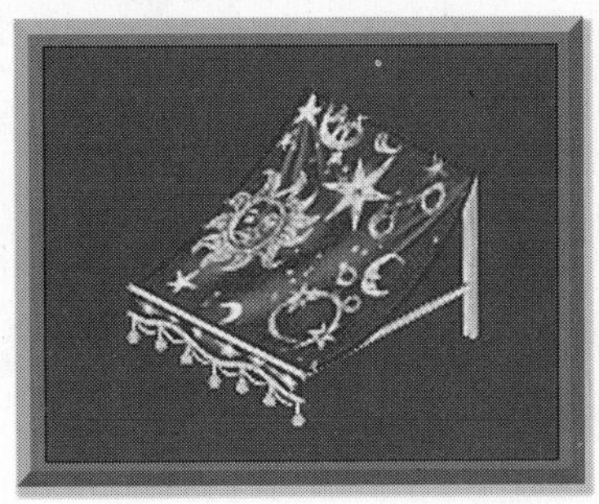

Cost: §74

Motive: N/A

All's Well That Ends Well (Fancy)

Cost: §2,333

Motive: Room (4)

Appliances

Stoves

Standard-Plus Brick Oven for Bakers

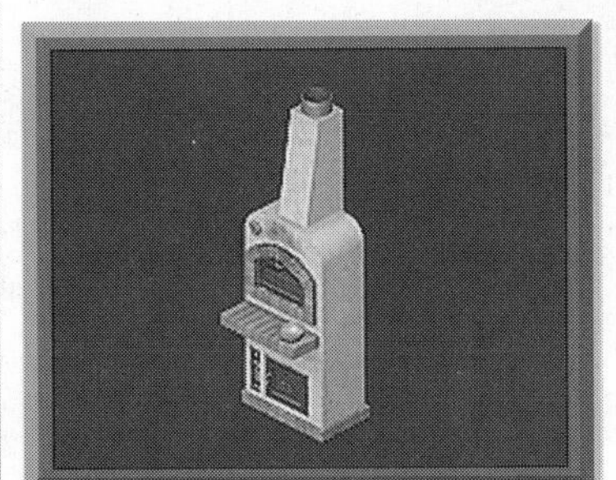

Cost: §899

Motive: Hunger (6)

Thermacotta Dual-Fuel Range

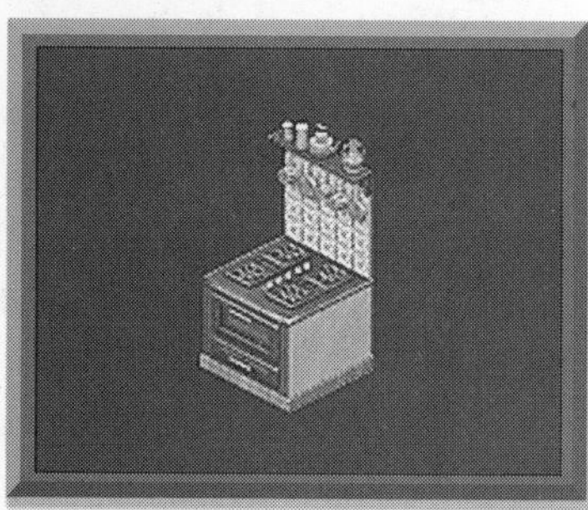

Cost: §1,900

Motive: Hunger (9), Room (1)

Refrigerators

La Frigorifero by Belconi

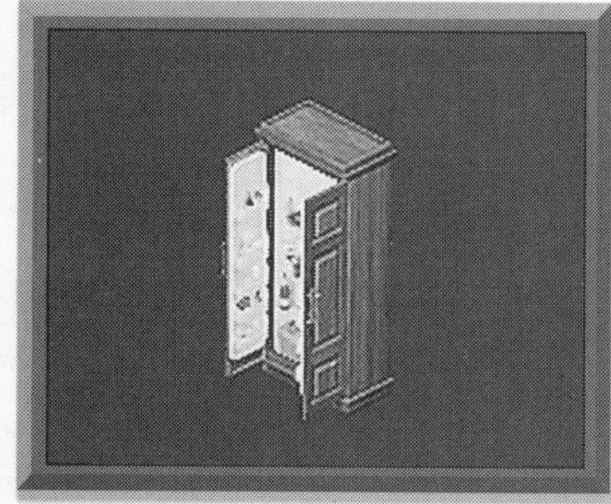

Cost: §2,950

Motive: Hunger (10), Room (1)

Small Appliances

Colonial Duties Tea Set

Cost: §300

Motive: Energy (2), Bladder (-2)

Notes: Can be used only by adults

Large Appliances

StinkSmasher 20X6

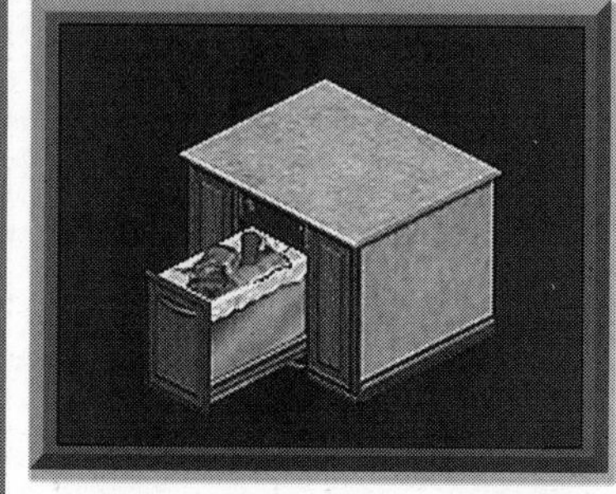

Cost: §575

Motive: Room (1)

Whimsy Wash Dishwasher by KitchenArt

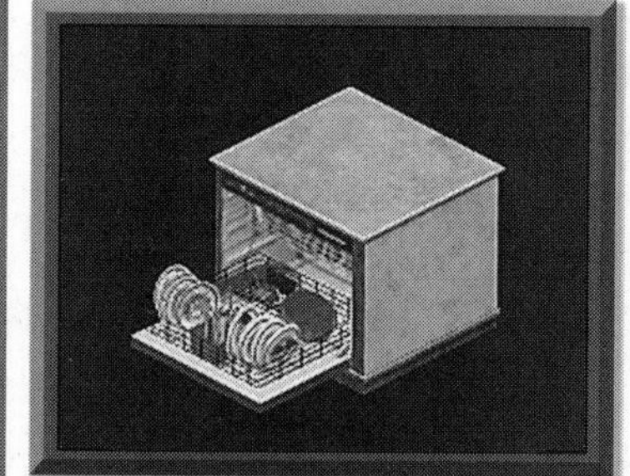

Cost: §1,150

Motive: Room (1)

Other

Pops O' Corn Deluxe Stand

Cost: §519

Motive: Hunger (2)

Plumbing

inks

eally Rustic Kitchen Sink

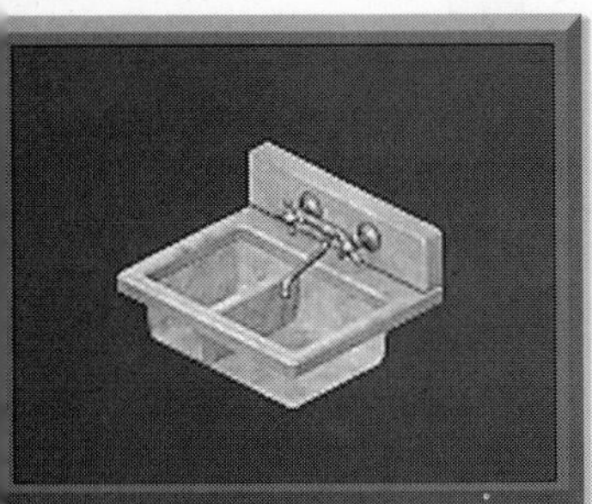

Cost: §699

Motive: Hygiene (3), Room (2)

ther

he B.A. Drain Outhouse

Cost: §319

Motives: Hygiene (-1), Bladder (4)

ighting

Vall Lamps

aux Gas Glass Light

Cost: §199

Motive: Room (1)

Romani Candle Lantern

Cost: §285

Motive: Room (1)

Other

Carni-Brite Carnival Lights

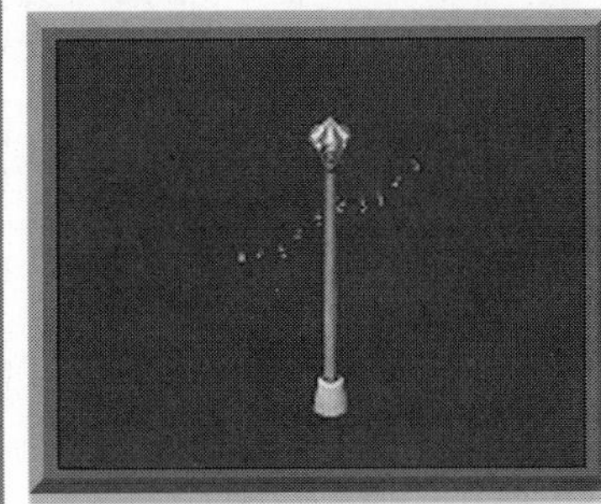

Cost: §65

Motive: N/A

Standing Torch by Fiehr

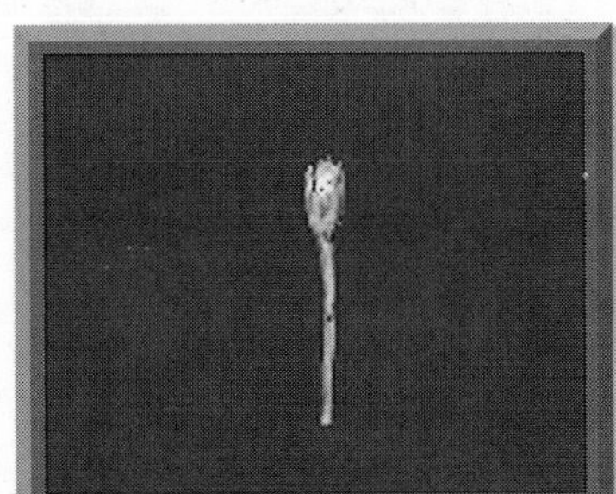

Cost: §99

Motive: N/A

Miscellaneous

Recreation

Visions of Sugarplums

Cost: §325

Motive: Fun (3)

Notes: Can only be used by kids

Knowledge

A Sim's Guide to Cooking

Cost: §89

Motive: N/A

Notes: Can be used only by adults

Checker Set Too

Cost: §399

Motive: Fun (2), + Logic

Notes: Group activity

Creativity

Craft-A-Gargoyle

Cost: §1,120

Motive: + Mechanical

Notes: Can be used only by adults

Magic

A Hole in the Ground

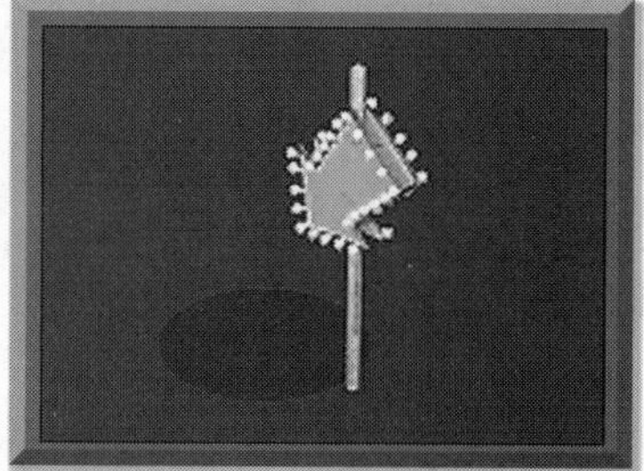

Cost: §89

Motive: N/A

The MagiCo NeoMagical Newt

Cost: §99

Motive: N/A

Note: Can be used only by kids

Spellbound Wand Charger by MagiCo

Cost: §129

Motive: N/A

Notes: Can be used only by adults

e Start Here Spell Book, Version 2.0

Cost: §149

Motive: N/A

e Start Here Spell Book, Original

Cost: §159

Motive: N/A

verAfter Crafter

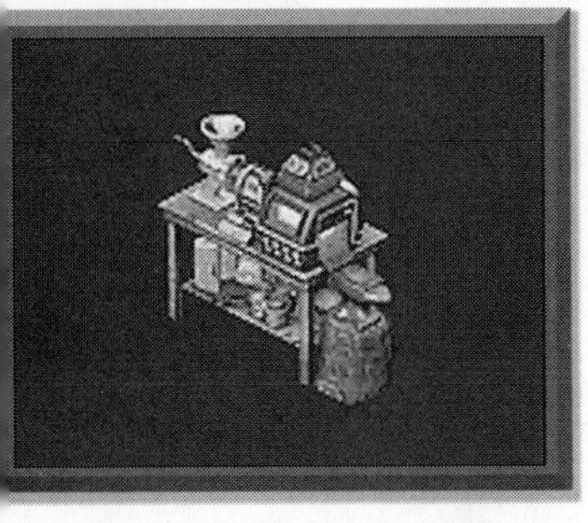

Cost: §199

Motive: N/A

otes: Can be used only by adults

rick-Me-Not Spinning Wheel

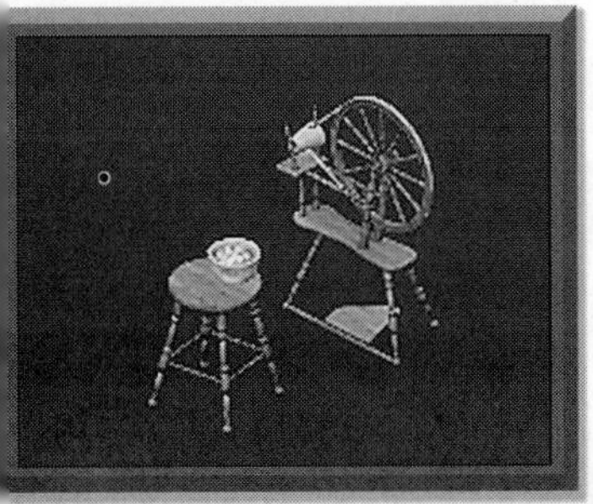

Cost: §417

Motive: + Mechanical

Alacazam Stand by MagiCo Inc.

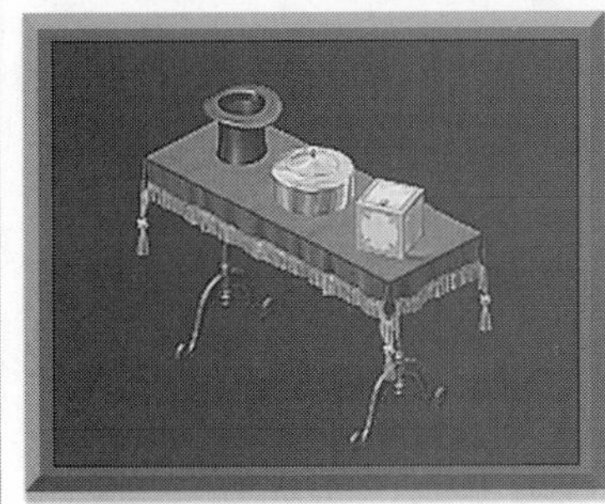

Cost: §562

Motive: Fun (5)

Notes: Group activity

"Bag-O-Bones" Skeleton Closet

Cost: §3,999

Motive: N/A

Other

Old-Fashioned Butter Churn

Cost: §447

Motive: + Cooking

Notes: Can be used only by adults

A Pressing Feeling

Cost: §599

Motive: N/A

Wax n' Honey Maker

Cost: §875

Motive: + Cooking

Notes: Can be used only by adults

Taste of the Vine Nectar Bar

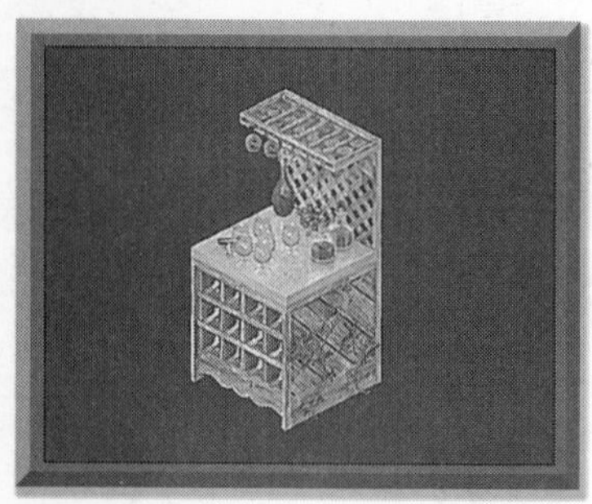

Cost: §899

Motive: Room (2)

Notes: Can be used only by adults

Build Mode

Wall and Fence Tool

Flags on a Wire

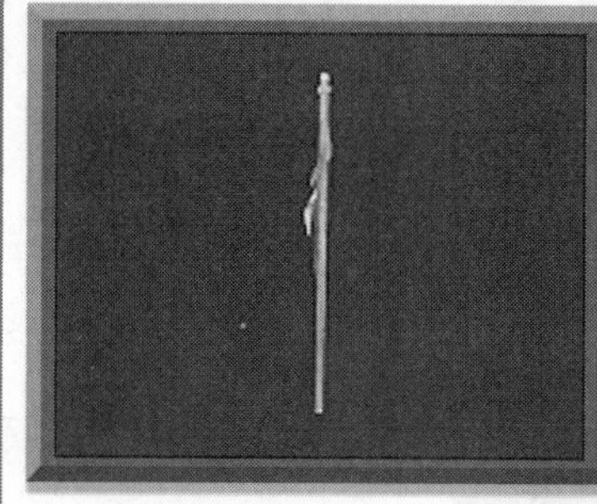

Cost: §19

Motive: N/A

Pile O' Logs Fence by McRoural

Cost: §24

Motive: N/A

Simbini's Tribute

Cost: §75

Motive: N/A

ffrighting Archway

Cost: §230

Motive: N/A

Knotsonu Wallpaper

Cost: §4

Motives: N/A

Wallpaper Tool

Debutante" Wall Covering

Cost: §4

Motives: N/A

andy Coated Siding

Cost: §4

Motives: N/A

Suburban Sprawl Siding

Cost: §4

Motives: N/A

Tuff N' Fun Wall Panel

Cost: §4

Motives: N/A

Wooden Clapboard Wall

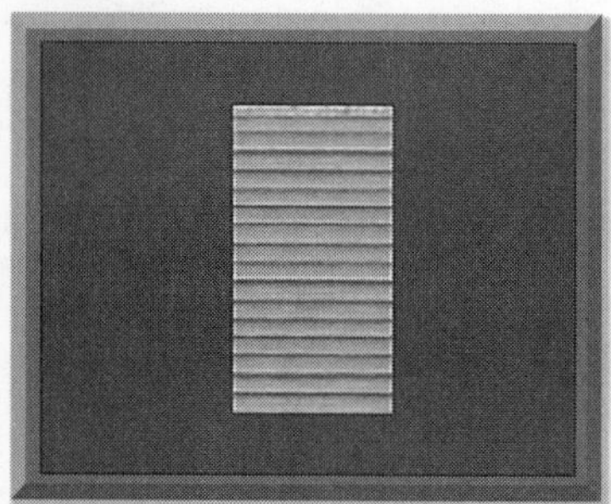

Cost: §4

Motives: N/A

"Caprice" Wall Cover

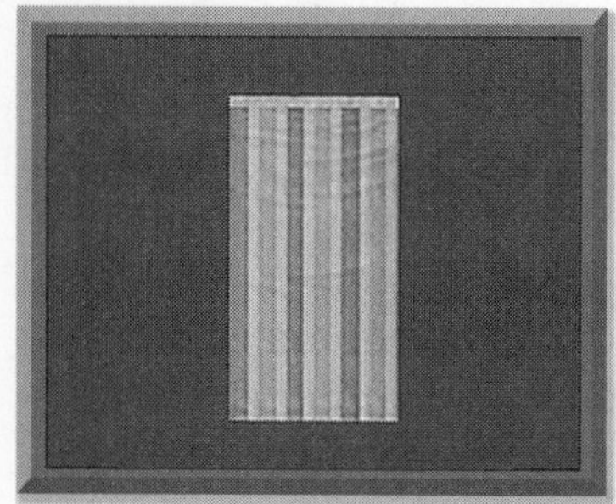

Cost: §5

Motives: N/A

"Sugarplum" Wallpaper

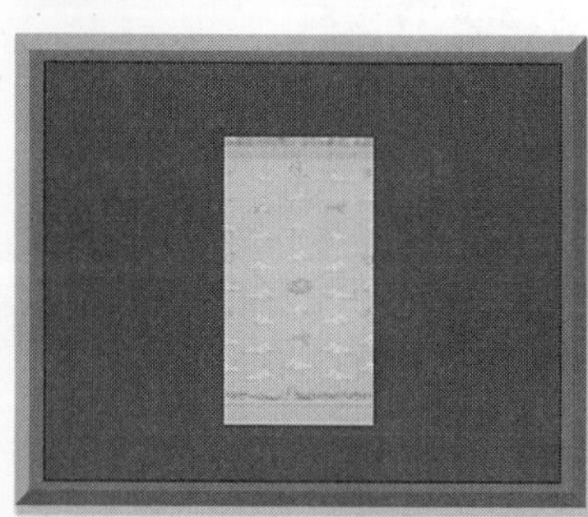

Cost: §5

Motives: N/A

Behind the Facade

Cost: §5

Motives: N/A

Beside the Facade

Cost: §5

Motives: N/A

Koordinated Colors

Cost: §5

Motives: N/A

azy Carnival Canvas

Cost: §5

Motives: N/A

atzLite! Wall Panel

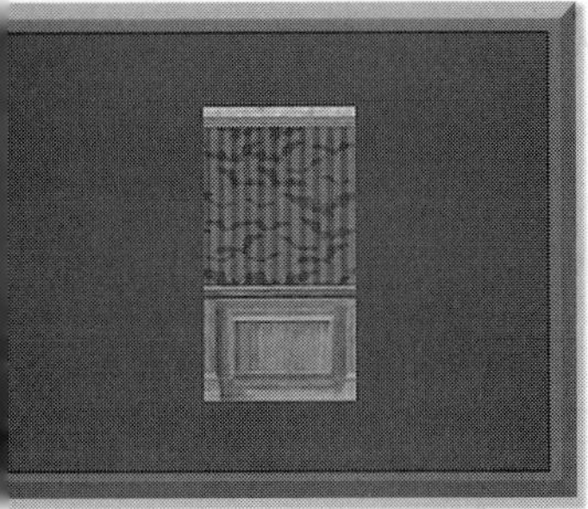

Cost: §6

Motives: N/A

atz! Wallpaper by MagiCo Inc.

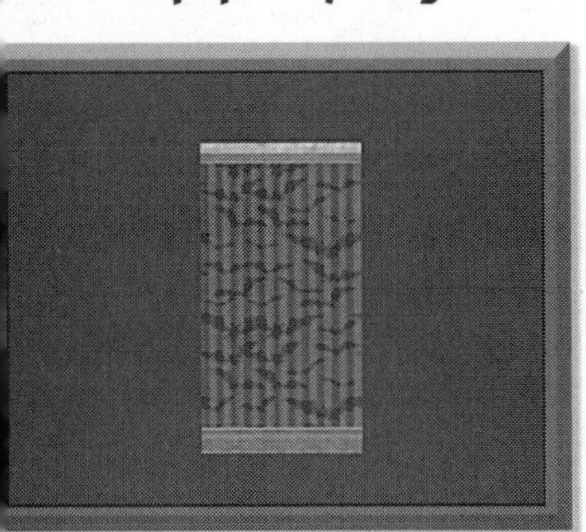

Cost: §6

Motives: N/A

Divine Grape Wallpaper

Cost: §6

Motives: N/A

Repurposed Wall of Fun

Cost: §6

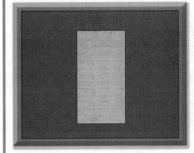

Motives: N/A

Straight Up Planks Wall

Cost: §6

Motives: N/A

"Nomad Nomore" Wall Panel

Cost: §7

Motives: N/A

EZ Wood Wall Panels

Cost: §7

Motives: N/A

Falling Tudor Wall

Cost: §7

Motives: N/A

Instant Relief Arch

Cost: §7

Motives: N/A

Leaning Tudor Wall

Cost: §7

Motives: N/A

Scalloped Wood Shingle

Cost: §7

Motives: N/A

lightly Suspicious Siding

Cost: §7

Motives: N/A

Wood and Stucco Combo

Cost: §7

Motives: N/A

a Bella Fresco in "Gilded"

Cost: §8

Motives: N/A

La Bella Fresco in "Vista"

Cost: §8

Motives: N/A

Old Wood Wall Shingle

Cost: §8

Motives: N/A

Classic Cellar Wall

Cost: §9

Motives: N/A

Creeping Ivy and Stone

Cost: §9

Motives: N/A

Parlor Wainscot

Cost: §9

Motives: N/A

Stuckno Stucco

Cost: §9

Motives: N/A

Malachi Wood Panels

Cost: §10

Motives: N/A

Panel Wainscot

Cost: §10

Motives: N/A

Stucco Wainscot

Cost: §10

Motives: N/A

ll Timbers Wall

Cost: §10

Motives: N/A

oble Velvet Wall

Cost: §11

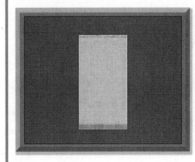

Motives: N/A

rimal Stone

Cost: §11

Motives: N/A

Stucco of Tuscany

Cost: §11

Motives: N/A

Tuscany Brick Trim

Cost: §11

Motives: N/A

Tuscan Basic by Stile

Cost: §12

Motives: N/A

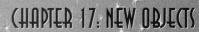

Tuscan Trim by Stile

Cost: §12

Motives: N/A

U.O.F Stucco/Tile Wall

Cost: §12

Motives: N/A

Weathered Ivy Wall

Cost: §12

Motives: N/A

Fabulous Fibular Wall Panel

Cost: §13

Motives: N/A

Wagon Wall

Cost: §13

Motives: N/A

"Rowena" Fabric Panels

Cost: §14

Motives: N/A

Ancient Draco Wall

Cost: §14

Motives: N/A

Earthish Stone Wall

Cost: §15

Motives: N/A

Old Stone Block

Cost: §15

Motives: N/A

Ruf-Hune Facade

Cost: §15

Motives: N/A

Wide Open Space

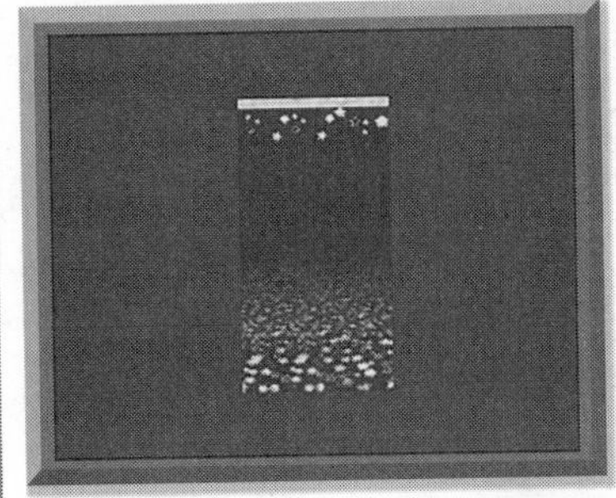

Cost: §16

Motives: N/A

Uber Tubers

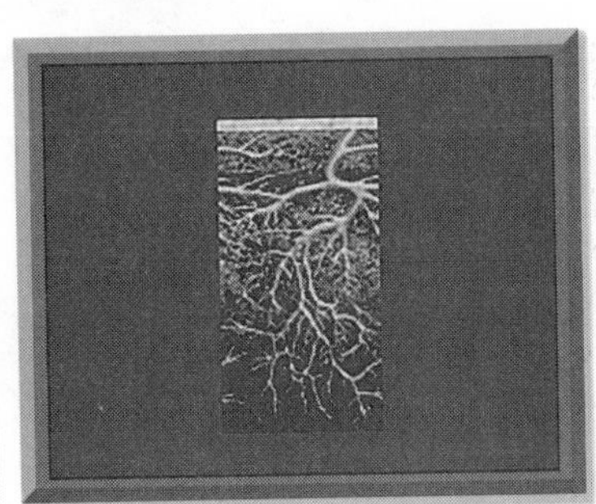

Cost: §17

Motives: N/A

Stair Tool

Reeking Creaking Stairway

Cost: §899

Motives: N/A

Downstairs UpStairs by MagiCo

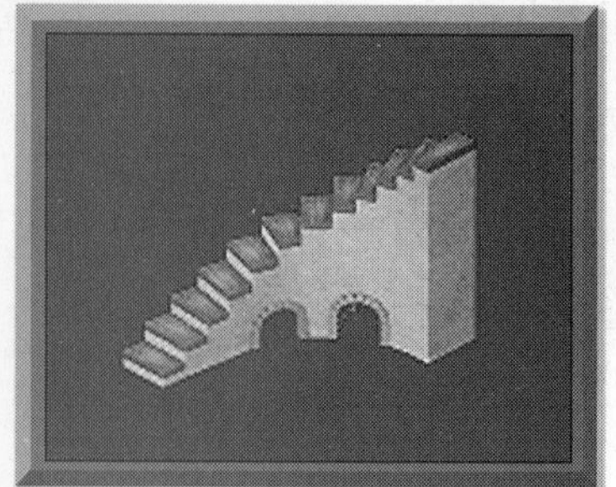

Cost: §2,699

Motives: N/A

12 Steps in Stone

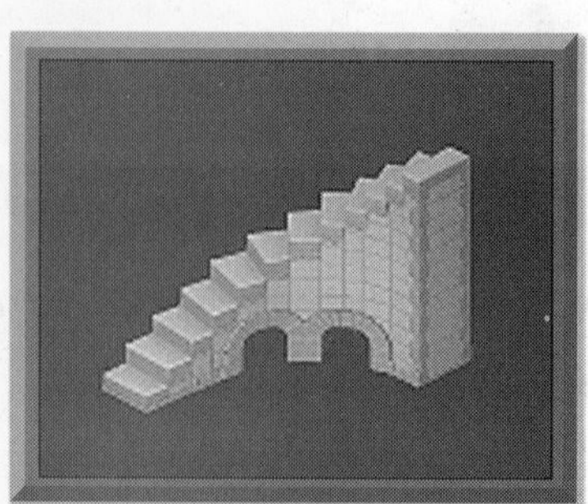

Cost: §2,999

Motives: N/A

Plant Tool

Common Feverfew

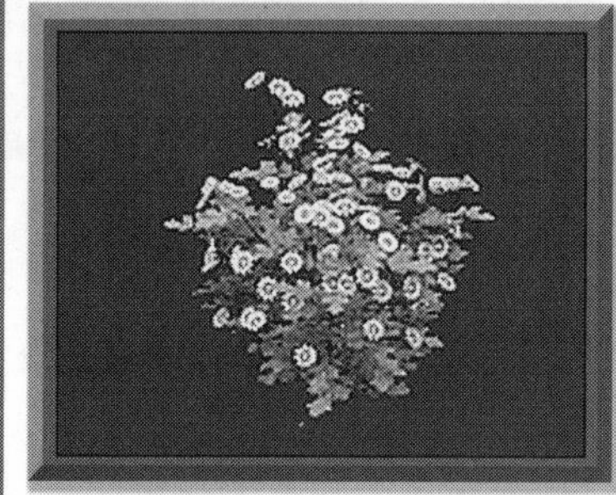

Cost: §40

Motives: N/A

Riley's Thistle

Cost: §45

Motive: N/A

As the Plot Thickens

Cost: §65

Motive: N/A

[N]everGreen Shrubbery by MagiCo

Cost: §111

Motive: N/A

[T]he Origins of the Shrub

Cost: §159

Motive: N/A

The Depressed Deciduous

Cost: §300

Motive: N/A

The Ever-Autumn Grougler Tree

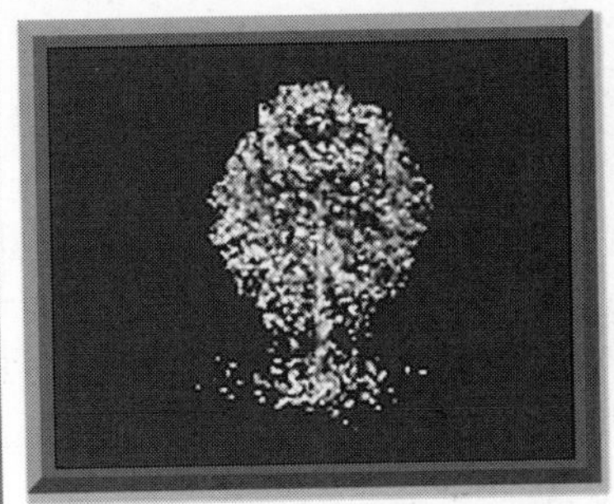

Cost: §399

Motive: N/A

Labermort Tree

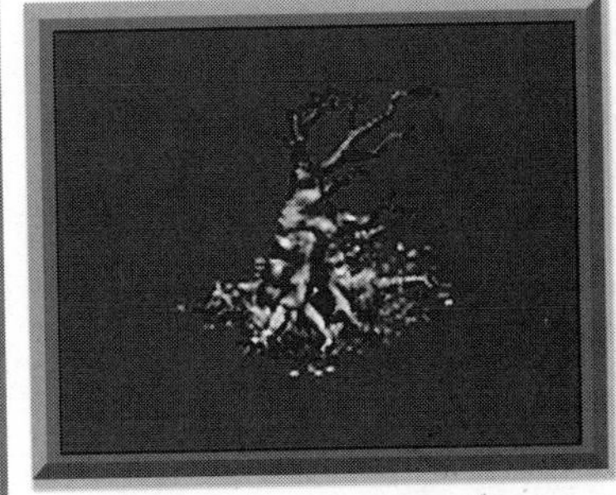

Cost: §559

Motive: N/A

Floor Tool

"High Society" Carpeting

Cost: §4

Motive: N/A

"Wither the Water?" Stepping Stone

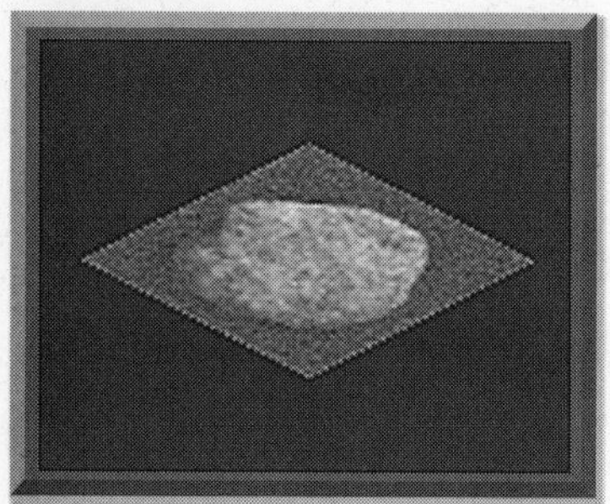

Cost: §4

Motive: N/A

A Path in Time Saves Grime

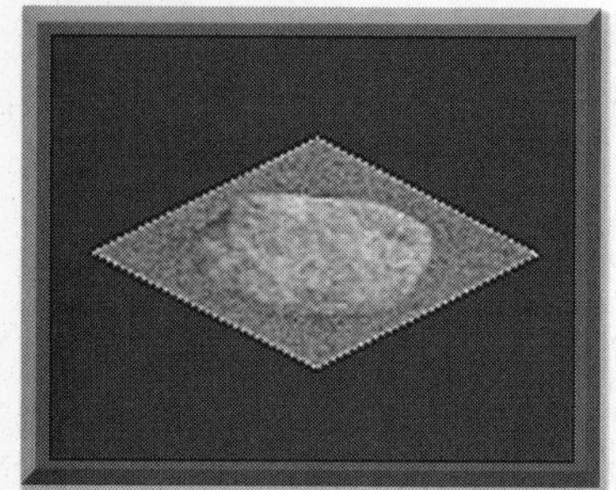

Cost: §4

Motive: N/A

Meandering Mossy Stone

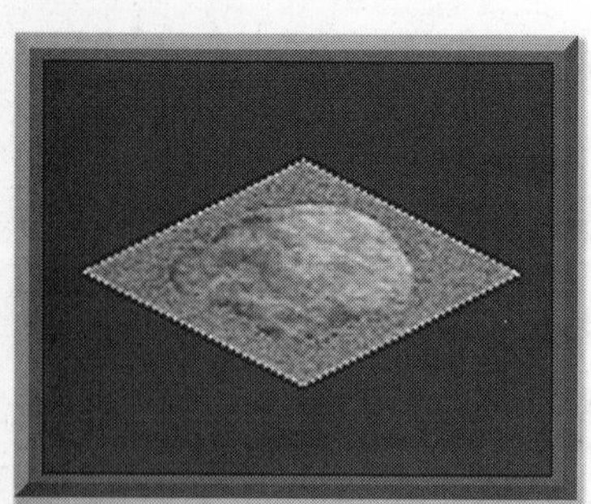

Cost: §4

Motive: N/A

Stone of Grassy Doom

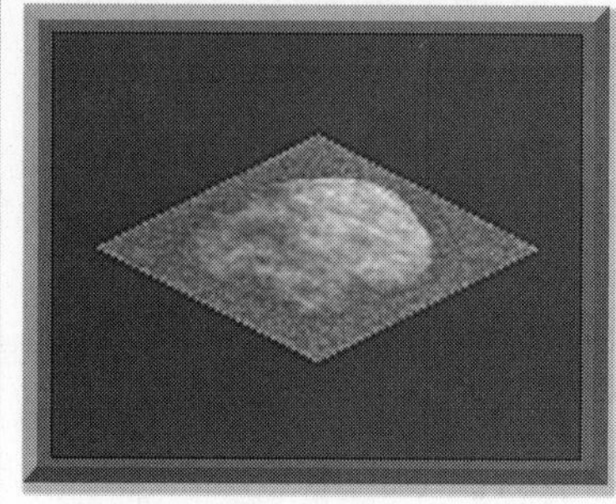

Cost: §4

Motive: N/A

Version IV

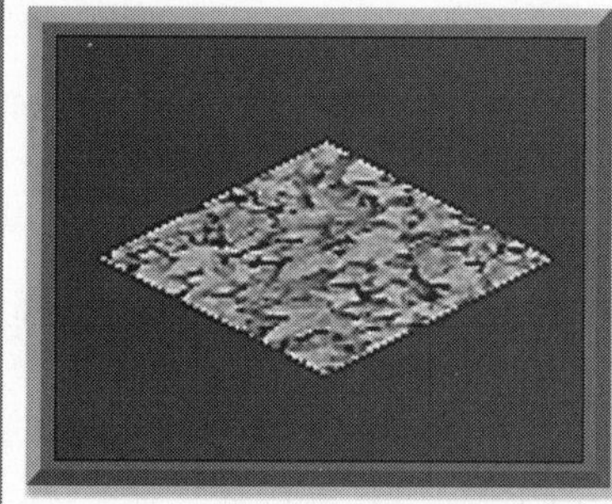

Cost: §4

Motive: N/A

Mr. TinkyDinky's Footpath

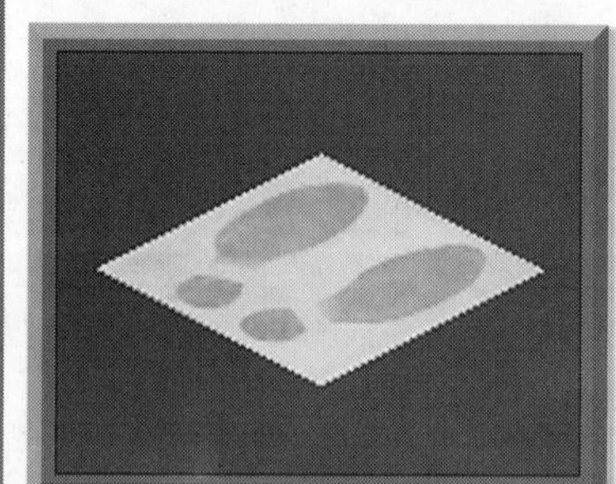

Cost: §5

Motive: N/A

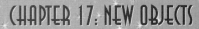

Happy Treads Flooring in "Popcorn"

Cost: §5

Motive: N/A

Happy Treads Flooring in "Clown Nose"

Cost: §5

Motive: N/A

Grassy Floor Cover by SirPlus!

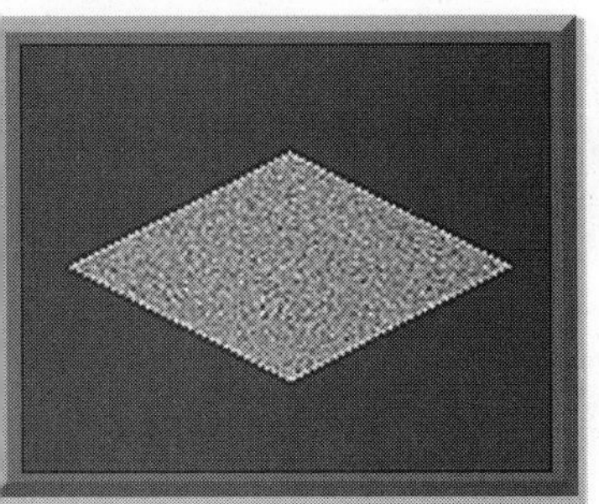

Cost: §5

Motive: N/A

"Hay Fever!" Flooring

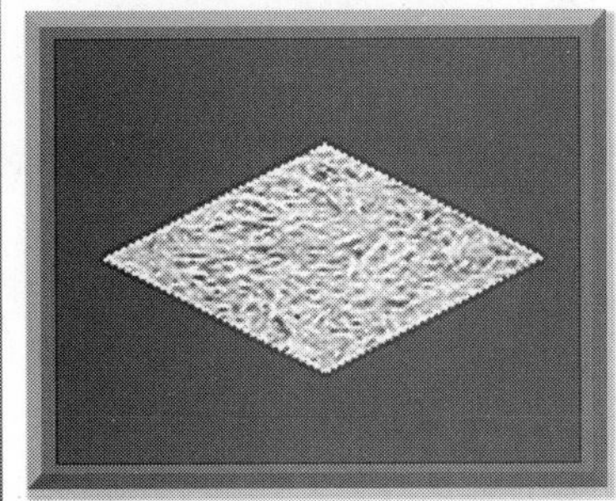

Cost: §6

Motive: N/A

FloorScape

Cost: §6

Motive: N/A

The Last Straw

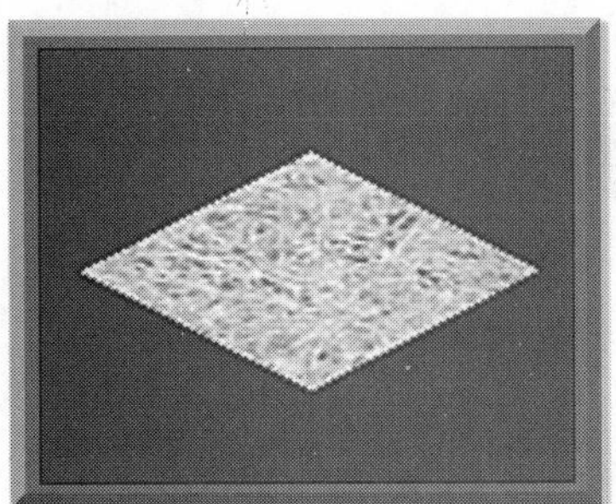

Cost: §6

Motive: N/A

Terrafirma Terracotta

Cost: §7

Motive: N/A

Teeantee Slatted Floor

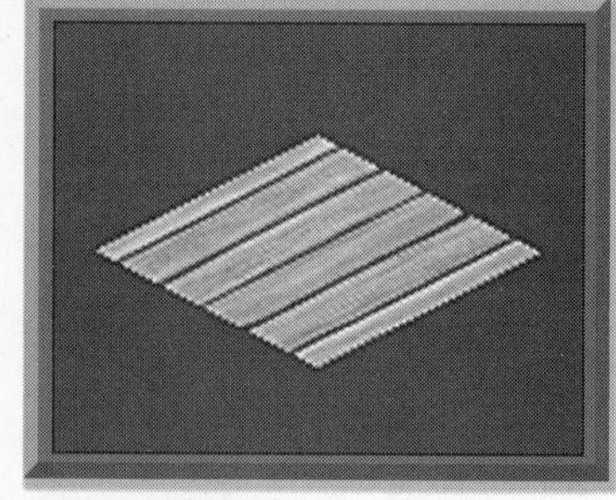

Cost: §7

Motive: N/A

"Fancy Footwork" Floorboards

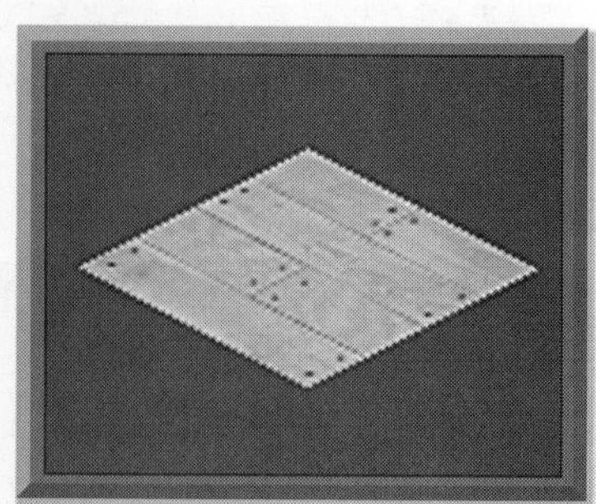

Cost: §7

Motive: N/A

Gypsyland Auction: Lot #927

Cost: §8

Motive: N/A

"Crumpets" Carpeting

Cost: §9

Motive: N/A

Commission Floor

Cost: §9

Motive: N/A

ypsyland Auction: Lot #330

Cost: §10

Motive: N/A

Herringbone Patio Bricks

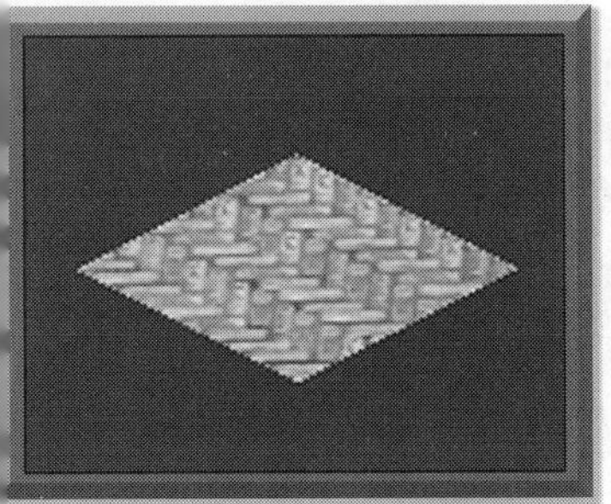

Cost: §11

Motive: N/A

Carpet Your Wagon

Cost: §12

Motive: N/A

Imitation Romany

Cost: §12

Motive: N/A

Tuscany Floor by Stile

Cost: §13

Motive: N/A

MagiCo's Fancy

Cost: §14

Motive: N/A

MagiCo's Mystic

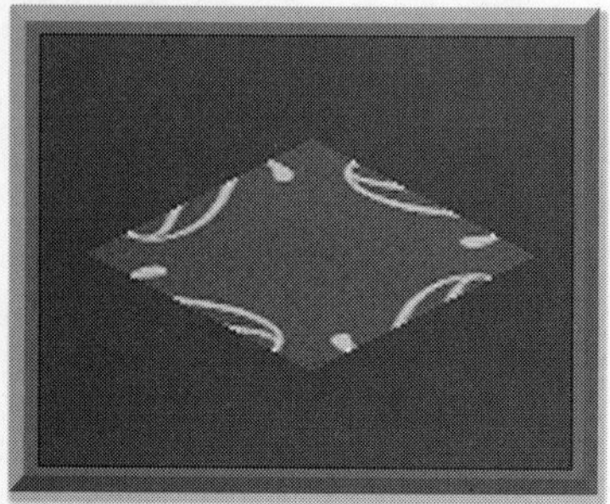

Cost: §14

Motive: N/A

Aged Dignity Marbling

Cost: §17

Motive: N/A

SkeleTastic Flooring

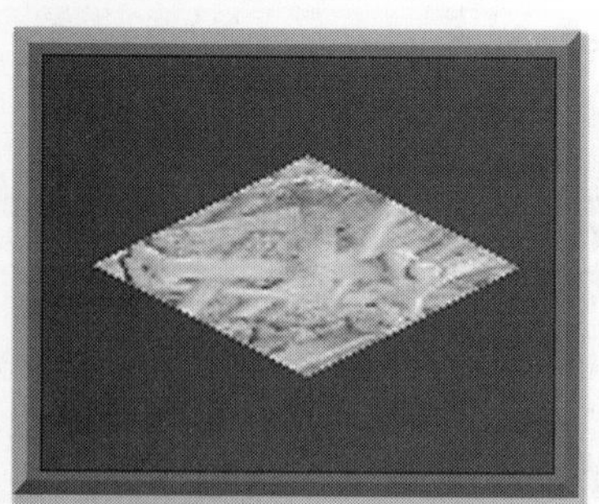

Cost: §18

Motive: N/A

Bonding Core Floor

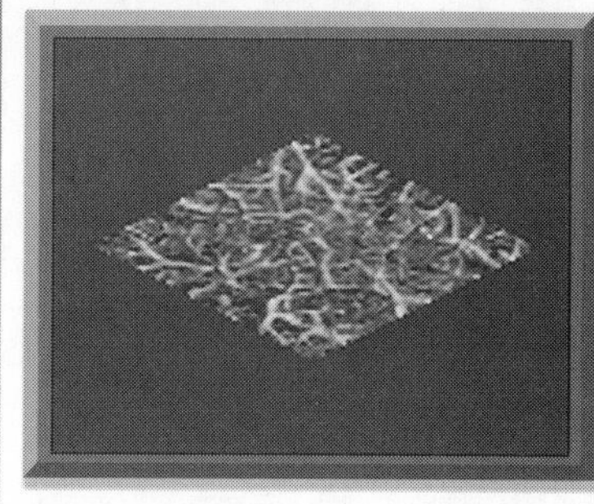

Cost: §19

Motive: N/A

Roots Squared

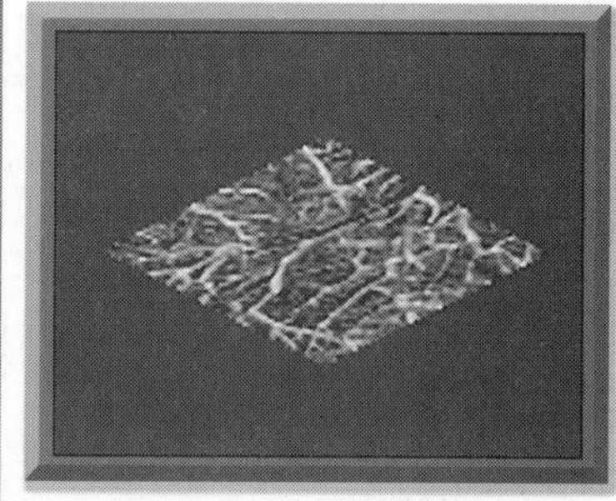

Cost: §19

Motive: N/A

Bumpy Boulevard Cobblestones

Cost: §20

Motive: N/A

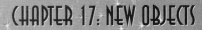

Timeless Stone Floor

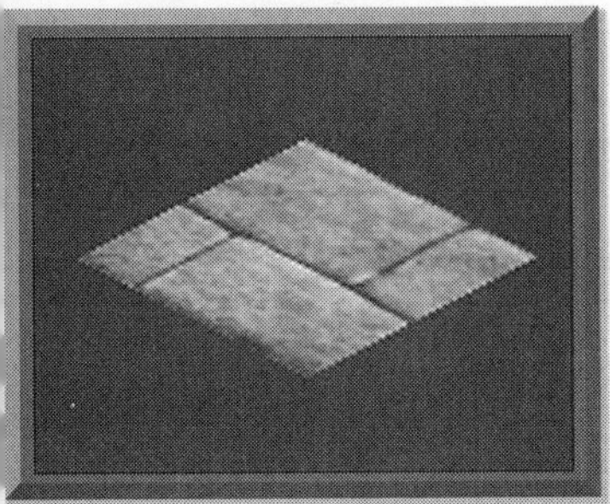

Cost: §22

Motive: N/A

Door Tool

Outdoor Indoor Door

Cost: §65

Motive: N/A

Gaily Gilded Gypsy Door

Cost: §281

Motive: N/A

Threshold of Trepidation

Cost: §409

Motive: N/A

Windows

Midway Memories Window

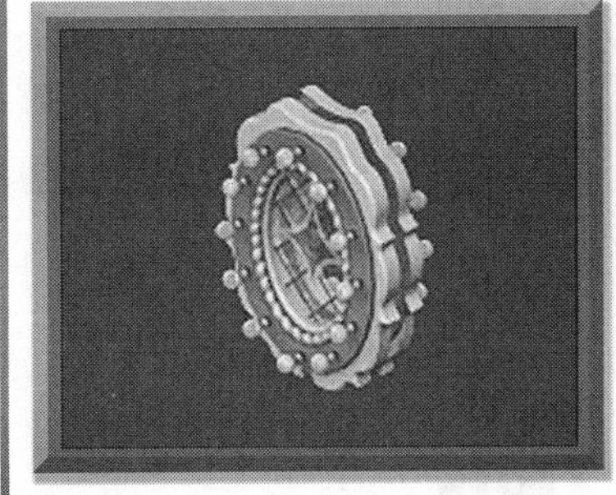

Cost: §89

Motives: N/A

Rowena's Waiting Window

Cost: §99

Motives: N/A

Candlematic Casement

Cost: §119

Motives: N/A

Shutter at the Thought

Cost: §149

Motives: N/A

Magic Town Only

Food

Decorative

Balloon Sculpture

Cost: §23

Motives: N/A

Thattaway Pointing Sign

Cost: §33

Motives: Room (1)

"Swami Slicer and the Box of Mystery"

Cost: §39

Motives: Room (1)

Extra Rickety Ride Sign

Cost: §39

Motives: Room (1)

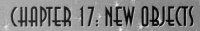

Commercial-grade Sublimisign

Cost: §99

Motives: Room (1)

Mr. Bones' Favorite Haunt

Cost: §99

Motives: N/A

Subliminal Suggestion Signage

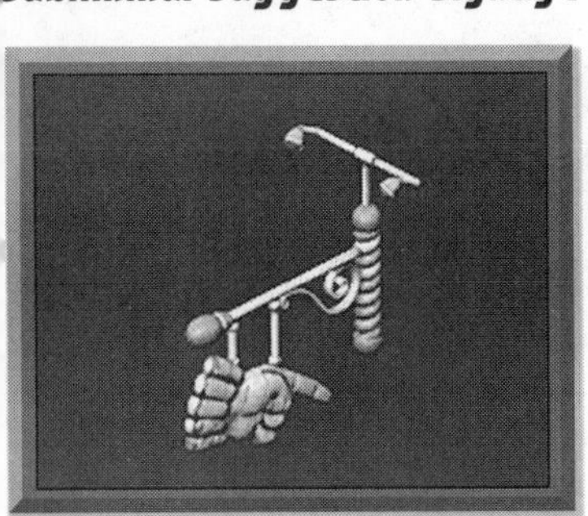

Cost: §99

Motives: N/A

Solar Powered Geraniums

Cost: §149

Motives: N/A

Doctor Sebastian Hyde, Self Portrait

Cost: §199

Motives: Room (1)

Notes: Purchased from the Painting Display

The Root of the Problem

Cost: §199

Motives: N/A

Notes: Magic Growth (earned from Spell Casting)

Leslie Giggham Fluttersbeak, October Hunt

Cost: §209

Motives: Room (1)

Notes: Purchased from the Painting Display

August J. Stuffiman IV, Legendary Gentleman

Cost: §229

Motives: Room (1)

Notes: Purchased from the Painting Display

Agnes Elizabeth Steadman, A Portrait

Cost: §239

Motives: Room (1)

Notes: Purchased from the Painting Display

Justa Beanstalk

Cost: §399

Motives: N/A

Notes: Magic Growth (earned from Spell Casting)

Appliances

Deluxe "Air-Puft" Candy Floss Cart

Cost: §342

Motives: Hunger (2)

Madame Magyar's Gulyas Goulash

Cost: §4,545

Motives: Hunger (4)

Ghoulish Graveyard Gumbo

Cost: §5,555

Motives: Hunger (5)

Miscellaneous

Trick or Trash Receptacle

Cost: §19

Motives: N/A

Shops

Miscellaneous

Kurrency Kiosk LX

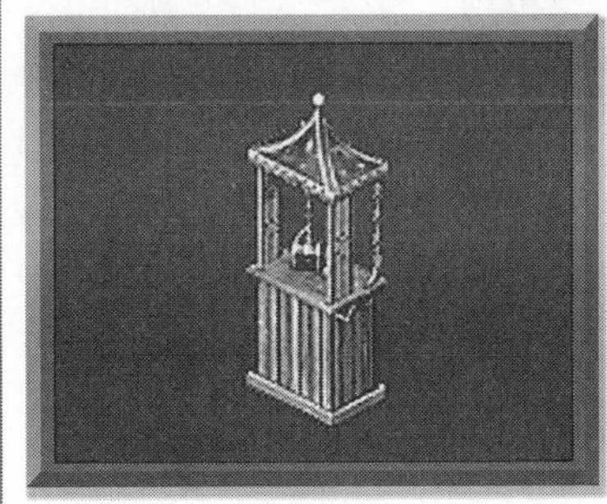

Cost: §99

Motives: N/A

Lotta's Foodstuffs

Cost: §649

Motives: N/A

Notes: Can be used only by adults

Meriklime Berry Display

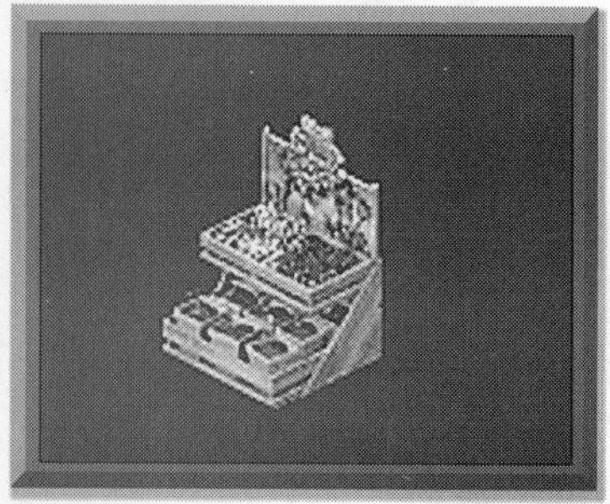

Cost: §699

Motives: N/A

Notes: Can be used only by adults

Hidimant Food Display

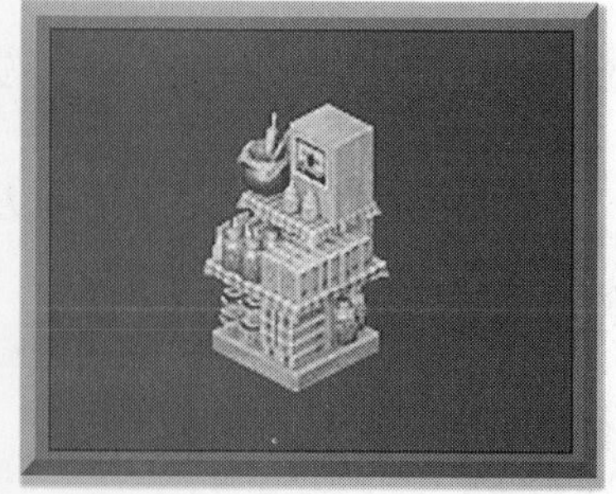

Cost: §949

Motives: N/A

Notes: Can be used only by adults

Golden Meriklime Display

Cost: §999

Motives: N/A

Notes: Can be used only by adults

Creepy Classics Painting Display by MagiCo

Cost: §1,612

Motives: N/A

Notes: Can be used only by adults

Faerie Mara's Odds and Ends

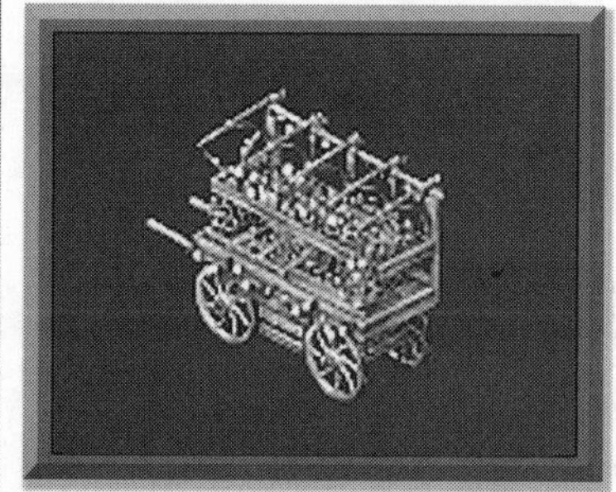

Cost: §8,000

Motives: N/A

Notes: Can be used only by adults

Wagon O'Wares

Cost: §8,100

Motives: N/A

Notes: Can be used only by adults

All Things Draconic

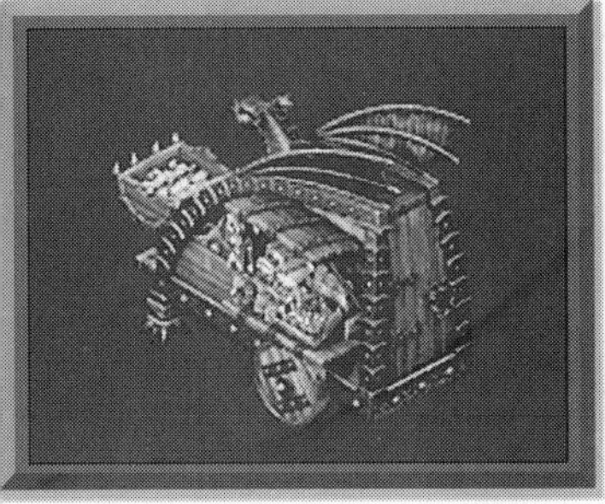

Cost: §8,200

Motives: N/A

Notes: Can be used only by adults

MagiCo

Electronics

Final Word Fortune Machine

Cost: §1,199

Motives: Fun (4)

Notes: Group activity

Blind the Cyclops

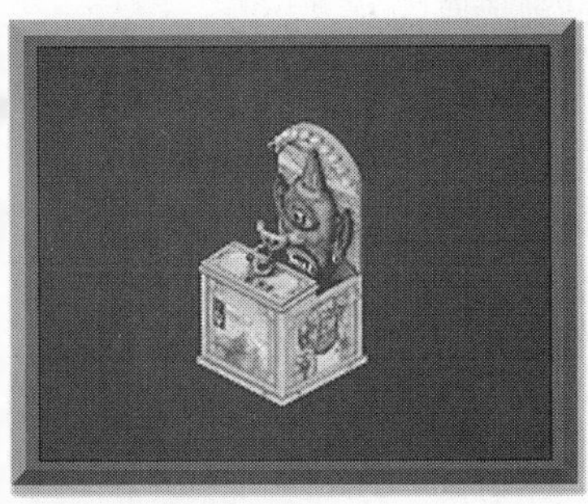

Cost: §1,999

Motives: Fun (6)

Notes: Group activity

Miscellaneous

The Left Bank

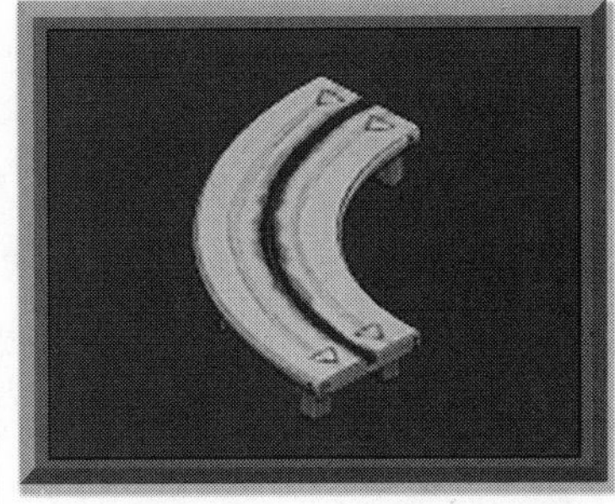

Cost: §399

Motives: N/A

The Right Most Taken

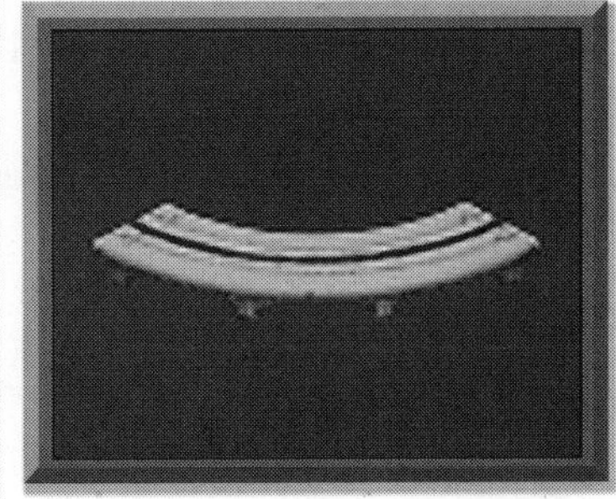

Cost: §399

Motives: N/A

The Straight and Narrow

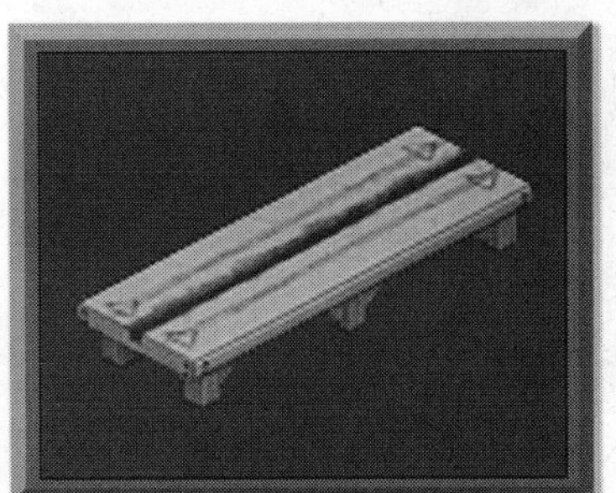

Cost: §399

Motives: N/A

Nagganaste and His Pet Cobra Cyril

Cost: §888

Motives: N/A

Spoooky Tombstone Puzzle

Cost: §5,996

Motives: N/A

Even More Magic Than Before

Cost: §17,777

Motives: N/A

Notes: Group activity

Diametric Dueling Device

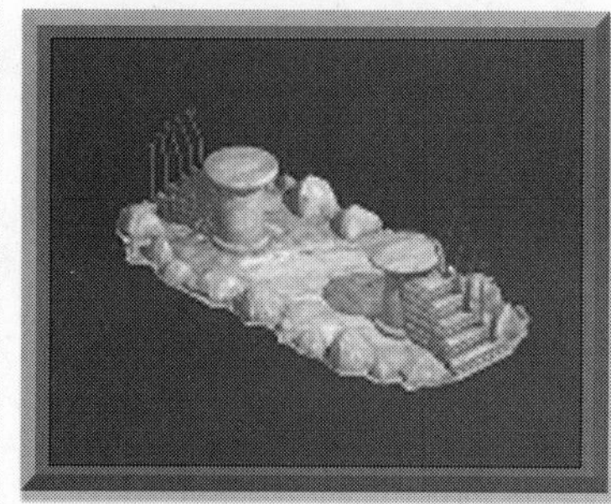

Cost: §21,000

Motives: N/A

Electro's Spooky Laboratory

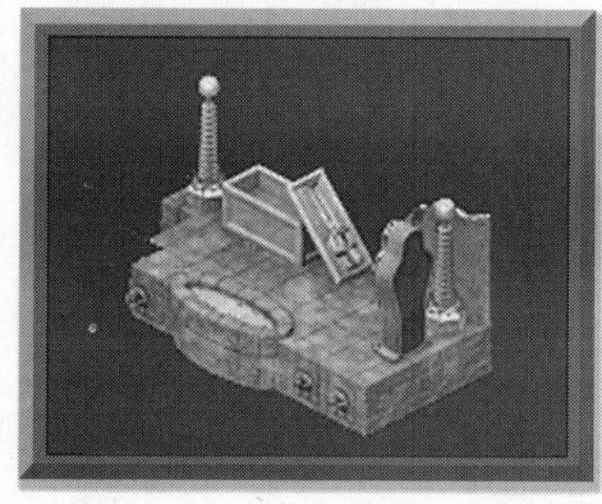

Cost: §23,339

Motives: N/A

The Haunted Belfry Ride

Cost: §26,999

Motives: Fun (10)

The Haunted Gatehouse Ride

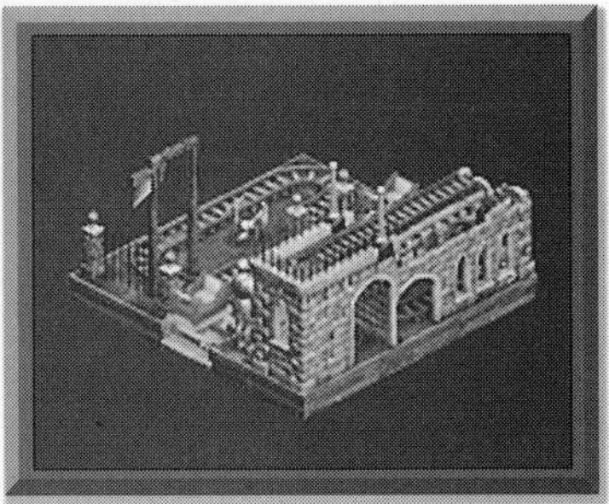

Cost: §26,999

Motives: Fun (10)

The Haunted Graveyard Ride

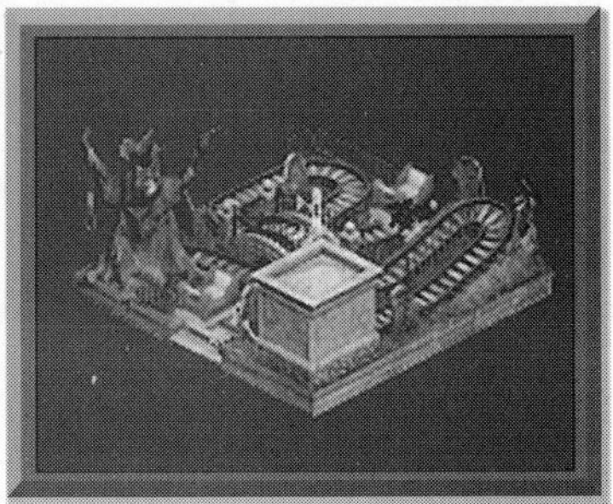

Cost: §26,999

Motives: Fun (10)

Awfully Fun House Coaster

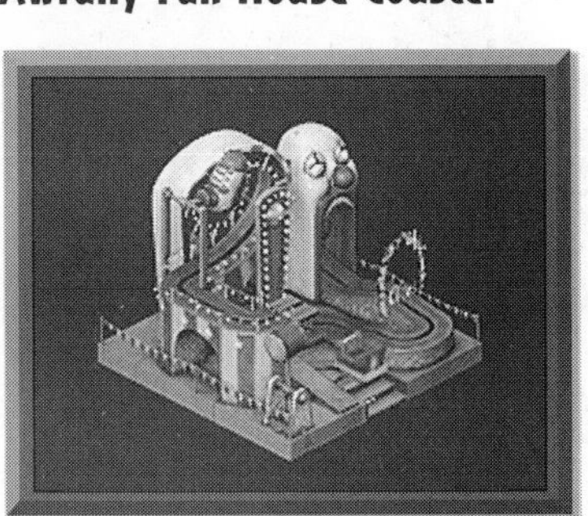

Cost: §27,999

Motives: Fun (10)

Clowning Around Mayhem Coaster

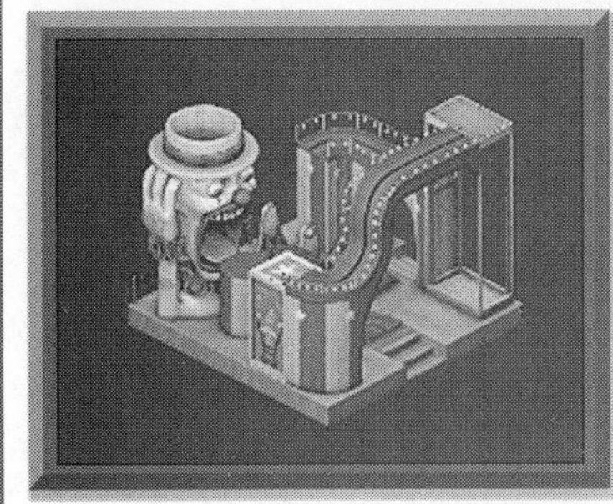

Cost: §27,999

Motives: Fun (10)

The Mind of a Cereal Killer Coaster

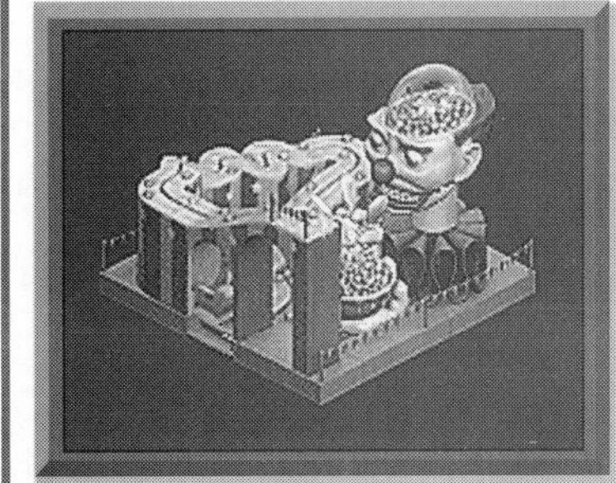

Cost: §27,999

Motives: Fun (10)

Outdoors

Miscellaneous

Hole of Harmony Mini-Golf

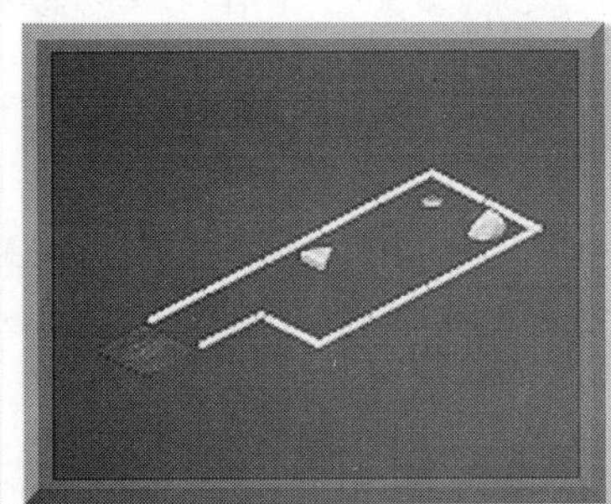

Cost: §1,300

Motives: Fun (7)

Veel Geluk Windmill Green

Cost: §1,400

Motives: Fun (7)

Clown O' Tears Mini Golf

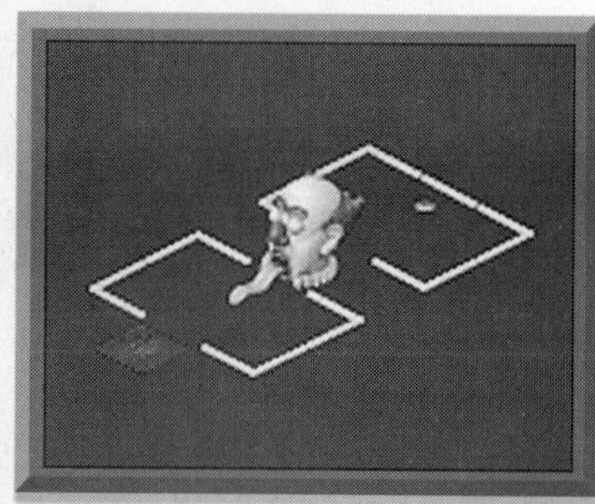

Cost: §1,450

Motives: Fun (7)

Princess Run Golf Trap

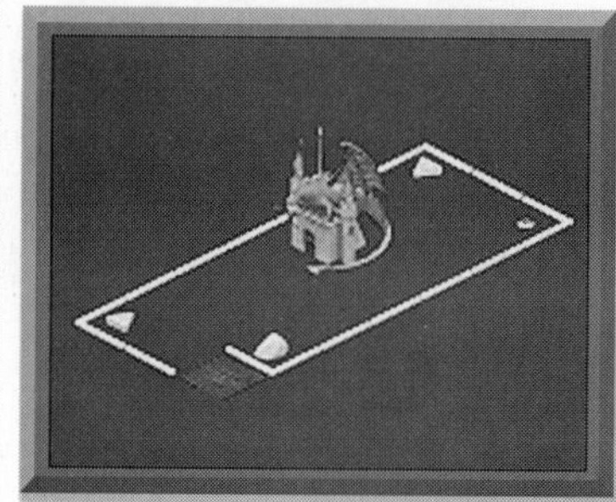

Cost: §1,500

Motives: Fun (7)

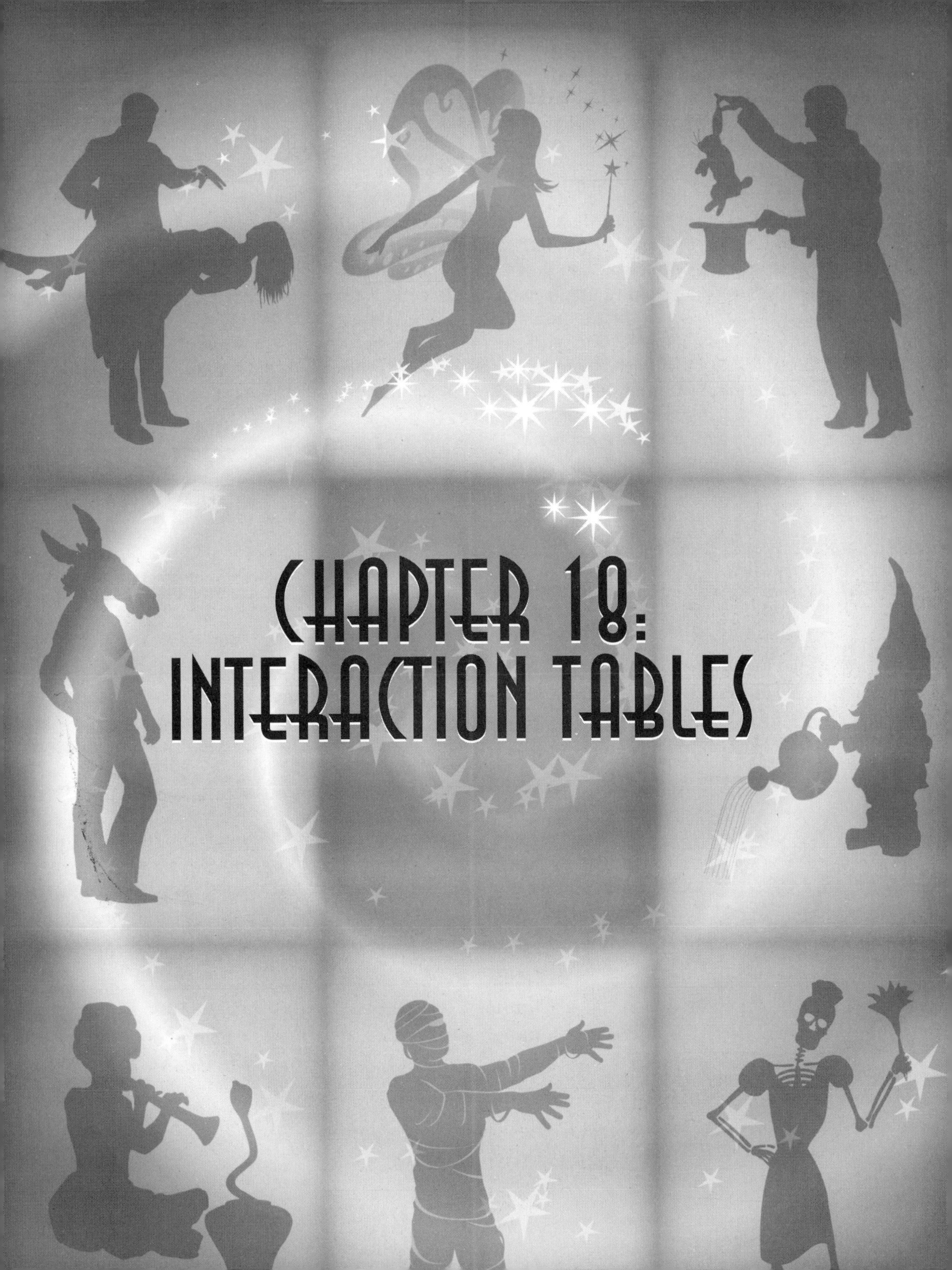

CHAPTER 18: INTERACTION TABLES

Introduction

The following tables contain relevant data for every interaction in *The Sims Makin' Magic*, including Short Term and Long Term Relationships. The interactions are broken down into four sections: adult to adult, adult to child, child to adult, and child to child. Each section contains three tables. The first table describes the general requirements for a successful interaction, and the second lists the effects of all possible results of each interaction. The third lists the conditions that determine whether or not a specific interaction shows up as an option in your menus. Use these tables to gauge your chance of success with each interaction.

Adult-to-Adult Interactions

Key

>	**Greater than**
≥	**Greater than or equal to**
<	**Less than**
≤	**Less than or equal to**

Adult Interaction Success Requirements

CATEGORY	INTERACTION	INITIATOR REQUIREMENTS	RECIPIENT REQUIREMENTS
Ask	How Are You?	None	Mood ≥ -80
	How's Work?	None	Mood ≥ -30
	Move In	None	Lifetime ≥ 60, Mood ≥ 45, Daily ≥ 85
	Propose	Different Genders	Love, Lifetime > 80, Daily > 75, Mood > 60
	What Are You Into?	None	Mood ≥ -30
Attack	Fight	Body ≥ Recipient's Body	None
	Shove	Body ≥ Recipient's Body +2	None
	Slap	Body > Recipient's Body	None
	Slap Fight	None	Daily ≥ 20, Mood ≥ 10, Playful ≥ 6
Brag	Boast	None	Daily between 0 and 25, Mood > 10
	Flex	None	Nice ≥ 9
		Body > Recipient's Body +5	None
		None	Daily ≥ 30
		None	Mood ≥ 25
	Primp	None	Daily ≥ 50
		None	Daily > 0, Outgoing > 6
		None	Daily > 0, Mood ≥ 35

Adult Interaction Success Requirements, continued

CATEGORY	INTERACTION	INITIATOR REQUIREMENTS	RECIPIENT REQUIREMENTS
Cheer Up	Comfort	None	Daily ≥ 65
		None	Daily > 55, Outgoing ≤ 3
	Encourage	None	Outgoing > 7
		None	Mood ≥ -25
	With Puppet	None	Playful > 7
		None	Nice ≥ 4, Mood ≥ -30
		None	Nice < 4, Mood ≥ -40
Compliment	Admire	None	Nice ≤ 3, Mood > 60
		None	Nice > 3, Daily > -25
		None	Nice > 3, Mood > 10
	Worship	None	Daily ≥ 20, Charisma ≥ 7
		None	Daily ≥ 20, Outgoing ≤ 3, Mood > 60
		None	Daily ≥ 20, Outgoing > 3, Nice > 4
		None	Daily ≥ 20, Outgoing > 3, Nice ≤ 3, Mood > 60
Dance	Lively	None	Daily > -10, Energy ≥ 10, Mood ≥ 0, Outgoing > 3
		None	Daily > -10, Energy ≥ 10, Mood ≥ 0, Outgoing ≤ 3, Mood > 40
		None	Daily > -10, Energy ≥ 10, Mood ≥ 0, Outgoing ≤ 3, Daily > 30
	Slow	Hygiene > 20	Energy > 10, Mood > 20, Daily > -10, Outgoing > 3
		Hygiene > 20	Energy > 10, Mood > 20, Daily > -10, Lifetime ≥ 35
		Hygiene > 20	Energy > 10, Mood > 40, Outgoing ≤ 3
		Hygiene > 20	Energy > 10, Mood > 20, Daily > 30, Lifetime ≥ 35

Adult Interaction Success Requirements, continued

CATEGORY	INTERACTION	INITIATOR REQUIREMENTS	RECIPIENT REQUIREMENTS
Entertain	Joke	None	Playful > 7
		None	Playful < 3, Daily > 30
		None	Playful ≥ 3, Mood > 50, Daily > 30
	(Mild Accept)	None	Playful ≥ 3, Daily < -10
	(Mild Accept)	None	Playful < 3, Mood > 50, Daily < -10
	Juggle	None	Playful > 7
		None	Playful ≥ 3, Daily > 20
		None	Playful < 3, Mood > 50, Daily > 20
	With Puppet	None	Nice < 4, Mood > 50
		None	Nice ≥ 3, Playful ≥ 7
		None	Nice ≥ 3, Playful < 3, Mood > 50
Flirt	Check Out	None	Mood ≥ -10, Outgoing ≥ 7
		None	Mood ≥ -10, Outgoing > 2, Mood > 40
		None	Mood ≥ -10, Outgoing > 2, Daily > 20
		None	Mood ≥ -10, Outgoing ≤ 2, Charisma ≥ 3
		None	Mood ≥ -10, Outgoing ≤ 2, Body ≥ 5
		None	Mood ≥ -10, Outgoing ≤ 2, Mood > 30
		None	Mood ≥ -10, Outgoing ≤ 2, Daily > 15
	Growl	None	Mood ≥ 20, Outgoing ≥ 9
		None	Mood < 20, Lifetime ≥ 30
		None	Outgoing ≥ 4
		None	Mood > 50
		None	Daily > 25
	Back Rub	None	Mood > 20, Daily or Lifetime > 35
		None	Mood > 20, Outgoing ≥ 6
		None	Mood > 20, Daily > 30
	Sweet Talk	None	Daily or Lifetime ≥ 40
Greet	Wave	None	Lifetime > -40
	Shake Hands	None	Lifetime ≥ -20
	Air Kiss	None	Lifetime ≥ 20
	Kiss Cheek	None	Lifetime ≥ 20
	Hug	None	Lifetime > -20
	Romantic Kiss	None	Lifetime ≥ 50
		In Love	In Love
	Suave Kiss	None	Lifetime > 15

Adult Interaction Success Requirements, continued

CATEGORY	INTERACTION	INITIATOR REQUIREMENTS	RECIPIENT REQUIREMENTS
Hug	Friendly	Hygiene ≥ -40	Mood > 50
		Hygiene ≥ -40	Daily > 30
		Hygiene ≥ -40	Nice ≥ 2, Mood > 10
	Intimate	Hygiene ≥ -40	Nice ≥ 3, Daily > 20
		Hygiene ≥ -40	Nice < 3, Mood > 60
		Hygiene ≥ -40	Nice < 3, Daily or Lifetime > 30
	Leap into Arms	Hygiene ≥ -40	Nice or Playful ≥ 7
		Hygiene ≥ -40	Mood > 40
		Hygiene ≥ -40	Daily > 45
		Hygiene ≥ -40	Lifetime > 30
	Romantic	Hygiene ≥ -40	Nice < 3, Mood > 60
		Hygiene ≥ -40	Nice < 3, Daily > 50
		Hygiene ≥ -40	Nice < 3, Lifetime > 40
		Hygiene ≥ -40	Nice ≥ 3, Daily > 30
		Hygiene ≥ -40	Nice ≥ 3, Lifetime > 35
Insult	Shake Fist	None	Nice ≥ 4, -30 < Mood < 0
		None	Nice ≥ 4, Mood > 0, Daily ≤ 20
	Poke	None	Nice < 4
		None	Nice ≥ 4, Mood ≤ 0
		None	Nice ≥ 4, Mood > 0, Daily < 20
Kiss	Peck	None	Mood > 0, Lifetime ≥ 10, Daily ≥ 20
		None	Mood > 0, Daily ≥ 20
	Polite	None	Daily ≥ 20, Lifetime > 10, Mood ≥ 25
	Suave	None	Mood >0, Lifetime ≥ 15, Daily ≥ 30
	Romantic	None	Crush
		None	Daily > 60, Mood > 40
		None	Lifetime > 60
	Passionate	None	Lifetime > 40, Daily ≥ 50, Mood ≥ 30
	Deep Kiss	None	Love, Mood ≥ 40
Nag	About Friends	None	Mood > 40
		None	Mood ≥ 0, Nice ≥ 7
	About House	None	Mood > 40
		None	Mood ≥ 0, Nice ≥ 7
	About Money	None	Mood > 40
		None	Mood ≥ 0, Nice ≥ 7

Adult Interaction Success Requirements, continued

CATEGORY	INTERACTION	INITIATOR REQUIREMENTS	RECIPIENT REQUIREMENTS
Plead	Apologize	None	Mood > -5
		None	Lifetime ≥ 25
	Grovel	None	Mood ≥ -15
		None	Lifetime ≥ 25
Say Good-bye	Shoo	None	Daily ≤ 10
	Shake Hands	None	Daily ≥ 20
		None	Lifetime ≥ 10
	Wave	None	Daily or Lifetime ≤ 20
	Kiss Cheek	None	Daily ≥ 20
		None	Lifetime ≥ 30
	Hug	None	Daily or Lifetime ≥ 30
	Kiss Hand	None	Nice ≤ 3, Daily ≥ 60
		None	Nice ≤ 3, Lifetime ≥ 50
		None	Nice > 3, Daily or Lifetime ≥ 40
	Polite Kiss	None	Outgoing ≥ 6, Daily ≥ 40
		None	Outgoing ≥ 6, Lifetime ≥ 60
		None	Outgoing < 6, Daily or Lifetime ≥ 60
	Passionate Kiss	None	Outgoing ≥ 7, Daily ≥ 60
		None	Outgoing ≥ 7, Lifetime ≥ 65
		None	Outgoing < 7, Daily ≥ 80
		None	Outgoing < 7, Lifetime ≥ 65
Talk	About Interests	(Always Accepted)	None
	Change Subject	(Always Accepted)	None
	Gossip	None	Daily > 40
	About Magic	None	Must have wand to accept
Tease	Imitate	None	Playful > 6, Mood > 50
		None	Playful > 6, Mood < 0
		None	Daily ≥ -15, Lifetime > 50, Playful ≤ 6
	Taunt	None	Mood or Daily > -20
	Raspberry	None	Mood or Daily ≥ -20, Lifetime > 25
	Scare	None	Playful ≥ 5
		None	Mood > 25
Tickle	Ribs	None	Playful > 5
		None	Mood > 50
	Extreme	None	Playful > 5
		None	Mood > 50

Adult Social Interaction Results

INTERACTION	RESPONSE	DAILY RELATIONSHIP CHANGE	LIFETIME RELATIONSHIP CHANGE	SOCIAL SCORE CHANGE
ATTACKS				
Slap	Cry	0	0	3
	Slap Back	-10	-3	-7
Be Slapped	Cry	-20	-10	-17
	Slap Back	-15	-7	3
Sissy Fight	Cry	0	0	3
	Fight Back	-8	-2	-5
Be Sissy Fought	Cry	-16	-8	-13
	Fight Back	-13	-5	3
Shove	Cry	0	0	3
	Shove Back	-8	-2	-5
Be Shoved	Cry	-16	-8	-13
	Shove Back	-13	-5	3
BRAGGING				
Brag	Good	5	0	10
	Bad	-5	0	0
Be Bragged To	Good	3	0	5
	Bad	-5	0	0
INSULTS				
Insult	Cry	-6	-3	0
	Stoic	0	-1	3
	Angry	-10	-1	5
Be Insulted	Cry	-12	-5	-10
	Stoic	-8	0	-5
	Angry	-14	-2	-7
TEASING				
Taunt	Giggle	4	0	7
	Cry	0	0	3
Be Taunted	Giggle	4	0	7
	Cry	-10	0	-7

Adult Social Interaction Results, continued

Interaction	Response	Daily Relationship Change	Lifetime Relationship Change	Social Score Change
Imitate with Puppet	Giggle	4	0	7
	Cry	0	0	3
Be Imitated with Puppet	Giggle	4	0	7
	Cry	-10	0	-7
Scare	Laugh	5	0	10
	Angry	-5	0	0
Be Scared	Laugh	5	0	8
	Angry	-10	0	0
TICKLING				
Tickle	Laugh	8	0	10
	Refuse	-5	-1	0
Be Tickled	Laugh	5	0	10
	Refuse	-8	-2	0
Extreme Tickle	Laugh	8	0	10
	Refuse	-5	-1	0
Be Extreme Tickled	Laugh	5	0	10
	Refuse	-5	-1	0
CHEERING				
Motivate	Good	5	0	7
	Mild	0	0	5
	Bad	-3	0	0
Be Motivated	Good	10	0	10
	Mild	0	0	5
	Bad	-10	0	0
Cheer Up with Puppet	Good	5	0	7 (Sensitive: 6)
	Mild	0	0	5
	Bad	-3	0	0
Be Cheered Up with Puppet	Good	6	0	10
	Mild	0	0	5
	Bad	-10	0	0

Adult Social Interaction Results, continued

Interaction	Response	Daily Relationship Change	Lifetime Relationship Change	Social Score Change
COMPLIMENTS				
Admire	Accept	4	1	5
	Reject	-10	-1	0
Be Admired	Accept	3	2	11
	Reject	-7	-2	0
Worship	Accept	3	1	5
	Reject	-15	-5	0
Be Worshiped	Accept	4	2	15
	Reject	-10	-4	0
DANCING				
Dance Lively	Accept	6	0	13
	Reject	-5	0	0
Be Danced with Lively	Accept	6	0	13
	Reject	-5	0	0
Dance Slow	Accept	8	2	15
	Reject	-10	-3	-4
Be Danced with Slowly	Accept	8	2	15
	Reject	-7	-2	0
ENTERTAINING				
Joke	Laugh	3	0	9
	Giggle	2	0	7
	Fail	-6	0	0
Hear Joke	Laugh	4	0	10
	Giggle	3	0	7
	Fail	-7	0	0
Juggle or Puppet	Laugh	3	0	7
	Fail	-10	0	0
Watch Juggle	Laugh	4	0	10
	Fail	-7	0	0
Watch Puppet	Laugh	4	0	13
	Fail	-7	0	0

Adult Social Interaction Results, continued

Interaction	Response	Daily Relationship Change	Lifetime Relationship Change	Social Score Change
FLIRTATION				
Give Backrub	Accept	3	2	7
	Reject	-7	-2	0
Receive Backrub	Accept	5	3	10
	Reject	-10	-3	0
Give Suggestion	Accept	4	1	10
	Ignore	-5	0	0
	Reject	-5	-1	-10
Receive Suggestion	Accept	6	1	10
	Ignore	-3	0	0
	Reject	-7	-2	0
Check Out	Accept	5	2	10
	Ignore	-5	0	0
	Reject	-8	-1	-10
Be Checked Out	Accept	5	2	10
	Ignore	-3	0	0
	Reject	-10	-3	0
Growl	Accept	5	2	10
	Ignore	-5	0	0
	Reject	-8	-2	-10
Receive Growl	Accept	6	2	10
	Ignore	-3	0	0
	Reject	-10	-3	0
GOOD-BYES				
Shake Hand	Good	2	0	0
	Bad	-2	0	0
Have Hand Shaken	Good	2	0	0
	Bad	-2	0	0
Hug	Good	5	0	0
	Bad	-5	0	0
Be Hugged	Good	5	0	0
	Bad	-5	0	0

Adult Social Interaction Results, continued

INTERACTION	RESPONSE	DAILY RELATIONSHIP CHANGE	LIFETIME RELATIONSHIP CHANGE	SOCIAL SCORE CHANGE
Polite Kiss	Good	7	2	0
	Bad	-7	-3	0
Be Politely Kissed	Good	7	3	0
	Bad	-7	-2	0
Kiss Cheek	Good	3	0	0
	Bad	-3	0	0
Have Cheek Kissed	Good	3	0	0
	Bad	-3	0	0
Kiss Hand	Good	3	1	0
	Bad	-3	-3	0
Have Hand Kissed	Good	3	2	0
	Bad	-3	-2	0
Passionate Kiss	Good	10	5	0
	Bad	-10	-6	0
Be Passionately Kissed	Good	10	5	0
	Bad	-10	-6	0
Wave	Good	1	0	0
	Bad	-1	0	0
Be Waved To	Good	1	0	0
	Bad	-1	0	0
Shoo	Good	1	0	0
	Neutral	0	0	0
	Bad	0	0	0
Be Shooed	Good	1	0	0
	Neutral	0	0	0
	Bad	-3	0	0
GREETINGS				
Wave	Good	1	0	2
	Bad	–2	0	2
Shake Hand	Good	1	0	2
	Bad	-2	-2	0

Adult Social Interaction Results, continued

INTERACTION	RESPONSE	DAILY RELATIONSHIP CHANGE	LIFETIME RELATIONSHIP CHANGE	SOCIAL SCORE CHANGE
Have Hand Shaken	Good	2	1	0
	Bad	-2	-2	0
Air Kiss	Good	2	0	3
	Bad	-4	0	-3
Be Air Kissed	Good	2	0	3
	Bad	-4	0	-3
Polite Kiss	Good	5	1	5
	Bad	-8	-2	-4
Be Politely Kissed	Good	5	5	1
	Bad	-6	-1	-3
Kiss Hand	Good	5	1	5
	Bad	-6	-2	-5
Have Hand Kissed	Good	5	1	10
	Bad	-6	-1	-3
Hug	Good	8	2	8
	Bad	-8	-2	-4
Be Hugged	Good	8	2	8
	Bad	-8	-1	-3
Romantic Kiss	Good	12	3	12
	Bad	-12	-2	-5
Be Romantically Kissed	Good	12	3	12
	Bad	-12	-2	-3
HUGS				
Friendly Hug	Accept	4	1	8
	Tentative	2	0	5
	Refuse	–5	-1	0
Receive Friendly Hug	Accept	5	1	8
	Tentative	4	0	5
	Refuse	–5	-1	0
Body Hug	Accept	5	2	10
	Tentative	5	0	7
	Refuse	-10	-3	0

Adult Social Interaction Results, continued

Interaction	Response	Daily Relationship Change	Lifetime Relationship Change	Social Score Change
Be Body Hugged	Accept	8	2	10
	Tentative	4	0	7
	Refuse	-10	-2	0
Romantic Hug	Accept	5	2	10
	Tentative	5	0	7
	Reject	-10	-3	0
Be Romantically Hugged	Accept	8	2	10
	Tentative	4	0	7
	Reject	-10	-2	0
Flying Hug	Accept	9	2	10
	Refuse	-15	-4	0
Receive Flying Hug	Accept	8	2	10
	Tentative	4	0	7
	Refuse	-10	-2	0
KISSES				
Kiss Hand	Passionate	5	0	5
	Polite	4	0	4
	Deny	-5	-1	4
Have Hand Kissed	Passionate	5	0	5
	Polite	4	0	4
	Deny	-5	0	0
Kiss Polite	Passionate	6	1	7
	Polite	5	0	5
	Deny	-7	-1	4
Be Kissed Politely	Passionate	6	1	7
	Polite	5	0	5
	Deny	-6	-1	0
Kiss Tentatively	Passionate	8	2	8
	Polite	6	1	6
	Deny	-9	-2	4

Adult Social Interaction Results, continued

INTERACTION	RESPONSE	DAILY RELATIONSHIP CHANGE	LIFETIME RELATIONSHIP CHANGE	SOCIAL SCORE CHANGE
Be Kissed Tentatively	Passionate	8	2	8
	Polite	6	1	6
	Deny	-8	-2	0
Kiss Passionately	Passionate	13	4	10
	Polite	8	2	8
	Deny	-10	-3	4
Be Kissed Passionately	Passionate	13	3	10
	Polite	8	2	8
	Deny	-10	-4	0
Dip Kiss	Passionate	15	5	15
	Polite	10	2	10
	Deny	-15	-5	4
Be Dip Kissed	Passionate	15	5	15
	Polite	10	2	10
	Deny	-15	-5	0
NAGGING				
Nag	Giggle	-1	0	3
	Cry	-4	-1	3
Be Nagged	Giggle	-3	0	4
	Cry	-8	-2	-5
PLEADING				
Apologize	Accept	8	0	8
	Reject	-8	0	3
Be Apologized To	Accept	8	0	8
	Reject	-5	0	3
Grovel	Accept	12	0	8
	Reject	-12	0	3
Be Groveled To	Accept	12	0	8
	Reject	-5	0	3

Adult Interaction Menu Triggers

CATEGORY	INTERACTION	RELATIONSHIP REQUIREMENTS	DISPOSITION REQUIREMENTS
Ask	How Are You?	Daily > -80	Mood > -70
	How's Work?	Daily between –5 and 35, Lifetime < 40	Mood > 0
	Move In	Lifetime > 50, Daily > 50	Same Gender
	Propose	Daily > 75	Different Genders, In Love
	What Are You Into?	Daily between –5 and 35, Lifetime < 40	Mood > 0
Attack	Fight	Daily < -40, Lifetime < 0	Mood < 0
	Shove	Lifetime ≤ 30, Daily < -40	Mood < 0
	Slap	Lifetime ≤ 30, Daily < -40	Mood < 0
	Slapfight	Daily < -40	Playful ≥ 7, Mood < 0
Brag	Boast	None	Daily < 50, Lifetime < 40
	Flex	Daily < 50, Lifetime < 40	Body ≥ 4
	Primp	Daily < 50, Lifetime < 40	Charisma ≥ 2
Cheer Up	Comfort	Lifetime > 25, Friends	Outgoing > 3, Mood > 25, Subject's Mood < 0
		Lifetime > 5, Friends	Outgoing ≤ 3, Mood > 20, Subject's Mood < 0
	Encourage	Lifetime > 25, Friends	Charisma ≥ 2, Mood > 25
	With Puppet	Friends	Playful ≥ 6, Outgoing ≥ 4, Mood > 25, Subject's Mood < 0
Compliment	Admire	Daily between -10 and 40	Mood > 20
	Worship	Daily between -10 and 40, Lifetime between 20 and 80,	Nice > 3, Outgoing > 3 Mood > 20
Dance	Lively	Daily > 30, Lifetime > -25	Energy > 20, Mood > -20, Outgoing > 3
	Slow	Lifetime > 20	Energy > 10
Entertain	Joke	Daily > 0, Lifetime between –25 and 70	Playful ≥3, Mood > -10
	Juggle	Daily > -25, Lifetime between 0 and 70	Outgoing > 3, Playful > 4 Mood > 0
	With Puppet	Daily > -25, Lifetime between 0 and 70	Outgoing > 3, Playful > 3 Mood > 0

Adult Interaction Menu Triggers, continued

CATEGORY	INTERACTION	RELATIONSHIP REQUIREMENTS	DISPOSITION REQUIREMENTS
Flirt	Check Out	Lifetime between –10 and 10, Daily between 5 and 60	Mood > -20
	Growl	Lifetime between –10 and 10, Daily between 5 and 60	Mood > -20
	Backrub	Daily between 30 and 60, Lifetime > 30	Mood > 30
	Sweet Talk	Daily between 25 and 60, Lifetime > -50	Outgoing ≥ 7, Mood > 30
		Daily between 40 and 60, Lifetime > -50	Outgoing < 7, Mood > 30
Greet	Wave	Always Available	
	Shake Hands	Always Available	
	Air Kiss	Lifetime ≥ 5	None
	Kiss Cheek	Lifetime ≥ 20	None
	Hug	Crush	None
	Romantic Kiss	Crush	None
	Suave Kiss	Lifetime > 15	Outgoing ≥ 3
Hug	Friendly	Lifetime > 0, Daily > 15	Mood > 10
	Intimate	Lifetime > 10, Daily > 15	Mood > 20
	Leap into Arms	Daily > 40, Lifetime > 30	Mood > 25, Outgoing > 5
	Romantic	Daily > 40, Lifetime > 40	Mood > 35, Outgoing > 3
Insult	Shake Fist	Lifetime < 50	Nice ≤ 3
		None	Mood < 0
	Poke	Lifetime < 50	Nice < 3
		None	Mood ≤ 0
Kiss	Peck	Daily ≥ 20, Lifetime > 0	Mood > 0
	Polite	Daily ≥ 35, Lifetime > 15	Mood > 15
	Suave	Daily ≥ 25, Lifetime > 10	Mood > 0
	Romantic	Daily ≥ 55, Lifetime > 25	Mood > 25
	Passionate	Daily ≥ 45, Lifetime > 25	Mood > 15
	Deep Kiss	Love	Mood > 25

dult Interaction Menu Triggers, continued

CATEGORY	INTERACTION	RELATIONSHIP REQUIREMENTS	DISPOSITION REQUIREMENTS
Nag	About Friends	Lifetime > 40	Mood ≤ -30
	About House	Lifetime > 40	Mood ≤ -30
	About Money	Lifetime > 40	Mood ≤ -3, Cash < §1,000
Plead	Apologize	Daily ≤ -10 Lifetime > 5	Mood ≤ -20
	Grovel	Daily > -20, Lifetime > 10	Mood ≤ -40
Say Good-bye	Shoo	Daily < -50	None
	Shake Hands	Daily > -50	None
	Wave	Daily > -50	None
	Kiss Cheek	Daily > -10	None
	Hug	Daily > 0	None
	Kiss Hand	Daily > 20	None
	Polite Kiss	Daily ≥ 20	None
	Passionate Kiss	Daily > 20	Outgoing ≥ 7
		Daily > 40	Outgoing < 7
Talk	About Interests	None	Available in Ongoing Conversation
	Change Subject	None	Available in Ongoing Conversation
	Gossip	None	Mood > -25
Tease	Imitate	None	Playful > 5, Mood < 15
		Daily < -20	Playful > 5, Nice < 5
	Taunt	None	Mood < 30, Nice < 5
		Daily < -20	Nice < 5
	Raspberry	None	Mood < 15, Nice < 5
		Daily < -20	Nice < 5
	Scare	None	Playful ≥ 5, Mood < 30, Nice < 5
Tickle	Ribs	Daily > 10	Playful ≥4, Nice > 4
	Extreme	Daily > 10, Lifetime between 20 and 70	Playful > 3, Nice > 4

Adult-to-Child Interactions

Adult-to-Child Interaction Success Requirements

Category	Interaction	Recipient Requirements
Brag		Mood > 50, Daily > 50
Cheer Up		Social ≤ 0
		Daily ≥ 0
Entertain	Joke	Playful ≥ 2
		Mood ≥ 30
	Juggle	Playful ≥ 2
		Mood ≥ 30
Hug	Nice	Mood ≥ 20
		Daily ≥ 10
	Friendly	Mood ≥ 20
		Daily ≥ 10

Category	Interaction	Recipient Requirements
Insult		Daily ≥ 25
Play	Rough House	Mood ≥ 20
Scold		Mood ≥ -25
Tease	Scare	Mood between -10 and 15
	Taunt	Daily ≥ 10
Tickle		Mood ≥ 15, Playful ≥ 1

Adult-to-Child Interaction Results

Interaction	Response	Daily Relationship Change	Lifetime Relationship Change	Social Score Change
Brag	Accept	5	0	10
	Reject	-5	-1	0
Be Bragged To	Accept	3	0	5
	Reject	-5	-1	0
Cheer Up	Accept	5	0	7
	Reject	-3	0	0
Be Cheered Up	Accept	10	2	7
	Reject	-10	-2	0
Entertain—Joke	Accept	3	1	9
	Reject	-6	0	0
Be Entertained—Joke	Accept	4	2	10
	Reject	-7	0	0
Entertain—Juggle	Accept	3	1	7
	Reject	-10	-2	0
Be Entertained—Juggle	Accept	4	2	10
	Reject	-7	-1	0
Hug—Nice	Accept	4	1	8
	Reject	-5	-1	0
Be Hugged—Nice	Accept	4	1	8
	Reject	-5	-1	0

Adult-to-Child Interaction Results, continued

Interaction	Response	Daily Relationship Change	Lifetime Relationship Change	Social Score Change
Hug—Friendly	Accept	5	2	10
	Reject	-10	-3	0
Be Hugged—Friendly	Accept	5	2	10
	Reject	-10	-2	-2
Insult	Accept	-10	-1	5
	Reject	-6	-3	0
Be Insulted	Accept	-14	-3	-7
	Reject	-12	-5	-10
Play—Rough House	Accept	3	1	9
	Reject	-6	0	0
Be Played With—Rough House	Accept	4	2	10
	Reject	-7	0	0
Scold	Accept	5	3	5
	Reject	-8	-3	2
Be Scolded	Accept	5	3	10
	Reject	-10	-2	-2
Tease—Scare	Accept	5	1	10
	Reject	-5	-1	0
Be Teased—Scare	Accept	5	1	8
	Reject	-10	-2	0
Tease—Taunt	Accept	4	0	7
	Reject	-3	0	-3
Be Teased—Taunt	Accept	4	1	7
	Reject	-10	-1	-7
Tickle	Accept	8	1	10
	Reject	-5	-1	0
Be Tickled	Accept	5	1	10
	Reject	-8	-2	0

Adult-to-Child Interaction Menu Triggers

Category	Interaction	Initiator Requirements	Recipient Requirements
Brag		Mood < 10, Daily ≥ 10, Daily ≤ 50	None
Cheer Up		Mood ≥ 25, Daily ≥ 25	Mood ≤ 0
Entertain	Joke	Playful ≥ 4, Mood ≥ 40	None
		Mood > 50	None
	Juggle	Playful ≥ 5, Mood ≥ 40	None
		Mood ≥ 50	None
Hug	Nice	Daily ≥ 30, Mood > 30	None
	Friendly	Daily ≥ 35, Mood > 35	None
Insult		Mood ≤ -10	None

Adult-to-Child Interaction Menu Triggers, continued

Category	Interaction	Initiator Requirements	Recipient Requirements
Play	Rough House	Playful ≥ 4, Mood ≥ 20	None
		Mood ≥ 40	None
Scold		None	Mood ≤ -10
Tease	Scare	Mood ≤ 5	None
		Daily ≤ -5	None
	Taunt	Mood ≤ 15	None
		Daily ≤ -5	None
Tickle		Playful ≥ 2, Mood ≥ 0	None
		Mood > 30	None

Child-to-Adult Interactions

Child-to-Adult Interaction Menu Triggers

Category	Interaction	Initiator Requirements	Recipient Requirements
Brag		Daily ≥ 10, Mood ≥ 20	None
Cheer Up		Daily ≥ 5, Mood ≥ 0	Mood ≤ 0
Entertain	Crazy Dance	None	Social ≤ 50
	Handstand	None	Social ≤ 30
	Joke	Mood ≥ 0	None
	Perform Trick	Mood ≥ 10	None
Hug	Nice	Mood ≥ 30, Daily ≥ 30	None
	Friendly	Mood ≥ 35, Daily ≥ 35	None
Insult		Mood ≥ -10, Daily ≥ -5	None
Play	Rock-Paper-Scissors	Mood ≥ 50	None
Talk	Jabber	Daily ≥ 10	None
Tease	Scare	Daily < 10, Mood ≤ -10	None
	Taunt	Daily < 15, Mood ≤ -15	None
Tickle		Mood > 5	None

hild-to-Adult Interaction Results

Interaction	Response	Daily Relationship Change	Lifetime Relationship Change	Social Score Change
Brag	Accept	5	0	10
	Reject	-5	-1	0
Be Bragged To	Accept	3	0	5
	Reject	-5	-1	0
Cheer Up	Accept	5	0	7
	Reject	-3	0	0
Be Cheered Up	Accept	10	2	7
	Reject	-10	-2	0
Entertain—Joke	Accept	3	1	9
	Reject	-6	0	0
Be Entertained—Joke	Accept	4	2	10
	Reject	-7	0	0
Entertain—Perform Trick	Accept	3	1	7
	Reject	-5	-1	0
Be Entertained—Perform Trick	Accept	4	2	10
	Reject	-7	-1	0
Entertain—Crazy Dance	Accept	4	2	6
	Reject	-6	-1	0
Be Entertained—Crazy Dance	Accept	3	1	5
	Reject	-5	0	0
Hug—Nice	Accept	4	1	8
	Reject	-5	-1	0
Be Hugged—Nice	Accept	4	1	8
	Reject	-5	-1	0
Hug—Friendly	Accept	5	2	10
	Reject	-10	-3	0
Be Hugged—Friendly	Accept	5	2	10
	Reject	-10	-2	-2
Insult	Accept	-10	-1	5
	Reject	-6	-3	0
Be Insulted	Accept	-14	-3	-7
	Reject	-12	-5	-10
Play—Rock-Paper-Scissors	Accept	5	1	6
	Reject	-5	-1	-2
Be Played With—Rock-Paper-Scissors	Accept	7	2	6
	Reject	-9	-3	-2
Talk—Jabber	Accept	4	1	5
	Reject	-4	-2	-1

Child-to-Adult Interaction Results, continued

Interaction	Response	Daily Relationship Change	Lifetime Relationship Change	Social Score Change
Hear Talk—Jabber	Accept	4	0	5
	Reject	-3	0	0
Tease—Scare	Accept	5	1	10
	Reject	-5	-1	0
Be Teased—Scare	Accept	5	1	8
	Reject	-10	-2	0
Tease—Taunt	Accept	4	0	7
	Reject	-3	0	-3
Be Teased—Taunt	Accept	4	1	7
	Reject	-10	-1	-7
Tickle	Accept	8	1	10
	Reject	-5	-1	0
Be Tickled	Accept	5	1	10
	Reject	-8	-2	0

Child-to-Adult Interaction Success Requirements

Category	Interaction	Initiator Requirements	Recipient Requirements
Brag		Mood ≥ 20, Daily ≥ 10	None
Cheer Up		Mood ≥ 0, Daily ≥ 5	Mood ≤ 0
Entertain	Crazy Dance	None	Social ≤ 0
	Handstand	None	Social ≤ 0
	Joke	Mood ≥ 0	None
Hug	Nice	Daily ≥ 30, Mood > 30	None
	Friendly	Daily ≥ 35, Mood > 35	None
Insult		Mood ≤ -10	None
		Daily ≤ -5	None
Play	Rock-Paper-Scissors	Mood ≥ 50	None
Talk	Jabber	Daily ≥ 10	None
Tease	Scare	Mood ≤ 10	None
		Daily ≤ 10	None
	Taunt	Mood ≤ 15	None
		Daily ≤ 15	None
Tickle		Mood ≥ 5	None

hild-to-Child Interactions

hild-to-Child Interaction Success Requirements

CATEGORY	INTERACTION	RECIPIENT REQUIREMENTS
Annoy	Poke	Mood ≥ 0, Daily ≥ 15
	Push	Mood ≥ 0, Daily ≥ 10
	Kick Shin	Mood ≥ 0, Daily ≥ 5
Brag		Daily ≥ 20
Cheer Up		Daily ≥ 20
Entertain	Joke	Mood ≥ 20, Daily > -25
	Perform Trick	Mood ≥ 15, Daily ≥ -15
Hug	Nice	Mood ≥ 20, Daily ≥ 10
	Friendly	Mood ≥ 20, Daily ≥ 10
Insult		Mood > 0, Daily > 20
Play	Rock-Paper-Scissors	Mood ≥ 15
	Tag	Mood ≥ 15
Talk	Jabber	Mood ≥ 20, Social ≤ 5
	Whisper	No Data
Tease	Scare	Daily ≥ 30
	Taunt	Daily > 10 Nice > 3
Tickle		Mood ≥ 25, Daily ≥ 30

Child-to-Child Interaction Results

Interaction	Response	Daily Relationship Change	Lifetime Relationship Change	Social Score Change
Annoy—Push	Accept	-6	-1	6
	Reject	-6	-2	1
Be Annoyed—Push	Accept	-3	-1	6
	Reject	-7	-3	-1
Annoy—Poke	Accept	-4	0	7
	Reject	-4	-1	0
Be Annoyed—Poke	Accept	-2	0	3
	Reject	-5	-1	0
Annoy—Kick Shin	Accept	-8	-2	10
	Reject	-8	-5	2
Be Annoyed—Kick Shin	Accept	-6	-2	9
	Reject	-10	-8	-2
Brag	Accept	5	0	10
	Reject	-5	-1	0
Be Bragged To	Accept	3	0	5
	Reject	-5	-1	0
Cheer Up	Accept	5	0	7
	Reject	-3	0	0
Be Cheered Up	Accept	10	2	7
	Reject	-10	-2	0
Entertain—Joke	Accept	3	1	9
	Reject	-6	0	0
Be Entertained—Joke	Accept	4	2	10
	Reject	-7	0	0
Entertain—Perform Trick	Accept	3	1	7
	Reject	-10	-2	0
Be Entertained—Perform Trick	Accept	4	2	10
	Reject	-7	-1	0
Hug—Nice	Accept	4	1	8
	Reject	-5	-1	0
Be Hugged—Nice	Accept	4	1	8
	Reject	-5	-1	0
Hug—Friendly	Accept	5	2	10
	Reject	-10	-3	0
Be Hugged—Friendly	Accept	5	2	10
	Reject	-10	-2	-2

hild-to-Child Interaction Results, coontinued

Interaction	Response	Daily Relationship Change	Lifetime Relationship Change	Social Score Change
Insult	Accept	-10	-1	5
	Reject	-6	-3	0
Be Insulted	Accept	-14	-3	-7
	Reject	-12	-5	-10
Play—Rock-Paper-Scissors	Accept	5	1	6
	Reject	-2	-1	0
Be Played With—Rock-Paper-Scissors	Accept	7	2	6
	Reject	-9	-3	-2
Play—Tag	Accept	No Data		
	Reject	No Data		
Be Played With—Tag	Accept	No Data		
	Reject	No Data		
Talk—Jabber	Accept	4	1	5
	Reject	-4	-1	-1
Hear Talk—Jabber	Accept	4	0	5
	Reject	-3	0	0
Tease—Scare	Accept	5	1	10
	Reject	-3	0	0
Be Teased—Scare	Accept	5	1	8
	Reject	-10	1	0
Tease—Taunt	Accept	4	0	7
	Reject	-5	-1	-3
Be Teased—Taunt	Accept	4	1	7
	Reject	-10	2	-7
Tickle	Accept	8	1	10
	Reject	-5	-1	0
Be Tickled	Accept	5	1	10
	Reject	-8	-2	0

Child-to-Child Interaction Menu Triggers

CATEGORY	INTERACTION	INITIATOR REQUIREMENTS	RECIPIENT REQUIREMENTS
Annoy	Poke	Mood ≤ -20	None
	Push	Mood ≤ -10	None
	Kick Shin	Mood ≤ -30	None
Brag		Daily ≥ 10, Mood ≤ 20	None
Cheer Up		Mood ≥ 0	Mood ≤ 0
Entertain	Joke	Mood ≥ 25	None
	Perform Trick	Mood ≥ 25	None
Hug	Nice	Mood ≥ 30, Daily ≥ 30	None
	Friendly	Mood ≥ 35, Daily ≥ 35	None
Insult		Mood ≤ 0	None
		Daily ≤ -10	None
Play	Rock-Paper-Scissors	Mood ≥ 50, Daily ≥ 25	None
	Tag	Mood ≥ 0, Daily ≥ 30	None
Talk	Jabber	Daily ≥ 10	None
	Whisper	Mood ≥ 15, Daily ≥ 15	None
Tease	Scare	Mood ≥ 20	None
		Daily > 0	None
	Taunt	Mood ≤ 15	None
		Daily > 15	None
Tickle		Mood ≥ 5	None